Elizabeth Stuart Phelps

Elizabeth Stuart Phelps

Selected Tales, Essays, and Poems

Edited by Elizabeth Duquette and Cheryl Tevlin

Introduction by Elizabeth Duquette

University of Nebraska Press

Lincoln and London

LIBRARY OF CONGRESS
Cataloging-in-Publication Data

Phelps, Elizabeth Stuart, 1844-1911, author.
[Works. Selections]
Elizabeth Stuart Phelps: selected tales,
essays, and poems / edited by Elizabeth
Duquette and Cheryl Tevlin; introduction
by Elizabeth Duquette.
pages   cm.—(Legacies of
Nineteenth-Century American
Women Writers)

ISBN 978-0-8032-4397-2 (paperback)
ISBN 978-0-8032-5422-0 (epub)
ISBN 978-0-8032-5423-7 (mobi)
ISBN 978-0-8032-5421-3 (pdf)
I. Duquette, Elizabeth, 1963, editor of
compilation. II. Tevlin, Cheryl, editor
of compilation. III. Title.
PS3141.D87 2014
813'.4—dc23   2014001163

Set in Adobe Carlson Pro by
Renni Johnson.
Designed by A. Shahan.

Contents

POEMS

Acknowledgments

Every book is the culmination of the efforts of many people, this one perhaps more than most. We began the volume as professor and student and end as colleagues and coeditors; it has been an exciting process, and we are deeply grateful to the people and institutions that supported us along the way, especially those willing to see the possibilities in an arrangement that deviates from the norm.

Gettysburg College has been unflaggingly supportive and generous, providing funds for travel and transcription, remote computer support, and constant cheerleading and enthusiasm. It's hard to imagine a more congenial place for the kind of collaboration that yielded this volume than the English Department. Linda Miller assisted in countless ways, keeping us on track and calm. Also crucial was the assistance of the excellent staff at Musselman Library, unfailingly generous with their time and knowledge. The volume would not exist without the extra efforts of Kerri Odess-Harnish, Meggan Smith, and Janelle Wertzberger, reference and instruction librarians. Special thanks as well to the Gettysburg College students who provided research assistance for the project: Victoria Belinsky and Eric Kozlik.

Sharon Harris, Cindy Weinstein, and Theresa Gaul provided excellent editorial support and guidance for the project, even before it began: Cindy encouraged us to submit the proposal; Sherry gave shape to the volume with timely and pertinent advice; and Theresa offered excellent feedback on the final product. Anonymous readers chimed in with useful suggestions, which improved the volume greatly. Our editor at University of Nebraska Press, Kristen Elias Rowley, has been equally helpful. Ann Baker and Judith Hoover helped give the volume its final shape.

In learning about Phelps's life, times, and works, we have relied on the collections of multiple libraries and archives, including the New

York Public Library, Rutgers University–Camden's Paul Robeson Library, and Temple University's Samuel L. Paley's Library. An early research trip to Boston included visits to Boston University and the Peabody Collection.

Individuals as well as institutions have been crucial to the completion of the volume, particularly the many scholars, friends, and family who have provided both of us with intellectual and emotional support. Elizabeth has been talking about Phelps for years at conferences like the SSAWW and MLA, as well as with friends both in and out of the academy. Participants in the Nineteenth-Century American Women Writers Study Group provided insights and much-needed final encouragement during a discussion of Phelps's *Doctor Zay*; special thanks to Cynthia Davis, Sari Edelstein, Holly Jackson, Marianne Noble, and Jane Thrailkill. Elizabeth has also benefited from the wisdom and encouragement of Kate Adams, Erin Forbes, Travis Foster, Katja Garloff, Howard Horwitz, Bob Levine, Stacey Margolis, and Matt Sandler. Friends and family have been equally important: members of the Breen and Duquette families (Ali, Sean, Maria, John, Merinda, Tom), David Garrett, and Bridget and Brady Rymer. But the greatest debt is to Michael Breen, whose intelligence, humor, and love create the conditions of possibility for achievements of all kinds, both big and small.

Cheryl is similarly grateful for the support of mentors, friends and family. Temma Berg provided important intellectual guidance as a thesis director. Thanks to Mary Stephens and Amy Meros for many hours of discussion about Phelps during the past three years. Lee Gatto, Gracie Raver, Angie Barney, and Meghan Kelly were models of patience during weeks of Phelps submersion. Most important, however, has been the constant support of Cheryl's parents, David and Laurie Tevlin, who have shared, and humored, her enthusiasm for Phelps, adapting vacation schedules and lending key assistance with some of Phelps's more obscure biblical references. This book is dedicated to them.

Editor's Introduction

From December 1907 to November 1908, *Harper's Bazar* published *The Whole Family*, a project conceived by the author and editor William Dean Howells and executed by Howells and eleven other prominent authors. Each writer contributed a chapter in the voice of a different member of an American family, developing the plot from previously completed sections. Howells wrote the first chapter, setting the story in motion and introducing the family members. Many noteworthy authors agreed to participate, including Henry James, Mary E. Wilkins Freeman, and Elizabeth Stuart Phelps. As part of the fun, *Bazar* published the installments anonymously, encouraging readers to match the author of each chapter to the list of twelve contributors. But, as a commentator noted, the list of contributors made it is hard to imagine the family as anything but dysfunctional: "The man—or woman—who could draw Mr. Howells, and Mr. James, and Mrs. Phelps Ward, and Dr. Van Dyke into such a scheme, and hold them to playing the game with straight faces in public" "deserves" to have his name "written on brass" (Howard, 53).[1] The gathered authors had won their reputations in a dizzying range of styles and genres, including regionalism, sentimentalism, children's literature, religious fiction, reform writing, and realism. As a result, *The Whole Family* is characterized by a chaotic style and lurching plot, so much so that a *New York Times* reviewer dubbed it a "comedy of confusion" (Kelly). But then, as now, the real accomplishment of the project lay in bringing the complexity of the late nineteenth-century literary world into stark relief.

Twenty-first-century readers are accustomed to tidy accounts of postbellum literary history, organized around the dyad of realism and naturalism, with a quick nod to local color or regionalist writers. There is little sign of the multiple styles included in *The Whole Family*. Where did the "comedy of confusion" go? The critical priorities and professional anxieties that shaped postbellum literary history derive from the (often fierce) late-century debates about realism and the changing status of writers and their critics.[2] Even though women writers participated in these debates, few were included either in the literary histories written during the period or the canon they established. Elizabeth Stuart Phelps was not one of the few. This might have surprised postbellum readers, who were accustomed to encountering Phelps's writings alongside works by Howells, James, and Mark Twain in prominent and elite periodicals such as the *Atlantic Monthly*, *Harper's Monthly*, *Century*, and the *North American Review*. Phelps's home was profiled in Richard Stoddard's *Poets' Homes* (1879); her literary contributions were detailed in *Our Famous Women* (1888); and her advice to writers was included in *The Art of Authorship* (1890). Helen Gray Cone confidently asserted that women writers belonged "among their brother authors, in classes determined by method, local background, or any other basis of arrangement which is artistic rather than personal," pointing to Phelps's achievements to support her claim (928). Phelps was, in other words, a popular and respected author across the postbellum period, even if, as scholars have detailed, it became increasingly difficult for her to maintain her position as the business of literature evolved. One of the aims of this collection of stories, essays, and poems is to return Phelps to the prominence she once enjoyed, thus bringing to view both the chaos of the postbellum literary world and the vital contributions Phelps made to it.

Phelps was close to the end of her career when she contributed to *The Whole Family*. She was assigned "The Married Daughter," and her chapter was scheduled to follow Henry James's contribution, "The Married Son." According to June Jordan, the *Bazar* editor in charge of the project, Phelps bristled at what she took to be James's attacks on "her" character. "I shall defend Maria from the aspersions of being 'a manger,'" she promised Jordan (*Three Rousing Cheers*, 277). Unsurprisingly her chapter begins on a defensive note: "We start in life with the most preposterous of all human claims—that one should be understood. We get bravely over that after awhile; but not until the idea has been knocked out of us by the hardest. I used to worry a good deal, myself, because nobody—distinctly not one person—in our family understood me; that is, me in my relation to themselves; nothing else, of course, mattered so much" (*The Whole Family*, 185). Maria Price may be speaking, but it is easy enough to hear the author herself in this lament. Indeed, as Alfred Habegger has observed, "The authors [of *The Whole Family*] often revealed a deep sympathy for their assigned characters" (Howells et al., *The Whole Family*, xxvi). This is especially true in Phelps's case, and it raises an important question: What would it take for contemporary readers to understand Phelps?

A first step would be to revise our approach to postbellum writing by devoting less attention to the novel. Decades ago Nina Baym observed, "If critics ever permit the woman's novel to join the main body of 'American literature,' then all our theories about American fiction . . . will have to be radically revised" (36–37). Feminist scholars have regularly reiterated Baym's trenchant observation, achieving only modest success with the field at large.[3] To finally enact these much-needed changes to literary history, a slight revision to Baym's argument is needed: it is not just the "woman's novel" but also the vast number of short works, including essays, tales, and poems, published by women after the Civil War that must be added to "the main body of 'American literature.'"[4] The handful of Phelps's novels familiar to scholars represents only a small portion of her impressive body of work. While some may be familiar with *The Gates Ajar* (1868), *The Silent Partner* (1871), *The Story of Avis* (1877), or *A Singular Life* (1895), few know the short works that echo and complicate the narratives presented in the novels. Phelps's longer works gesture to the diversity of her interests and the range of her talent, yet they cannot capture the whole of her achievement, articulated across the hundreds of stories, essays, and poems she wrote during her nearly five-decade-long career.

Phelps herself would likely have endorsed a shift in emphasis to short works. Like male authors of the period, Phelps wrote essays about literature, and hers make a powerful case for the artistic value of short stories. "The short story is to literature what the opal is to jewels," she asserts in one essay. When done well, the story is "the most delightful" form of fiction, but in the wrong hands it can be "the dreariest of things" ("George Eliot's Short Stories," 1). Ideally suited to the pace of postbellum life, "the short story is, without question," Phelps writes, "the literary favorite of our time" ("The Short Story," this volume). Too often, she explains, tales are not given their proper due, for they cannot be accurately assessed by standards developed for longer-form fiction; only "judges" "trained" in their particular features can fully appreciate the artistry of stories ("Stories that Stay," 118). In an effort to transform readers into "judges," Phelps lists four qualities that help stories to make a lasting impression: "originality, humanity, force, and finish" (123). Sounding like Edgar Allan Poe, who also lauded the power of short fiction, Phelps explains that stories should have "some surprise or shock of novelty; some hell or heaven of human feeling; or some grip of absolute strength" (123). Because of their brevity, stories can jolt readers in a way novels cannot, providing edifying and entertaining access to the extremes of human experience.

Phelps moderates her interest in the power of "novelty," however, when she asserts that literature's main charge is the depiction of "life as it is" (*Chapters*, 263). For readers who know Phelps from her best-selling novel *The Gates Ajar*, which describes heaven as embodied, domestic, and familiar, the claim that she draws her subjects from "life as it is" may be a surprise. Yet Phelps is clear that art cannot be divorced from the moral demands of mortal life. As she explains in her autobiography, *Chapters from a Life* (1896):

> the province of the artist is to portray life as it is; and life *is* moral responsibility. Life is several other things, we do not deny. It is beauty, it is joy, it is tragedy, it is comedy, it is psychical and physical pleasure, it is the interplay of a thousand rude or delicate motions and emotions, it is the grimmest and merriest motley of phantasmagoria that could appeal to the gravest or the maddest brush ever put to palette; but it is steadily and sturdily and always moral responsibility. An artist can no more fling off the moral sense from his work than he can oust it from his private life. (263)

To hold that "moral responsibility" is the first, and final, duty of the artist in an era that struggled to understand changing paradigms of responsibility from legal interpretation to arguments for evolution, indicates one of the key challenges associated with reading Phelps; to do so after modernism's campaigns to reject the social utility of art is even more difficult.[5] As the short works collected here demonstrate, Phelps's commitment to purposive fiction was a fundamental component of her thought; her works both argue and plead for social reform, changed economic priorities, and revised moral norms.[6]

It is not just to fiction that readers should turn to understand Elizabeth Stuart Phelps, however. She also wrote learned essay on theology, philosophy, and literary history, as well as polemical essays on contemporary social and political concerns. Not only do her essays, some of which are included in this volume, provide new perspectives on key subjects for the postbellum period, such as the definition of the fact or the aims of realism, they also challenge the prevailing assumption that affect was the primary means women writers used to engage readers or ideas. While Phelps was certainly capable of manipulating her readers' emotions, her essays make clear that she was also adept at crafting abstract arguments. Her immense erudition, on display in all of her work but especially the essays, complicates established conventions and counters lingering prejudices about the nature of women's writing during the period.

Like many nineteenth-century authors, Phelps wrote poetry as well as prose, composing key occasional pieces, such as a poem for the first graduation ceremony of Smith College in 1879 ("Victurae Salutamus"), as well as ballads and lyrics. In his *Poets of America* (1885), Edmund Stedman posits that Phelps is "essentially a poet," a quality he suggests is evident even in her prose (446). Subsequent readers have not always shared Stedman's assessment and, like much of the poetry written by women in the nineteenth century, Phelps's poetry has been largely ignored. This critical neglect might not have surprised the author, however, for she wrote in 1876, "My poetry is a great mystery to me. I accept criticism upon it with the meekness of perplexity. If people didn't read it, I shouldn't blame them, but as long as they do, I suppose I shall print it. But it seems so very *clear* to me that I am fain to cast about for greater reticence, half the time" (Bennett, 98). When compared to her prose, Phelps's poetry is admittedly limited in subject matter. Rather than ranging widely, Phelps returns to a handful of themes and images in her verse, focusing especially on issues of love, loss, and the promise of eternal life. In recent years scholars have returned to her poems, discovering new ways to appreciate the "beauties in them" (Howells, "Recent Literature," 108). To assist in this important work, this edition provides a sample of Phelps's poetic styles and themes, particularly her ongoing interest in a "Love so godlike that it could not die" ("Stranger than Death," this volume).

Phelps's short works command attention for a final reason: they productively unsettle current accounts of sentimentalism. In the past twenty years scholars have developed sophisticated arguments about the work of antebellum women writers, clarifying both their reformist aims and their formal complexity. As critics have made clear, these works often fused sentimentality and domestic ideology as a way to establish their claims. After the Civil War, however, this combination became less important, an observation that helped to justify the narrative of realism's rise. But scholars have been too hasty in dismissing postbellum sentimentalism. Not only is it a more important element of late nineteenth-century writing than has been acknowledged, but it is often deployed as a means of attacking the very domestic ideology it supported in the years before the Civil War. Because approaches to antebellum literature encourage scholars and students to conflate sentiment and domestic ideology, it has been difficult to appreciate the works of writers like Phelps who rely on sentiment to challenge, and even dismantle, the constraints of domesticity. As June Howard explains, "Sentimentality, although not always stigmatized, is always suspect, always questionable; the appearance of the term marks a site where values are contested" (223). Because reform fiction exists to challenge and change social values and norms, it must mobilize sentimentality if it is to succeed; this does not mean, however, that all uses of sentiment share the same political or social aim.

A full reconsideration of Phelps's place in American literary history requires, in other words, a thorough revision of established ways of approaching sentimentalism, realism, and the decades *before* the "rise" of realism in the 1880s.[7] Renewed emphasis on Phelps's short works should make it easier to begin this important work and to understand her considerable contributions to late nineteenth-century American literature. Its history may become somewhat more chaotic as a result, but it is long past due that we abandon the paradigms that exclude women like Phelps from the canon in the first place.

Life

Born into a New England family with roots dating back to the early seventeenth century, Elizabeth Stuart Phelps reminded many of New England's Puritan past. Poet John Greenleaf Whittier described her as "a Puritan with the passion and fire of Sappho" (187), and Rebecca Harding Davis observed that her friend could draw "the educated Puritan woman from life" (1). Critics made a similar connection: "There is a strong breeze out of the Puritan quarter in all her books," opined a reviewer for *Century*, "and it is thoroughly stimulating" ("Miss Phelps's 'Dr. Zay,'" 624). By the early twentieth century, the connection, still acknowledged, was no longer a compliment; Vernon Parrington slights Phelps's *The Silent Partner*, calling it an "emotional Puritan document" already "out of date when it came from the press" (62). Phelps never shrank from the association, counseling readers of *Chapters* to "Fear less to seem 'Puritan' than to be inadequate" (262). For Phelps, the daughter and granddaughter of highly regarded ministers, "seem[ing] 'Puritan'" meant devoting oneself to the reform of society along the lines of a Christianity committed to dignity, love, and respect for all. In this regard, she followed her paternal grandfather, Eliakim Phelps, who authored temperance tracts, worked with the Underground Railroad, and organized one of the earliest Sunday schools in the nation.

But the more severe side of Puritanism, the stern divines of popular culture, also shaped Phelps's development, even if her theological views diverged from their orthodox teachings. Both her maternal grandfather, Moses Stuart, and her father, Austin Phelps, served as faculty at the Andover Theological Seminary, which opened in 1808 as a bulwark against the perception of a creeping liberalism in American Protestantism. Phelps is comparatively reticent about Andover's theological atmosphere in *Chapters*, eliding her opinion in a dash's pause and speaking elliptically about the challenges it created for her, but the seminary was widely known as "the bosom of orthodoxy" ("Miss Phelps's 'Dr. Zay,'" 623). To underscore "the brevity of life," for example, students in attendance during Phelps's childhood were required to construct coffins (Rowe, 2). Not until later in the century did Andover incorporate more progressive doctrines into its theology, a move Phelps's father resisted from his retirement.[8]

Her parents met at Andover when he attended the Seminary as a resident licentiate; the couple, Elizabeth Stuart and Austin Phelps, married in September 1842. Austin had by this time accepted a position at Boston's Pine Street Church, where the family remained for six years. Their first child, Mary Gray Phelps, the future author, was born on August 31, 1844. In 1848 Austin was invited to return to Andover as Professor of Sacred Rhetoric and Homiletic and, although his wife was unenthusiastic about the move, he accepted. He was elected president of Andover in 1869, a position he held until 1879, when ill health forced him to resign. Andover proved a congenial environment for Austin; while there he wrote a number of books, including *The Still Hour* (1850), and his rhetoric lectures became important textbooks (*Theory of Preaching* [1881] and *English Style in Public Discourse* [1883]).

But Austin Phelps was not the only author in the immediate family; his wife was also an accomplished writer of stories and novels. Under the pseudonym H. Trusta, Elizabeth published several best-selling works, among them *Sunny Side* (1851) and *A Peep at "Number Five": or, A Chapter in the Life of a City Pastor* (1852), which presented pious and cheery pictures of the lives of ministers and their families. The crushing burdens of Andover life, motherhood, housekeeping, and authorship sadly proved too much for Elizabeth, who died shortly after the birth of their third child in 1852. After her mother's death, her first-born, Mary, changed her name to Elizabeth Stuart Phelps and, because "it was as natural to her daughter to write as to breathe," eventually followed her mother into a literary career. Of the elder Elizabeth Stuart Phelps, the daughter observed sadly, "She lived one of those rich and piteous lives such as only gifted women know; torn by the civil war of the dual nature which can be given to women only" (*Chapters*, 12). That writing could be fatal for women became one of Phelps's reiterated claims, made in essay ("What Shall They Do?" [1867]) and story ("The Rejected Manuscript" [1893]) alike.

Austin Phelps remarried twice, first to his wife's consumptive sister, Mary Stuart, and then in 1858 to Mary Johnson. Additional children soon followed, and with them came more housework for his oldest child. Phelps complained bitterly about the tedium of housework in her writings, recalling in *Chapters* that she wondered, "Must I cut out underclothes forever? Is *this* LIFE?" (104). But her father's attitude toward women "always retained something of a feudal view" about what they "should" find "natural," she explains in *Austin Phelps: A Memoir* (1891), and it was only thanks to her eventual critical success that she was able to put aside domestic chores (87).

Phelps could not attend either of the highly regarded schools in Andover, a fact that surely contributed to her later agitation for co-education, but she nonetheless received an education far superior to that available to most young women in the 1850s. The curriculum at Mrs. Edwards' School for Young Ladies nearly matched that of Phillips Academy, minus Greek and trigonometry. The erudition Phelps displays in many of her works reflects this formal education, as well as the intellectual environment of her home. In *Chapters*, Phelps recalls, "I learned to read and to love reading, not because I was made to, but because I could not help it. It was the atmosphere I breathed" (17).

Like her mother, Phelps began writing at an early age, composing works for children and Sunday school publications. *Chapters* records the thrill she felt at receiving her first payment for a story but still dismisses much of her early writing as "hack work" she was happy to abandon (81). Although she contributed to children's periodicals, such as *The Youth's Companion*, across the decades, the mainstream success Phelps achieved in the late 1860s allowed her to become more selective in her efforts, wrestling from her reluctant family the liberty to focus more fully on her writing. Two works in particular are responsible for establishing Phelps's reputation with readers and editors. In March 1868 "The Tenth of January" appeared in the *Atlantic Monthly*. Based on a disastrous fire at the Pemberton Mill eight years earlier, Phelps's grim depiction of the tragedy won her "first recognition" from literary notables like John Greenleaf Whittier and Thomas Wentworth Higginson (*Chapters*, 92).

Later the same year Phelps published *The Gates Ajar* with the prestigious Boston publisher Ticknor and Fields. The novel catapulted the young author into the spotlight. Phelps would later claim that she wrote *The Gates Ajar* because "our country was dark with sorrowing women," a group to which she herself belonged (*Chapters*, 96). Samuel Hopkins Taylor, a member of the Philips Academy class of 1862, was killed at Antietam just a few short months after his graduation. Although no formal arrangement existed between the two, Phelps was devastated by his death; her late story "The Oath of Allegiance" (1894) appears to draw on details of their relationship. Surely much of the power of *The Gates Ajar* derives from Phelps's own experience with grief and loss.

Phelps hoped *The Gates Ajar* would "say something that would comfort some few . . . of the women whose misery crowded the land," but the book far exceeded expectations: readers flocked to it (*Chapters*, 97). Critics were less enthusiastic, however, attacking its theology and accusing Phelps of "heresy" and "atrocity" (119). "Religious papers waged war across that girl's notions of the life to come," Phelps recalls, "as if she had been an evil spirit let loose upon accepted theology for the destruction of the world. The secular press was scarcely less disturbed about the matter; which it treated, however, with the more amused good-humor of a man of the world puzzled by a religious disagreement" (118). Complicating matters, Phelps dedicated the novel to her father, a move she later admitted had been unwise, for "certain citadels of stupidity" thus assumed "the views of the book" were his (107). Nothing could have been further from the case. Although his daughter boldly challenged restrictive and alienating religious dogma, Austin's commitment to Protestant orthodoxy remained unchanged throughout his life.

The Gates Ajar never matched the influence of the nineteenth century's most famous best seller, Harriet Beecher Stowe's *Uncle Tom's Cabin* (1852), but it too was a cultural phenomenon, inspiring pamphlets repudiating or defending its positions, grateful letters from readers, crossover products (patent medicines, funeral wreaths, cigars), and literary imitations, some parodic, like Mark Twain's "Captain Stormfield's Visit to Heaven" (1907), others celebratory, like Louis H. Pendleton's *Wedding Garment: A Tale of the Afterlife* (1894).[9] Phelps penned two additional novels and a poem on the subject (*Beyond the Gates* [1883], *Between the Gates* [1887], "The Gates Between" [1885]); the final novel was later adapted for the stage as *Within the Gates* (1901). Over the course of her career, Phelps published scores of stories and novels, essays, and poems, many of which would attract significant attention, but *The Gates Ajar* remained her most influential work.

Reflecting back on the novel's success in 1893, Phelps observed, "It may be called either a disadvantage or an advantage that, when a writer has begun his career with a large or a lofty subject of discussion he is never quite "let down" from it. Nothing lower or less is expected of him, nor, indeed, is ever really tolerated in him by his public" ("Immortality and Agnosticism," 567). In this regard she never disappointed her "public," demonstrating a consistent commitment to "lofty" goals in her writings, including expanded rights for women, the institution of temperance laws, and the prohibition of vivisection. These topics provided subject matter for her short stories and novels, as well as many essays. Her poetry likewise tackled "lofty" subjects but tended to be more explicitly religious than her prose. In the early 1870s Phelps regularly contributed polemical essays to the *Independent*, a New York religious weekly; these essays, many on subjects related to women's rights, were featured prominently on the paper's front page and helped to establish her credentials as an advocate for reform.

Although Phelps explores many themes in her writing, she returns most often to the condition of women in postbellum culture, showing how marriage forestalled their opportunities and squandered their talents, complaining about women's inability to establish independent lives, and demonstrating the need for religious practices that would comfort them more fully. While her essays argue for the expansion of women's opportunities, her fiction and occasionally her poetry depict women who reject marriage to pursue social reform or remain true to past promises, who suffer from the grinding cares associated with marriage and motherhood, or who compromise between competing demands, including those associated with professional choices.

In addition to her focus on the social challenges facing women, Phelps was also deeply and personally interested in the physical challenges both men and women had to confront when their health was compromised. On this subject, Phelps had a wealth of experience on which to draw. She was never physically strong, and her health deteriorated across the 1870s; until the end of her life she regularly suffered from debilitating illnesses, even calling herself a "professional invalid" in an 1884 letter to the famous physician S. Weir Mitchell. Like her father, Phelps suffered from acute insomnia; like her mother, she held that work contributed to her physical weakness. "I am not well enough even to earn my living!" she complains in 1890 (Curtis, 100). In a late essay, "Sympathy as a Remedy" (1909), Phelps writes bracingly to invalids, urging them to remember the "relativity of human misery" and insisting that they learn to do without "ease" and "sympathy" (743, 744). Although it is easy for the ill to forget, the healthy also have their cares and worries, so "nothing is more necessary," she asserts, "than for us to put ourselves in the places of the well" (745).

In 1888 Phelps surprised, and amused, the literary world when she agreed to marry Herbert Dickinson Ward (1861–1932), a man seventeen years her junior. Son of William Hayes Ward, editor of the *Independent*, Herbert had an advanced degree in theology but hoped to establish himself as a writer. Phelps's biographers have assumed that her ill health contributed both to her decision to wed and to the eventual decline of the marriage. The couple collaborated on several projects, including prize-winning children's fiction and two biblical romances (*The Master of the Magicians* [1890] and *Come Forth* [1891]), but it was not long before Phelps returned to publishing under her own name. In a 1903 letter to Harriet Spofford she confided, "Marriage is such tremendous material for the novel-writer! I wonder that it is not worn out in the using. But the married are hampered in what they can say" (Bennett, 83). Phelps found a way, however, to get around this limitation, publishing the withering *Confession of a Wife* (1902) under the pseudonym Mary Adams. In it a reluctant woman is wooed by a determined man, who tires of her quickly after the marriage; addicted to morphine, he decamps for Uruguay, returning a year later remorseful and damaged but hoping for reconciliation. Phelps's actual marriage did not end as happily as the fictional account; Herbert and Elizabeth spent most of their time apart, so much so that he was not present at her death.

Although still invited to participate in public forums and other projects, like *The Whole Family*, and celebrated in accounts of famous American women and famous American authors, including an article, "Nine Famous Women," in the *Ladies' Home Journal* in 1903, Phelps was no longer a literary celebrity when she died on January 28, 1911. Her previous prominence, however, guaranteed that her death was worthy of note. Obituaries celebrated her "breadth of mind and largeness of heart" ("Mrs. E. S. P. Ward Dies"), the "earnestness and intensity" that animated her best (and worst) literary efforts. "Indeed, for pure ability as well as for literary power," the *Independent* concluded, "she stood, notwithstanding her lifelong invalidism, at the head of our women writers" ("Elizabeth Stuart Phelps Ward," 269).

To Phelps, it had been an "incredible privilege" to speak to and for many readers, but popularity has often been met with suspicion in American literary history, taken as an indication of mediocrity, not merit (*Chapters*, 97). This was especially the case in the early decades of the twentieth century, as modernism solidified its intellectual position. Aided by the critical practices it invented to secure its spot atop the literary hierarchy, modernism "left women" like Phelps "out of the literary canon" and "made *sentimental* into a term of invective," Suzanne Clark explains (34–35). Not only did the modernists reject the fundamental relationship between art and morality, so central to Phelps's artistic practice, but they also made disinterestedness a chief critical principle, thus dismissing purposive writing as banal. Building on the literary histories written at the end of the nineteenth century, twentieth-century critics defined a predominantly masculine canon predicated on putatively timeless values. To fully appreciate Phelps's earnest "intensity," then, it is necessary to locate her more fully in her own moment, a moment when literary categories like realism and sentimentalism that seem so fixed today were very much in flux. A brief introduction to some of the subjects about which Phelps had strong opinions will help accomplish this goal and provide access to the selections of Phelps's writings collected here.

The Civil War

Literature during the Civil War sought to enlist men, women, and children into the conflict, defining the different ways they might participate and detailing methods of encouraging, or testing, universal patriotic engagement. Young men were to join the army, cheered on by wives, mothers, fathers, and sweethearts. While authors heaped fulsome praise on martial valor, they also detailed activities for those left at home, who were urged to write happy letters to the front, suppress their bonds of affection in the name of patriotism, buy war bonds, police their speech, volunteer at Sanitary Fairs or hospitals, and accept crushing loss bravely. "Such literature did not displace the importance of men in the conflict," historian Alice Fahs explains, "but it did sometimes ask for equal recognition of women's sacrifices, thus contributing to the diversity of claims to the war's meaning" (148–49).

In the suffering of those left behind during the Civil War, Phelps found inspiration for some of her best, and best-known, work, including *The Gates Ajar*. Her first major story, "A Sacrifice Consumed" (1864), spoke directly to the loss of hope and happiness many women struggle to manage.[10] Depicting the misery of a lonely seamstress after her fiancé is killed in battle, the story draws attention to the "martyrs at humble firesides" who "give up more" than the young soldiers who "face death with a smile." Women like the seamstress must endure "desolate" years from which "all the beauty, all the fragrance, all the song, has departed" (240). Here Phelps introduces a claim she develops at length in *The Gates Ajar*: there is no end to the war for those who suffer on the home front. Across her writings Phelps works to sketch a vision of heroism that could include the sacrifice of noncombatants, equating it to the more readily acknowledged efforts of the soldiers. In her last published story, "Comrades" (1911), as in her first, Phelps points to the contributions made by women to the Civil War. Here an elderly woman recalls how the war had "com[e] on" in her youth: "She thought of the day when he marched away—his arms, his lips, his groans. She remembered what the dregs of desolation were, and moral fear of unknown fate; the rack of the imagination; and inquisition of the nerve—the pangs that no man-soldier of them all could understand. 'It comes on women— war,' she thought" (39–40). Without diminishing the veteran's efforts, Phelps argues here, as in her other writings, that women's efforts are worthy of being remembered and celebrated.

When Phelps wrote "A Sacrifice Consumed," magazines and news-papers were filled with articles, stories, and poems written for families struggling with the war's unprecedented slaughter. But as Reconstruc-tion proceeded, Southern states were readmitted to the Union, and the fighting retreated into memory, writing about the Civil War shifted focus. Memoirs by famous generals and other kinds of battle remi-niscences, like those printed in the "Century War Series" (1884–87), dominated the market; such works tended to ignore or diminish the efforts of noncombatants, leaving less room for the heroism of women. Phelps's writings provide a critical counterpart to the explicitly gen-dered representation of the Civil War that became prominent across the postbellum period. Yet even as she stressed the importance of women's contributions, she never slighted the soldiers. In poems like "A Mes-sage" (1875) and stories like "The Oath of Allegiance," Phelps reminded readers that soldiers should figure prominently in the memory of the country for which they fought.

The Civil War was critical to Phelps's writing in a second way; it provided her with an important figure for the representation of con-flicting visions of gendered social organization. She shows women, like her own mother, suffering from internal conflict, unable to bring the warring sides of their nature into harmony. In *The Story of Avis*, for example, the title character likens love to "death. . . . It is civil war" (106). Later in her career, Phelps even compared unhappy marriage to civil conflict, transforming the home into a battlefield of daily emo-tional warfare.

Despite Phelps's serious engagement with the affective aftermath of the war, she seldom confronted the issues related to race that provided important material for other writers of the period, like Lydia Child, Rebecca Harding Davis, John De Forest, or Albion Tourgée, to name just a few. Where they engage with the promises and paradoxes of the Thirteenth, Fourteenth, and Fifteenth Amendments, Phelps tended to see slavery and its abolition as ways of thinking about women's rights.[11] At the end of "The Higher Claim" (1871), for example, Phelps argues that the extension of suffrage to women should have the same moral authority as the extension of suffrage to former slaves. On the subject of race, she is more likely to use a theoretical argument than to depict African American characters, although her short fiction does include some exceptions, like "How June Found Massa Linkum" (1868), to this general rule.

Religion

Phelps believed that abstract religious doctrines were cruel, for they obscured the important truths of Christianity from all people, but especially women. "Creeds and commentaries and sermons are made by men," she notes in *Chapters*, but "what can the doctrines do" for women (98)? Providing a satisfactory answer to this question was one of the chief motivations for her writing. According to Phelps, Christianity offered both the possibility of a rich future world and provided a useful guide for bettering the present one. "The important things— all that any of us need, all that most of us care for—are few, clear, and unquestionable," she explains in *The Story of Jesus Christ: An Interpretation* (1897). Chief among them, she continues, is that "Jesus Christ lived and died, and lived again after death. He lived a life explicable upon no other view of it than his. He founded a faith comprehensible upon no other interpretation of it than his own. . . . He is the greatest force in civilization: the highest motive power in philosophy, in art, in poetry, in science, in faith. He is the creator of human brotherhood. To apprehend him is to open the only way that has yet been found out of the trap of human misery" (ix). Like many nineteenth-century religious thinkers, Phelps stressed the importance of religious affections, particularly those inspired by the person of Jesus. "It all comes, in the end, perhaps, to a matter of feeling," she notes in "The Great Hope," "profound and high-minded feeling" (*In After Days*, 30). Although Phelps indicates that this "feeling" has a personal component, as in "A Jewish Legend" (1885) when she writes, "I like to think, for playmate / We have the Lord Christ still," it would be wrong to assume that her interests were exclusively private (38). On the contrary, Phelps's Jesus was "a holy exemplar of social reform," and her writings emphasize the central importance of Christian action in society, as well as private piety (Curtis, 17).[12]

In stressing the social aspects of Christianity, Phelps was very much of her time. The postbellum period was, Claudia Stokes reminds us, "a veritable golden age of religious fiction." Rather than a minor subfield, religious writing was an important element in mainstream American literature. Historical novels like Lew Wallace's *Ben-Hur* imagined the rich world of Roman antiquity, while others brought biblical figures or events to life; prominent examples include novels by Phelps and Ward (*The Master of the Magicians* [1890] and *Come Forth* [1891]), Harriet Beecher Stowe (*Woman in Sacred History* [1873]), and fellow member of *The Whole Family* Henry van Dyke (*The Other Wise Man* [1895]). Following the example set by Ernest Renan, whose 1863 *Life of Jesus* had an enormous transatlantic influence, authors offered fictional accounts of the life of Jesus, like Phelps's own *The Story of Jesus*. At the same time, pious poetry filled many periodicals. Enormously popular with readers although ignored by most literary histories, such works drew on progressive theological trends, as well as debates about the relationship between fact and fiction, to bring religion alive for readers.

Phelps shared many principles with adherents to the Social Gospel, a nondenominational Protestant tradition that emerged at the end of the nineteenth century and urged believers to ask themselves, "What Would Jesus Do?" This phrase, the subtitle of Charles M. Sheldon's 1896 novel *In His Steps*, encouraged the faithful to imagine themselves in the position of Jesus, an identification that leaders of the Social Gospel movement argued was central to a rich understanding of the New Testament. Optimistic even in the face of intransigent poverty and misery, the Social Gospel embraced the idea of human perfectibility, emphasizing the importance of placing community before self (Jackson, 155). In her representation of heroic ministers, sacrificing social position to combat drunkenness in Massachusetts or risking death to preach the gospel in the unreconstructed South, Phelps not only demonstrates the potential heroism of everyday existence but also traces important connections between Christianity and social justice.

Trying to separate Phelps's religious principles from her commitment to social change would be foolish; they are fundamentally connected. A key difference between her socially oriented Christianity and that of her antebellum predecessors, however, is the emphasis she placed on combining feeling with action. Drawing on the valorization of labor prevalent in Protestant culture, Phelps argued for the importance, economic and religious, of work for women. She repeatedly asserted that labor is a source of dignity and self-respect for both genders and, as such, is key to personal and spiritual health both in and out of marriage. Along the same vein, she constructed the argument for suffrage in "The Higher Claim" to culminate in a defense of the necessary correlation of Christianity and expanded civic participation.

One area where Phelps was especially active was in defending the right of women to preach. Although conservatives pointed to 1 Corinthians 14:34 to justify keeping women out of the pulpit, Phelps joined those who argued that women were better suited than men to share the truths of the Gospel with others. "A Woman's Pulpit" (1870) takes up this theme, expanding an idea already introduced in *The Gates Ajar*. As the essay "In Her Sphere" (1873) makes clear, Phelps had no doubt that the pulpit fell within women's "sphere." Years later Frances E. Willard, president of the Woman's Christian Temperance Union, published *Woman in the Pulpit* (1888), a defense of female ministers that included testimonials reminiscent of "A Woman's Pulpit."

Despite her progressive tendencies, there were limits to the challenge Phelps would mount against organized religion. For example, she took no part in the feminist revision of the Bible organized by Elizabeth Cady Stanton, published in 1895 and 1898 as *The Woman's Bible*. Written in part as a feminist response to disappointment in the Revised Version of the New Testament (1881), the controversial project demonstrated the gendered bias of scripture, including the way that religion had been used as a weapon in the battle to deny women their rights. Stanton's project dismayed many less radical activists, but it provides an important context for appreciating the prescience and topicality of Phelps's work, for many of its claims are anticipated or echoed in her polemical essays and religious tales.[13]

Phelps's religious thinking bears the impress, as well, of two notable experiences from her youth. She may have rejected much of the theology taught at Andover, the "sacred West Point," but its impact is evident in the nuanced representations of theological controversies and the diverse range of scholarly references that appear throughout her works, particularly in "What Is a Fact" and other essays collected in *The Struggle for Immortality* (1889) (Smith, ix). At the same time, Phelps's ideas were influenced by nineteenth-century spiritualism, the belief in the possible material presence of the dead, and specifically by her paternal grandfather's "seven months' affliction by spirits" (*Chapters*, 6). In an 1868 letter to Kate Fields, Phelps admits her belief "in the fact" of spiritual manifestations, which she maintains she holds "precisely on the principle by which I believe in the pyramids of Egypt" (Bennett, 5). Although she experimented with subjects adjacent to spirits and spiritualism, as in the story "Since I Died" (1873), Phelps's interests were ultimately more religious than sensational.

Women's Rights

Because *The Gates Ajar* is Phelps's most famous work, twentieth-century scholars tended to label her a religious writer. But, as should be clear, her religious commitments can be understood only in the context of her deep commitment to social justice, particularly for women. Writing to John Greenleaf Whittier in 1871, Phelps observed that the "'Woman Cause' . . . grows upon my conscience, as well as my enthusiasm, every day. It seems to me to be the first work God has to be done just now" (Bennett, 56–57). In advocating for women's rights, Phelps saw herself as doing God's work, and she was not alone in drawing this conclusion. Across the nineteenth century many thinkers and writers fused religion and social reform, grounding arguments for abolition, temperance, and women's rights in Christian precepts.

Phelps's ideas about women's rights were shaped by the writings of the British philosopher John Stuart Mill, as well as by her religion.[14]

In private correspondence, she expressed her admiration for Mill's work, particularly his treatise *The Subjection of Women* (1869); she cited the volume frequently, especially in essays arguing for greater equality in marriage.[15] As Mill provocatively points out, "The wife is the actual bond-servant of her husband: no less so, as far as legal obligation goes, than slaves commonly so called. She vows a livelong obedience to him at the altar, and is held to it all through her life by law" (31). In an ironic reversal, Mill used fiction, Stowe's *Uncle Tom's Cabin*, to argue that women were more fully subject to their masters than slaves had been. While this conclusion is doubtful, it is part of Mill's larger strategy, one that challenges readers to question the relationship between fact and fiction. Reasonable people assent to the subjugation of women, Mill argues, because an "artificial" view of the "nature of women," "the result of forced repression in some directions, unnatural stimulation in others," has been accepted as fact (22). Phelps drew on Mill both in terms of the content of his argument and the way he passionately questioned the ability to differentiate clearly between fact and fiction on contested issues.

Phelps, like many activists after the Civil War, was energized to improve the condition of women both in and out of the home. For many who embraced the cause, an expansion of voting rights was the main goal. The Fifteenth Amendment, which extended the vote to African American men, frustrated and angered women, many of whom believed that they were better equipped to participate in the electoral process. Reconstruction was therefore a chaotic and disappointing time for women's rights activists, split over the best way to continue after this defeat. More radical activists, like Elizabeth Cady Stanton and Susan B. Anthony, maintained that a constitutional amendment was necessary to secure women's rights permanently, and in 1869 Stanton and Anthony formed the National Women's Suffrage Association (NWSA).[16] But others disagreed, preferring a more gradual approach; these women joined the American Women's Suffrage Association (AWSA), with Julia Ward Howe and Lucy Stone at the helm, which adopted a state-by-state approach to the challenge. As sympathetic as she was to the aims of these groups, particularly the more conservative AWSA, Phelps seldom had anything but a remote relationship with reform organizations. On one rare occasion she did participate, contributing an essay to a volume Howe edited on the subject of women's education. Written in response to *Sex in Education* (1873), Dr. Edward H. Clarke's explanation of the dangers to women's health from expanded educational options, the essays in Howe's volume *Sex and Education* (1874) vigorously defended the importance of female education. Most often Phelps's reform activity took written form, either in prose pieces of her own or as part of forums, like the one included in this collection titled "Women's View of Divorce." Phelps seldom used poetry to express her reform goals, but she did pen a few poems about women's conditions in marriage, including "Congratulation" (1875) and "New Neighbors" (1885). Because her poor health limited her ability to appear in public, Phelps rarely engaged in other reform activities, such as lecturing or organizing events.

Over the course of her career, Phelps's interest in women's rights found expression in many causes, including her impassioned pleas for dress reform. Restrictive corsets, heavy skirts, and revealing bodices all met with her withering scorn. According to Phelps, prevailing fashions were not just ruinous to women's health, limiting the ability to move and twisting the body into unnatural and dangerous shapes, they also made women symbolically subservient to and dependent on men. In forwarding this argument, Phelps anticipates claims made by Thorstein Veblen, who famously argues for the symbolic function of women's clothing in *The Theory of the Leisure Class* (1899): "It may broadly be set down that the womanliness of woman's apparel resolves itself, in point of substantial fact, into the more effective hindrance to useful exertion offered by the garments peculiar to women" (172). Yet where Veblen's arguments have been celebrated as innovative, the same claims made by women reformers like Phelps have been largely ignored. Phelps developed her argument for dress reform across a series of articles in the *Independent*, later expanded into *What to Wear* (1873). In this campaign, as in her arguments in favor of coeducation and the expansion of economic opportunities for women, Phelps opposed the social construction of women to the rich abundance of women's possibility.

Phelps based her argument in favor of expanding women's options for education and employment on her reading of Mill, specifically his claim that women's abilities had yet to be tested. Women are trained to see themselves as weak and helpless, he argues, so a change in the perception of the capacities of both sexes would be necessary if women were to reach their full potential. Forwarding a similar argument, Phelps writes in "Men and Muscle" (1871), "A man is *trained* to be strong. A woman is *trained* not to be. Good health is *expected* of a man. Ill-health is *expected* of a woman." "The expectations of society," she concludes, "are to an all but mathematical extent the limits of the individual. What others look for in us, that we are" (1). Although she advocated for many professions, her interest in "the physical disabilities of women" pointed to the fundamental importance of medicine as a career for women (1). It is medical training that receives the most sustained attention in her writings, even though "What Shall They Do?" offers a full list of career options.

Form and Reform

Phelps argued directly for reform in her essays and only slightly less directly in her fiction. As a reviewer of *The Silent Partner* observed, the novel "is a terribly needed lesson" as much as an "interesting story" ("Editor's Literary Record," 301). But her commitment to social improvement has diminished her appeal to subsequent generations of readers. Trained to view purposive fiction as less literary, readers across the twentieth century generally ignored the works produced in the decades right after the Civil War, when Phelps achieved her greatest success. Only those works that "apparently prefigure the dilemmas facing 'modern' women" have continued to draw readers, Lisa Long rightly notes (265). The issues that engaged Phelps, such as dress reform, temperance, and antivivisection legislation, are easily enough viewed as quaint relics, even though these movements were instrumental in creating the conditions of possibility for the New Woman, the idealized independent and educated career woman of the turn of the century. A renewed appreciation for the work Phelps's fiction set out to do requires, however, a fuller sense of her aesthetic principles, the ways she thought form could help to forward the goals of reform.

"It is the duty of artist in fiction to-day," Phelps asserts unequivocally, "to paint life as it exists" (*Chapters*, 259). The stress on "duty" captures the moral urgency she brought to her literary practice. For Phelps, as for other writers of the period, an accurate representation of life often meant consulting either historical accounts or economic studies. Like Stephen Crane, who read testimonials about slum life while writing *Maggie, Girl of the Streets* (1893), Phelps scoured available records to guarantee the accuracy of her works, studying historical accounts of the Pemberton Mill fire for "The Tenth of January" and reports from the Massachusetts Bureau of Statistics of Labor for *The Silent Partner*. But where Crane seems to have done so to divorce accuracy from compassion, Phelps hoped to fuse them permanently, inspiring readers to take action. "Fear less to 'point your moral' than to miss your opportunity," she urged (*Chapters*, 265). As Susan S. Williams has recently argued, Phelps's style of writing may best be described as "ethical realism," for it takes the communication of ethical principles as one of its main aims (174). Although scholars often claim that hers is a utopian vision, Phelps herself hoped to intervene in the daily lives of readers, providing comfort and direction, while also presenting characters or scenes that challenged readers to expand their capacities for sympathy.

According to Phelps, literature that sought to reform readers required both accurate content and the proper form and tone. Phelps scolded Dr. E. H. Clarke for failing to recognize that "he is not in the lecture-room of the medical school" when addressing a general audience, urging him to work harder at gauging "the real effect" of his words (*Sex and Education*, 126). In this instance Phelps's advice was sarcastically intended: her constructive criticisms are part of an attack on his ideas. But the main thrust of the argument is one she repeated in other instances. In *The Gates Ajar*, for example, Winifred Forecythe explains to the narrator that she tailors her arguments to match the intellectual capacity of each auditor, thus guaranteeing greater success. As Phelps observed elsewhere, the "time" must be "ripe" and the audience receptive for didactic works to be effective (*Friends*, 126).

Like antebellum writers, Phelps believed that it was affect, not argument, that was most likely to motivate change. It is no surprise that she claimed her Andover neighbor Harriet Beecher Stowe as an important predecessor, calling her "the greatest of American women" and penning

"Birthday Verses" in honor of her seventieth birthday (*Chapters*, 131). Yet critics who conflate Phelps's writing with the domestic ideology of antebellum novelists like Stowe mistake her aims: Phelps's approach to the work of affect diverges importantly from that presented in antebellum reform fiction. She explicitly rejects the idea of "the true woman," arguing pointedly that women can be "true," fulfilled in themselves and fulfilling their divine purposes, only when they are allowed to explore a potential that is not linked in any necessary way to domesticity or maternity ("'The True Woman,'" 1). Indeed for many of Phelps's female characters, like the young woman depicted in "The Sacrifice of Antigone" (1891), fulfillment is more likely to be found in serious study than marriage and motherhood.

Even though Phelps appears ardently local, situating the majority of her works in New England and celebrating the virtues of provincialism in a review of Henry James's *Hawthorne* (1879), the two authors who had the most profound influence on her work were British: Elizabeth Barrett Browning and George Eliot. Browning's *Aurora Leigh* (1856) was personally important to Phelps and is prominently referenced in *The Story of Avis*, but Eliot is more fundamental to Phelps's evolution as a thinker and an artist. Phelps celebrated Eliot's achievement extravagantly in essays, poems, and an 1873 series of lectures at Boston University, the first given by a woman at the institution; the letters that remain between Eliot and Phelps convey the American's ardent, sometimes too ardent, admiration for the British author.[17] And it is not hard to see why Phelps valued Eliot's example, despite their divergent positions on Christianity.[18] In *Adam Bede* (1859), Eliot writes that the "secret of deep human sympathy" can be found in the lives of average people; when we pay proper attention to people, we get to the "truthfulness" of human existence: "It is for this rare, precious quality of truthfulness that I delight in many Dutch paintings, which lofty-minded people despise. I find a source of delicious sympathy in these faithful pictures of a monotonous homely existence, which has been the fate of so many more among my fellow-mortals than a life of pomp or of absolute indigence, of tragic suffering or of world-stirring actions" (161). Like Eliot, Phelps hoped to convey the "truthfulness" of the human condition in her fiction, fusing this aim with a moral commitment she likewise associated with Eliot. Although Eliot did not share Phelps's committed Christian perspective, the American found in her British counterpart an example of what morally complicated realism might achieve.

Passionately committed to the hope of human perfectibility, Elizabeth Stuart Phelps spent a lifetime advocating for change, personal and social, that would yield a better and more just society for women and men alike. In addition to the causes discussed above, she was also active in the postbellum temperance movement and the campaign to outlaw vivisection. For Phelps, the suffering of the individual, human or animal, always demanded action, attention, and compassion. Despite these laudable goals, Phelps's comparative conservatism, as well as her fundamental religious orientation and her investment in the Civil War, have made her difficult to place in literary history. As Lora Romero observed, scholars struggle "to entertain the possibility that traditions, or even individual texts, could be radical on some issues (market capitalism, for example) and reactionary on others (gender or race, for instance). Or that some discourses could be oppositional without being outright liberating. Or conservative without being outright enslaving" (4). Romero's observation is certainly true of Phelps's writing, which is sometimes radical, sometimes conservative. But if we can come to understand Phelps better, we will have a clearer sense of the complexity of the postbellum past, as well as a helpful guide for creating a finer future.

Notes

1. Elizabeth Stuart Phelps chose to publish under her married name, Elizabeth Stuart Phelps Ward, for only a few years after her 1888 marriage to Herbert Dickinson Ward; her decision to revert to her own name, unusual for the time, was not always respected by critics.
2. Stokes provides an indispensable overview of this history in *Writers in Retrospect*, 17–32.
3. Baym's claim was reiterated by Judith Fetterley in 1985, Elizabeth Ammons and Sharon Harris in 1991. Several recent scholars, including Susan

Williams, Anne Boyd, and Naomi Sofer, have detailed the exclusion of women both during the period and in the histories written about it.

4. Such a shift could also have a positive effect on the study of long-form fiction as well. As *The Whole Family* underscores, the distinction between story and novel in the period was far from fixed; novels were often published serially alongside or even comprise short stories.

5. For an overview of these changes, see Goodman, 65–97.

6. Claybaugh argues compellingly for the use of the term *purposive fiction* to describe a range of reform writing in the nineteenth-century Anglo-American world (*Novels of Purpose*).

7. There is a growing body of excellent work in this area, however, including books or articles by Glazener, Howard, Boyd, Williams, and Sofer. On changes to the publishing industry and their effect on Phelps, see Coultrap-McQuinn, 168–92.

8. In the 1880s, for example, he offered a spirited defense of the principle of infant damnation, an incident Phelps depicts in *A Singular Life*.

9. Twain's story did not appear until 1907, but he started writing it much earlier, probably around the time that *The Gates Ajar* appeared.

10. There is some dispute about an earlier publication. Scholars now attribute the unsigned "'Tenty Scran'" (*Atlantic Monthly*, November 1860) to Gail Hamilton, the pen name of Mary Abigail Dodge, but an index from 1889 identifies Phelps as its author.

11. The influence of John Stuart Mill on Phelps's thought is discussed later in this introduction, but it is worth noting that he is an important precursor of this idea. See, as well, Claybaugh, 91.

12. It is interesting to note how Phelps's definition of religious sentiment diverges from the one William James develops in *Varieties of Religious Experience* (1902). According to James, religion is "the feelings, acts, and experiences of individual men in their solitude, so far as they apprehend themselves to stand in relation to whatever they may consider the divine" (31).

13. Kessler argues, "Neither Phelps nor women who read [*A Singular Life*] are likely to have read Stanton's *Bible*. The novel is, nonetheless, a realistic representation of the implications for women of this *Bible*" (99).

14. Mill first drafted the book in 1861 and had to revise some of its sections, particularly those comparing the condition of women to that of slaves in the United States, to reflect the outcome of the American Civil War.

15. An especially pertinent example is "The New Earth," *Independent*, September 28, 1871, 1.

16. For an overview of the two organizations, see Clinton, 94.

17. Phelps destroyed much of her own correspondence late in her life; the materials that remain are scattered through multiple archives, often held in the papers of her correspondents.
18. In her poems about Eliot, Phelps seeks to convert the British author, suggesting that Eliot was accompanied by Jesus, "though she knew [Him] not" ("George Eliot," 43).

Bibliography

Ahlstrom, Sydney E. *A Religious History of the American People.* New Haven: Yale University Press, 1972.

Ammons, Elizabeth. *Conflicting Stories: American Women Writers at the Turn into the Twentieth Century.* New York: Oxford University Press, 1991.

Baym, Nina. *Woman's Fiction: A Guide to Novels by and about Women in America, 1820–1870.* Urbana: University of Illinois Press, 1993.

Bennett, Mary Angela. *Elizabeth Stuart Phelps.* Philadelphia: University of Pennsylvania Press, 1939.

Boyd, Anne E. *Writing for Immortality: Women Writers and the Emergence of High Literary Culture in America.* Baltimore: Johns Hopkins University Press, 2004.

Clark, Suzanne. *Sentimental Modernism: Women Writers and the Revolution of the Word.* Bloomington: Indiana University Press, 1991.

Claybaugh, Amanda. *The Novel of Purpose: Literature and Social Reform in the Anglo-American World.* Ithaca NY: Cornell University Press, 2007.

Clinton, Catherine. *The Other Civil War: American Women in the Nineteenth Century.* Revised edition. New York: Hill and Wang, 1999.

Cone, Helen Gray. "Woman in American Literature." *Century,* October 1890, 921–30.

Coultrap-McQuinn, Susan. *Doing Literary Business: American Women Writers in the Nineteenth Century.* Chapel Hill: University of North Carolina Press, 1990.

Curtis, Susan. *A Consuming Faith: The Social Gospel and Modern American Culture.* Baltimore: Johns Hopkins University Press, 1991.

Davis, Rebecca Harding. "Women in Literature." *Independent,* May 7, 1891, 1.

"Editor's Literary Record: Fiction." *Harper's Monthly Magazine,* July 1871, 300–301.

Eliot, George. *Adam Bede.* New York: Oxford University Press, 2008.

"Elizabeth Stuart Phelps Ward." *Independent,* February 2, 1911, 269.

Fahs, Alice. *The Imagined Civil War: Popular Literature of the North and South, 1861–1865.* Chapel Hill: University of North Carolina Press, 2001.

Fetterley, Judith, ed. *Provisions: A Reader from 19th-Century American Women*. Indianapolis: Indiana University Press, 1985.

Glazener, Nancy. *Reading for Realism: The History of a U.S. Literary Institution, 1850–1910*. Durham NC: Duke University Press, 1997.

Goodman, Nan. *Shifting the Blame: Literature, Law, and the Theory of Accidents in Nineteenth-Century America*. Princeton NJ: Princeton University Press, 1999.

Griffith, George. "An Epistolary Friendship: The Letters of Elizabeth Stuart Phelps to George Eliot." *Legacy* 18.1 (2001): 94–100.

Harris, Sharon M. *Rebecca Harding Davis and American Realism*. Philadelphia: University of Pennsylvania Press, 1991.

Howard, June. *Publishing the Family*. Durham NC: Duke University Press, 2001.

Howe, Julia Ward, ed. *Sex and Education: A Reply to Dr. E. H. Clarke's "Sex in Education."* Boston: Roberts Brothers, 1874.

Howells, William Dean. "Recent Literature: Miss Phelps's Poetic Studies." *Atlantic Monthly*, July 1875, 108–9.

Howells, William Dean, et al. *In After Days: Thoughts on the Future Life*. New York: Harper & Brothers, 1910.

Howells, William Dean, et al. *The Whole Family: A Novel by Twelve Authors*. Ed. Alfred Habegger. New York: Ungar, 1986.

Jackson, Gregory S. *The Word and Its Witness: The Spiritualization of American Realism*. Chicago: University of Chicago Press, 2009.

James, William. *The Varieties of Religious Experience*. New York: Penguin, 1982.

Jordan, June. *Three Rousing Cheers*. New York: D. Appleton-Century, 1938.

Kelly, Florence Finch. "'The Whole Family' and Its Troubles." *New York Times*, October 23, 1908.

Kessler, Carol. *Elizabeth Stuart Phelps*. Boston: Twayne, 1982.

Long, Lisa A. "The Postbellum Reform Writings of Rebecca Harding Davis and Elizabeth Stuart Phelps." In *The Cambridge Companion to Nineteenth-Century American Women's Writing*, edited by Dale M. Bauer and Philip Gould. Cambridge, U.K.: Cambridge University Press, 2001. 262–83.

Mill, John Stuart. *The Subjection of Women*. Introduction by Wendell Robert Carr. Cambridge MA: MIT Press, 1984.

"Miss Phelps's 'Doctor Zay.'" *Century*, February 1883, 623–24.

"Mrs. E. S. P. Ward Dies in 67th Year." *New York Times*, January 29, 1911.

Parrington, Vernon. *Main Currents in American Thought*. Vol. 3: *The Beginnings of Critical Realism in America, 1860–1920*. Norman: University of Oklahoma Press, 1987.

Phelps, Elizabeth Stuart. "At Bay." *Harper's New Monthly Magazine*, May 1867, 780–87.

———. *Austin Phelps: A Memoir*. New York: Charles Scribner's Sons, 1891.

———. *Chapters from a Life*. Boston: Houghton, Mifflin, 1896.

———. *Comrades*. New York: Harper & Brothers, 1911.

———. *Friends: A Duet*. Boston: Houghton, Mifflin, 1881.

———. "George Eliot." In *Songs of the Silent World*. Boston: Houghton, Mifflin, 1885. 42–43.

———. "George Eliot's Short Stories." *Independent*, April 30, 1885, 1.

———. "Immortality and Agnosticism I: The Gates Ajar—Twenty-Five Years After." *North American Review*, May 1893, 567–76.

———. "A Jewish Legend." *Songs of the Silent World*. Boston: Houghton, Mifflin, 1885. 37–38.

———. "Men and Muscle." *Independent*, August 31, 1871, 1.

———. "A Sacrifice Consumed." *Harper's Monthly*, January 1864, 235–40.

———. "Stories That Stay." *Century*, November 1910, 118–23.

———. *The Story of Avis*. 1877. New Brunswick NJ: Rutgers University Press, 1985.

———. *The Story of Jesus Christ: An Interpretation*. Boston: Houghton, Mifflin, 1897.

———. "Sympathy as a Remedy." *Harper's Bazar*, August 1909, 743–48.

———. "'The True Woman.'" *Independent*, October 12, 1871, 1.

Romero, Lora. *Home Fronts: Domesticity and Its Critics in the Antebellum United States*. Durham NC: Duke University Press, 1997.

Rowe, Henry K. *History of the Andover Theological Seminary*. Newton MA: Thomas Todd, 1933.

S.B.H. "Women and Business." *Century*, April 1882, 954.

Smith, Helen Sootin. Introduction to *The Gates Ajar*. Cambridge MA: Belknap Press, 1964.

Sofer, Naomi Z. *Making the America of Art: Cultural Nationalism and Nineteenth-Century Women Writers*. Columbus: Ohio State University Press, 2005.

Stedman, Edmund Clarence. *Poets of America*. Boston: Houghton, Mifflin, 1885.

Stokes, Claudia. "The Religious Novel." In *The Oxford History of the Novel in English*. Vol. 6: *The American Novel: 1870–1940*. Edited by Priscilla Wald and Michael A. Elliott. New York: Oxford University Press, forthcoming.

———. *Writers in Retrospect: The Rise of American Literary History, 1875–1910*. Chapel Hill: University of North Carolina Press, 2006.

Stuart, Ruth McEnery. "If They Had a Million Dollars: What Nine Famous Women Would Do If a Fortune Were Theirs." *Ladies' Home Journal*, September 1903, 10.

Tuttle, Jennifer S. "Letters from Elizabeth Stuart Phelps (Ward) to S. Weir Mitchell, M.D., 1884–1897." *Legacy* 17.1 (2000): 83–94.

Veblen, Thorstein. *The Theory of the Leisure Class*. New York: Penguin, 1994.

Whittier, John Greenleaf. *The Letters of John Greenleaf Whittier*. Vol. 3: *1861–1892*. Edited by John B. Pickard. Cambridge MA: Harvard University Press, 1975.

Williams, Susan S. *Reclaiming Authorship: Literary Women in America, 1850–1900*. Philadelphia: University of Pennsylvania Press, 2006.

Note on the Text

All of the texts selected for inclusion in this volume were published during Phelps's lifetime, many more than once. For each selection, we have included a full publication history. Because Phelps revised, sometimes significantly, for each reprinting, we have decided to include the last version of the story, essay, or poem over which she could be said to have had control. There are two notable exceptions to this general rule, however. Phelps substantially expanded her essays on dress reform, "Is It Healthful?" and "What Can Be Done about It?," for *What to Wear* (1873); so as to be able to present these arguments in their entirety, we have decided to include the earlier, more compact versions, originally published in the *Independent*. "The Moral Element of Fiction" is a redacted section of Phelps's autobiography, *Chapters from a Life*, originally published serially in *McClure's Magazine* (1895–96) and then as a volume (1896). This abbreviated section circulated at the same time, and we have chosen to include it, rather than a longer excerpt from the autobiography, because it appeared on its own during Phelps's lifetime.

We have made minimal changes to the texts, amending them only in the case of obvious printer error or intrusive and confusing anachronism. The vast majority of the footnotes in the volume are the editors', but a few were written by Phelps herself; these are presented as footnotes, not endnotes.

Elizabeth Stuart Phelps

TALES

The Tenth of January

The city of Lawrence is unique in its way.[1]

For simooms that scorch you and tempests that freeze;[2] for sand-heaps and sand-hillocks and sand-roads; for men digging sand, for women shaking off sand, for minute boys crawling in sand; for sand in the church-slips and the gingerbread-windows, for sand in your eyes, your nose, your mouth, down your neck, up your sleeves, under your *chignon*, down your throat;[3] for unexpected corners where tornadoes lie in wait; for "bleak, uncomforted" sidewalks, where they chase you, dog you, confront you, strangle you, twist you, blind you, turn your umbrella wrong side out;[4] for "dimmykhrats" and bad ice-cream;[5] for unutterable circus-bills and religious tea-parties; for uncleared ruins, and mills that spring up in a night; for jaded faces and busy feet; for an air of youth and incompleteness at which you laugh, and a consciousness of growth and greatness which you respect,—it—

I believe, when I commenced that sentence, I intended to say that it would be difficult to find Lawrence's equal.

Of the twenty-five thousand souls who inhabit that city, ten thousand are operatives in the factories. Of these ten thousand two thirds are girls.

These pages are written as one sets a bit of marble to mark a mound. I linger over them as we linger beside the grave of one who sleeps well; half sadly, half gladly,—more gladly than sadly,—but hushed.

The time to see Lawrence is when the mills open or close. So languidly the dull-colored, inexpectant crowd wind in! So briskly they come bounding out! Factory faces have a look of their own,—not only their common dinginess, and a general air of being in a hurry to find the wash-bowl, but an appearance of restlessness,—often of envious restlessness, not habitual in most departments of "healthy labor." Watch them closely: you can read their histories at a venture. A widow this, in the dusty black, with she can scarcely remember how many mouths to feed at home. Worse than widowed that one: she has put her baby out to board,—and humane people know what that means,—to keep the little thing beyond its besotted father's reach. There is a group who have "just come over." A child's face here, old before its time. That girl— she climbs five flights of stairs twice a day—will climb no more stairs for herself or another by the time the clover-leaves are green. "The best thing about one's grave is that it will be level," she was heard once to say. Somebody muses a little here,—she is to be married this winter. There is a face just behind her whose fixed eyes repel and attract you; there may be more love than guilt in them, more despair than either.

Had you stood in some unobserved corner of Essex Street, at four o'clock one Saturday afternoon towards the last of November, 1859, watching the impatient stream pour out of the Pemberton Mill, eager with a saddening eagerness for its few holiday hours, you would have observed one girl who did not bound.[6]

She was slightly built, and undersized; her neck and shoulders were closely muffled, though the day was mild; she wore a faded scarlet hood which heightened the pallor of what must at best have been a pallid face. It was a sickly face, shaded off with purple shadows, but with a certain wiry nervous strength about the muscles of the mouth and chin: it would have been a womanly, pleasant mouth, had it not been crossed by a white scar, which attracted more of one's attention than either the womanliness or pleasantness. Her eyes had light long lashes, and shone through them steadily.

You would have noticed as well, had you been used to analyzing crowds, another face,—the two were side by side,—dimpled with pink and white flushes, and framed with bright black hair. One would laugh at this girl and love her, scold her and pity her, caress her and pray for her,—then forget her perhaps.

The girls from behind called after her: "Del! Del Ivory! look over there!"

Pretty Del turned her head. She had just flung a smile at a young clerk who was petting his mustache in a shop-window, and the smile lingered.

One of the factory boys was walking alone across the Common in his factory clothes.

"Why, there's Dick! Sene, do you see?"

Sene's scarred mouth moved slightly, but she made no reply. She had seen him five minutes ago.

One never knows exactly whether to laugh or cry over them, catching their chatter as they file past the show-windows of the long, showy street.

"Look a' that pink silk with the figures on it!"

"I've seen them as is betther nor that in the ould counthree.—Patsy Malorrn, let alon' hangin' onto the shawl of me!"

"That's Mary Foster getting out of that carriage with the two white horses,—she that lives in the brown house with the cupilo."

"Look at her dress trailin' after her. I'd like my dresses trailin' after me."

"Well, may they be good,—these rich folks!"

"That's so. I'd be good if I was rich; would n't you, Moll?"

"You'd keep growing wilder than ever, if you went to hell, Meg Match; yes you would, because my teacher said so."

"So, then, he would n't marry her, after all; and she—"

"Going to the circus to-night, Bess?"

"I can't help crying, Jenny. You don't *know* how my head aches! It aches, and it aches, and it seems as if it would never stop aching. I wish—I wish I was dead, Jenny!"

They separated at last, going each her own way,—pretty Del Ivory to her boarding-place by the canal, her companion walking home alone.

This girl, Asenath Martyn, when left to herself, fell into a contented dream not common to girls who have reached her age,—especially girls who have seen the phases of life which she had seen.[7] Yet few of the faces in the streets that led her home were more gravely lined. She puzzled one at the first glance, and at the second. An artist, meeting her musing on a canal-bridge one day, went home and painted a Mayflower budding in February.

It was a damp, unwholesome place, the street in which she lived, cut short by a broken fence, a sudden steep, and the water; filled with children,—they ran from the gutters after her, as she passed,—and filled to the brim; it tipped now and then, like an over-full soup-plate, and spilled out two or three through the break in the fence.

Down in the corner, sharp upon the water, the east-winds broke about a little yellow house, where no children played; an old man's face watched at a window, and a nasturtium-vine crawled in the garden. The broken panes of glass about the place were well mended, and a clever little gate, extemporized from a wild grape-vine, swung at the entrance. It was not an old man's work.

Asenath went in with expectant eyes; they took in the room at a glance, and fell.

"Dick has n't come, father?"

"Come and gone, child; did n't want any supper, he said. You 're an hour before time, Senath."

"Yes. Did n't want any supper, you say? I don't see why not."

"No more do I, but it 's none of our concern as I knows on; very like the pickles hurt him for dinner; Dick never had an o'er-strong stomach, as you might say. But you don't tell me how it m' happen you 're let out at four o'clock, Senath," half complaining.

"O, something broke in the machinery, father; you know you would n't understand if I told you what."

He looked up from his bench,—he cobbled shoes there in the corner on his strongest days,—and after her as she turned quickly away and up stairs to change her dress. She was never exactly cross with her father; but her words rang impatiently sometimes.

She came down presently, transformed, as only factory-girls are transformed, by the simple little toilet she had been making; her thin, soft hair knotted smoothly, the tips of her fingers rosy from the water, her pale neck well toned by her gray staff dress and cape;—Asenath always wore a cape: there was one of crimson flannel, with a hood, that she had meant to wear to-night; she had thought about it coming home from the mill; she was apt to wear it on Saturdays and Sundays; Dick had more time at home. Going up stairs to-night, she had thrown it away into a drawer, and shut the drawer with a snap; then opened it softly, and cried a little; but she had not taken it out.

As she moved silently about the room, setting the supper-table for two, crossing and recrossing the broad belt of sunlight that fell upon the floor, it was easy to read the sad story of the little hooded capes.

They might have been graceful shoulders. The hand which had scarred her face had rounded and bent them,—her own mother's hand.

Of a bottle always on the shelf; of brutal scowls where smiles should be; of days when she wandered dinnerless and supperless in the streets through loathing of her home; of nights when she sat out in the snow-drifts through terror of her home; of a broken jug one day, a blow, a fall, then numbness, and the silence of the grave,—she had her distant memories; of waking on a sunny afternoon, in bed, with a little cracked glass upon the opposite wall; of creeping out and up to it in her night-dress; of the ghastly twisted thing that looked back at her. Through the open window she heard the children laughing and leaping in the sweet summer air. She crawled into bed and shut her eyes. She remembered stealing out at last, after many days, to the grocery around the corner for a pound of coffee. "Humpback! humpback!" cried the children,— the very children who could leap and laugh.

One day she and little Del Ivory made mud-houses after school.

"I'm going to have a house of my own, when I'm grown up," said pretty Del; "I shall have a red carpet and some curtains; my husband will buy me a piano."

"So will mine, I guess," said Sene, simply.

"*Yours!*" Del shook back her curls; "who do you suppose would ever marry *you?*"

One night there was a knocking at the door, and a hideous, sodden thing borne in upon a plank. The crowded street, tired of tipping out little children, had tipped her mother staggering through the broken fence. At the funeral she heard some one say, "How glad Sene must be!"

Since that, life had meant three things,—her father, the mills, and Richard Cross.

"You 're a bit put out that the young fellow did n't stay to supper,— eh, Senath?" the old man said, laying down his boot.

"Put out! Why should I be? His time is his own. It 's likely to be the Union that took him out,—such a fine day for the Union! I 'm sure I never expected him to go to walk with me *every* Saturday afternoon. I 'm not a fool to tie him up to the notions of a crippled girl. Supper is ready, father."

But her voice rasped bitterly. Life's pleasures were so new and late and important to her, poor thing! It went hard to miss the least of them. Very happy people will not understand exactly how hard.

Old Martyn took off his leather apron with a troubled face, and, as he passed his daughter, gently laid his tremulous, stained hand upon her head. He felt her least uneasiness, it would seem, as a chameleon feels a cloud upon the sun.

She turned her face softly and kissed him. But she did not smile.

She had planned a little for this holiday supper; saving three mellow-cheeked Louise Bonnes—expensive pears just then—to add to their bread and molasses. She brought them out from the closet, and watched her father eat them.

"Going out again Senath?" he asked, seeing that she went for her hat and shawl, "and not a mouthful have you eaten! Find your old father dull company hey? Well, well!"

She said something about needing the air; the mill was hot; she should soon be back; she spoke tenderly and she spoke truly, but she went out into the windy sunset with her little trouble, and forgot him. The old man, left alone, sat for a while with his head sunk upon his breast. She was all he had in the world,—this one little crippled girl that the world had dealt hardly with. She loved him; but he was not, probably would never be, to her exactly what she was to him. Usually he forgot this. Sometimes he quite understood it, as to-night.

Asenath, with the purpose only of avoiding Dick, and of finding a still spot where she might think her thoughts undisturbed, wandered away over the eastern bridge, and down to the river's brink. It was a moody place; such a one as only apathetic or healthy natures (I wonder if that is tautology!) can healthfully yield to. The bank sloped steeply; a fringe of stunted aspens and willows sprang from the frozen sand: it was a sickening, airless place in summer,—it was damp and desolate now. There was a sluggish wash of water under foot, and a stretch of dreary flats behind. Belated locomotives shrieked to each other across the river, and the wind bore down the current the roar and rage of the dam. Shadows were beginning to skulk under the huge brown bridge. The silent mills stared up and down and over the streams with a blank, unvarying stare. An oriflamme of scarlet burned in the west,[8] flickered dully in the dirty, curdling water, flared against the windows of the Pemberton, which quivered and dripped, Asenath thought, as if with blood.

She sat down on a gray stone, wrapped in her gray shawl, curtained about by the aspens from the eye of passers on the bridge. She had a fancy for this place when things went ill with her. She had always borne her troubles alone, but she must be alone to bear them.

She knew very well that she was tired and nervous that afternoon, and that, if she could reason quietly about this little neglect of Dick's, it would cease to annoy her. Indeed, why should she be annoyed? Had he not done everything for her, been everything to her, for two long, sweet years? She dropped her head with a shy smile. She was never tired of living over these two years. She took positive pleasure in recalling the wretchedness in which they found her, for the sake of their dear relief. Many a time, sitting with her happy face hidden in his arms, she had laughed softly, to remember the day on which he came to her. It was at twilight, and she was tired. Her reels had troubled her all the afternoon; the overseer was cross; the day was hot and long. Somebody on the way home had said in passing her: "Look at that girl! I'd kill myself if I looked like that": it was in a whisper, but she heard it. All life looked hot and long; the reels would always be out of order; the overseer would never be kind. Her temples would always throb, and her back would ache. People would always say, "Look at that girl!"

"Can you direct me to—" She looked up; she had been sitting on the door-step with her face in her hands. Dick stood there with his cap off. He forgot that he was to inquire the way to Newbury Street, when he saw the tears on her shrunken cheeks. Dick could never bear to see a woman suffer.

"I would n't cry," he said simply, sitting down beside her. Telling a girl not to cry is an infallible recipe for keeping her at it. What could the child do, but sob as if her heart would break? Of course he had the whole story in ten minutes, she his in another ten. It was common and short enough:—a "Down-East" boy,[9] fresh from his father's farm, hunting for work and board,—a bit homesick here in the strange, unhome-like city, it might be, and glad of some one to say so to.

What more natural than that, when her father came out and was pleased with the lad, there should be no more talk of Newbury Street; that the little yellow house should become his home; that he should swing the fantastic gate, and plant the nasturtiums; that his life should grow to be one with hers and the old man's, his future and theirs unite unconsciously?

She remembered—it was not exactly pleasant, somehow, to remember it to-night—just the look of his face when they came into the house that summer evening, and he for the first time saw what she was, her cape having fallen off, in the full lamplight. His kindly blue eyes widened with shocked surprise, and fell; when he raised them, a pity like a mother's had crept into them; it broadened and brightened as time slid by, but it never left them.

So you see, after that, life unfolded in a burst of little surprises for Asenath. If she came home very tired, some one said, "I am sorry." If she wore a pink ribbon, she heard a whisper, "It suits you." If she sang a little song, she knew that somebody listened.

"I did not know the world was like this!" cried the girl.

After a time there came a night that he chanced to be out late,—they had planned an arithmetic lesson together, which he had forgotten,—and she sat grieving by the kitchen fire.

"You missed me so much then?" he said regretfully, standing with his hand upon her chair. She was trying to shell some corn; she dropped the pan, and the yellow kernels rolled away on the floor.

"What should I have if I did n't have you?" she said, and caught her breath.

The young man paced to the window and back again. The firelight touched her shoulders, and the sad, white scar.

"You shall have me always, Asenath," he made answer. He took her face within his hands and kissed it; and so they shelled the corn together, and nothing more was said about it.

He had spoken this last spring of their marriage; but the girl, like all girls, was shyly silent, and he had not urged it.

Asenath started from her pleasant dreaming just as the oriflamme was furling into gray, suddenly conscious that she was not alone. Below her, quite on the brink of the water, a girl was sitting,—a girl with a bright plaid shawl, and a nodding red feather in her hat. Her head was bent, and her hair fell against a profile cut in pink-and-white.

"Del is too pretty to be here alone so late," thought Asenath, smiling tenderly. Good-natured Del was kind to her in a certain way, and she rather loved the girl. She rose to speak to her, but concluded, on a second glance through the aspens, that Miss Ivory was quite able to take care of herself.

Del was sitting on an old log that jutted into the stream, dabbling in the water with the tips of her feet. (Had she lived on The Avenue she could not have been more particular about her shoemaker.)[10] Some one—it was too dark to see distinctly—stood beside her, his eyes upon her face. Asenath could hear nothing, but she needed to hear nothing to know how the young fellow's eyes drank in the coquettish picture. Besides, it was an old story. Del counted her rejected lovers by the score.

"It 's no wonder," she thought in her honest way, standing still to watch them with a sense of puzzled pleasure much like that with which she watched the print-windows,—"it's no wonder they love her. I'd love her if I was a man: so pretty! so pretty! She's just good for nothing, Del is;—would let the kitchen fire go out, and would n't mend the baby's aprons; but I'd love her all the same; marry her, probably, and be sorry all my life."

Pretty Del! Poor Del! Asenath wondered whether she wished that she were like her; she could not quite make out; it would be pleasant to sit on a log and look like that; it would be more pleasant to be watched as Del was watched just now: it struck her suddenly that Dick had never looked like this at her.

The hum of their voices ceased while she stood there with her eyes upon them; Del turned her head away with a sudden movement, and the young man left her, apparently without bow or farewell, sprang up the bank at a bound, and crushed the undergrowth with quick, uneasy strides.

Asenath, with some vague idea that it would not be honorable to see his face,—poor fellow!—shrank back into the aspens and the shadow.

He towered tall in the twilight as he passed her, and a dull, umber gleam, the last of the sunset, struck him from the west.

Struck it out into her sight,—the haggard struggling face,—Richard Cross's face.

Of course you knew it from the beginning, but remember that the girl did not. She might have known it, perhaps, but she had not.

Asenath stood up, sat down again.

She had a distinct consciousness, for the moment, of seeing herself crouched down there under the aspens and the shadow, a humpbacked white creature, with distorted face and wide eyes. She remembered a picture she had somewhere seen of a little chattering goblin in a grave-yard, and was struck with the resemblance. Distinctly, too, she heard herself saying, with a laugh, she thought, "I might have known it; I might have known."

Then the blood came through her heart with a hot rush, and she saw Del on the log, smoothing the red feather of her hat. She heard a man's step, too, that rang over the bridge, passed the toll-house, grew faint, grew fainter, died in the sand by the Everett Mill.[11]

Richard's face! Richard's face, looking—God help her!—as it had never looked at her; struggling—God pity him!—as it had never strug-gled for her.

She shut her hands into each other, and sat still a little while. A faint hope came to her then perhaps, after all; her face lightened grayly, and she crept down the bank to Del.

"I won't be a fool," she said, "I'll make sure,—I 'll make as sure as death."

"Well, where did *you* drop down from, Sene?" said Del, with a guilty start.

"From over the bridge, to be sure. Did you think I swam, or flew, or blew?"

"You came on me so sudden!" said Del, petulantly; "you nearly fright-ened the wits out of me. You did n't meet anybody on the bridge?" with a quick look.

"Let me see." Asenath considered gravely. "There was one small boy making faces, and two—no, three—dogs, I believe; that was all."

"Oh!"

Del looked relieved, but fell silent.

"You're sober, Del. Been sending off a lover, as usual?"

"I don't know anything about its being usual," answered Del, in an aggrieved, coquettish way, "but there's been somebody here that liked me well enough."

"You like him, maybe? It's time you liked somebody, Del."

Del curled the red feather about her fingers, and put her hat on over her eyes, then a little cry broke from her, half sob, half anger.

"I might perhaps,—I don't know. He's good. I think he'd let me have a parlor and a door-bell. But he's going to marry somebody else, you see. I sha'n't tell you his name, so you need n't ask."

Asenath looked out straight upon the water. A dead leaf that had been caught in an eddy attracted her attention; it tossed about for a minute, then a tiny whirlpool sucked it down.

"I was n't going to ask; it's nothing to me, of course. He does n't care for her then,—this other girl?"

"Not so much as he does for me. He did n't mean to tell me, but he said that I—that I looked so—pretty, it came right out. But there! I must n't tell you any more."

Del began to be frightened; she looked up sideways at Asenath's quiet face. "I won't say another word," and so chattered on, growing a little cross; Asenath need not look so still, and sure of herself,—a mere humpbacked fright!

"He'll never break his engagement, not even for me; he's sorry for her, and all that. I think it's too bad. He's handsome. He makes me feel like saying my prayers, too, he's so good! Besides, I want to be married. I hate the mill. I hate to work. I'd rather be taken care of,—a sight rather. I feel bad enough about it to cry."

Two tears rolled over her cheeks, and fell on the soft plaid shawl. Del wiped them away carefully with her rounded fingers.

Asenath turned and looked at this Del Ivory long and steadily through the dusk. The pretty, shallow thing! The worthless, bewildering thing!

A fierce contempt for her pink-and-white, and tears and eyelashes and attitudes, came upon her; then a sudden sickening jealousy that turned her faint where she sat.

What did God mean,—Asenath believed in God, having so little else to believe in,—what did he mean, when he had blessed the girl all her happy life with such wealth of beauty, by filling her careless hands with this one best, last gift? Why, the child could not hold such golden love! She would throw it away by and by. What a waste it was!

Not that she had these words for her thought, but she had the thought distinctly through her dizzy pain.

"So there's nothing to do about it," said Del, pinning her shawl. "We can't have anything to say to each other,—unless anybody should die, or anything; and of course I'm not wicked enough to think of *that*.— Sene! Sene! what are you doing?"

Sene had risen slowly, stood upon the log, caught at an aspen-top, and swung out with it its whole length above the water. The slight tree writhed and quivered about the roots. Sene looked down and moved her marred lips without sound.

Del screamed and wrung her hands. It was an ugly sight!

"O don't, Sene, *don't!* You 'll drown yourself! you will be drowned! you will be—O, what a start you gave me! What *were* you doing, Sen-ath Martyn?"

Sene swung slowly back, and sat down.

"Amusing myself a little;—well, unless somebody died, you said? But I believe I won't talk any more to-night. My head aches. Go home, Del."

Del muttered a weak protest at leaving her there alone; but, with her bright face clouded and uncomfortable, went.

Asenath turned her head to listen for the last rustle of her dress, then folded her arms, and, with her eyes upon the sluggish current, sat still.

An hour and a half later, an Andover farmer, driving home across the bridge, observed on the river's edge—a shadow cut within a shadow— the outline of a woman's figure, sitting perfectly still with folded arms. He reined up and looked down; but it sat quite still.

"Hallo there!" he called; "you 'll fall in if you don't look out!" for the wind was strong, and it blew against the figure; but it did not move nor make reply. The Andover farmer looked over his shoulder with a sudden recollection of a ghost-story which he had charged his grandchildren not to believe last week, cracked his whip, and rumbled on.

Asenath began to understand by and by that she was cold, so climbed the bank, made her way over the windy flats, the railroad, and the western bridge confusedly with an idea of going home. She turned aside by the toll-gate. The keeper came out to see what she was doing, but she kept out of his sight behind the great willow and his little blue house,— the blue house with the green blinds and red moulding. The dam thundered that night, the wind and the water being high. She made her way up above it, and looked in. She had never seen it so black and smooth there. As she listened to the roar, she remembered something that she had read—was it in the Bible or the Ledger?—about seven thunders uttering their voices.[12]

"He's sorry for her, and all that," they said.

A dead bough shot down the current while she stood there, went over and down, and out of sight, throwing up its little branches like helpless hands.

It fell in with a thought of Asenath's, perhaps; at any rate she did not like the looks of it, and went home.

Over the bridge, and the canal, and the lighted streets, the falls called after her: "He 's sorry for her, and all that." The curtain was drawn aside when she came home, and she saw her father through the window, sitting alone, with his gray head bent.

It occurred to her that she had often left him alone,—poor old father! It occurred to her, also, that she understood now what it was to be alone. Had she forgotten him in these two comforted, companioned years?

She came in weakly, and looked about.

"Dick 's in, and gone to bed," said the old man, answering her look. "You 're tired, Senath."

"I am tired, father."

She sunk upon the floor,—the heat of the room made her a little faint,—and laid her head upon his knee; oddly enough, she noticed that the patch on it had given way,—wondered how many days it had been so,—whether he had felt ragged and neglected while she was busy about that blue neck-tie for Dick. She put her hand up and smoothed the corners of the rent.

"You shall be mended up to-morrow, poor father!"

He smiled, pleased like a child to be remembered. She looked up at him,—at his gray hair and shrivelled face, at his blackened hands and bent shoulders, and dusty, ill-kept coat. What would it be like, if the days brought her nothing but him?

"Something's the matter with my little gal? Tell father, can't ye?"

Her face flushed hot, as if she had done him wrong. She crept up into his arms, and put her hands behind his rough old neck.

"Would you kiss me, father? You don't think I 'm too ugly to kiss, maybe,—you?"

She felt better after that. She had not gone to sleep now for many a night unkissed; it had seemed hard at first.

When she had gone half-way up stairs, Dick came to the door of his room on the first floor, and called her. He held the little kerosene lamp over his head; his face was grave and pale.

"I have n't said good night, Sene."

She made no reply.

"Asenath, good night."

She stayed her steps upon the stairs without turning her head. Her father had kissed her to-night. Was not that enough?

"Why, Sene, what 's the matter with you?"

Dick mounted the stairs, and touched his lips to her forehead with a gently compassionate smile.

She fled from him with a cry like the cry of a suffocated creature, shut her door, and locked it with a ringing clang.

"She 's walked too far, and got a little nervous," said Dick, screwing up his lamp; "poor thing!"

Then he went into his room to look at Del's photograph awhile before he burned it up; for he meant to burn it up.

Asenath, when she had locked her door, put her lamp before the looking-glass and tore off her gray cape; tore it off so savagely that the button snapped and rolled away,—two little crystal semicircles like tears upon the floor.

There was no collar about the neck of her dress, and this heightened the plainness and the pallor of her face. She shrank instinctively at the first sight of herself, and opened the drawer where the crimson cape was folded, but shut it resolutely.

"I'll see the worst of it," she said with pinched lips. She turned herself about and about before the glass, letting the cruel light gloat over her shoulders, letting the sickly shadows grow purple on her face. Then she put her elbows on the table and her chin into her hands, and so, for a motionless half-hour, studied the unrounded, uncolored, unlightened face that stared back at her; her eyes darkening at its eyes, her hair touching its hair, her breath dimming the outline of its repulsive mouth.

By and by she dropped her head into hands. The poor, mistaken face! She felt as if she would like to blot it out of the world, as her tears used to blot out the wrong sums upon her slate. It had been so happy! But he was sorry for it, and all that. Why did a good God make such faces?

She slipped upon her knees, bewildered.

"He *can't* mean any harm nohow," she said, speaking fast, and knelt there and said it over till she felt sure of it.

Then she thought of Del once more,—of her colors and sinuous springs, and little cries and chatter.

After a time she found that she was growing faint, and so stole down into the kitchen for some food. She stayed a minute to warm her feet. The fire was red and the clock was ticking. It seemed to her home-like and comfortable, and she seemed to herself very homeless and lonely; so she sat down on the floor, with her head in a chair, and cried as hard as she ought to have done four hours ago.

She climbed into bed about one o'clock, having decided, in a dull way, to give Dick up to-morrow.

But when to-morrow came he was up with a bright face, and built the kitchen fire for her, and brought in all the water, and helped her fry the potatoes, and whistled a little about the house, and worried at her paleness, and so she said nothing about it.

"I'll wait till night," she planned, making ready for the mill.

"O, I can't!" she cried at night. So other mornings came, and other nights.

I am quite aware that, according to all romantic precedents, this conduct was preposterous in Asenath. Floracita,[13] in the novel, never so far forgets the whole duty of a heroine as to struggle, waver, doubt, delay. It is proud and proper to free the young fellow; proudly and properly she frees him; "suffers in silence"—till she marries another man; and (having had a convenient opportunity to refuse the original lover) overwhelms the reflective reader with a sense of poetic justice and the eternal fitness of things.

But I am not writing a novel, and, as the biographer of this simple factory girl, am offered few advantages.

Asenath was no heroine, you see. Such heroic elements as were in her—none could tell exactly what they were, or whether there were any: she was one of those people in whom it is easy to be quite mistaken;—her life had not been one to develop. She might have a certain pride of her own, under given circumstances; but plants grown in a cellar will turn to the sun at any cost; how could she go back into her dark?

As for the other man to marry, he was out of the question. Then, none love with the tenacity of the unhappy; no life is so lavish of itself as the denied life: to him that hath not shall be given,—and Asenath loved this Richard Cross.[14]

It might be altogether the grand and suitable thing to say to him, "I will not be your wife." It might be that she would thus regain a strong shade of lost self-respect. It might be that she would make him happy, and give pleasure to Del. It might be that the two young people would be her "friends," and love her in a way.

But all this meant that Dick must go out of her life. Practically, she must make up her mind to build the fires, and pump the water, and mend the windows alone. In dreary fact, he would not listen when she sung; would not say, "You are tired, Sene"; would never kiss away an undried tear. There would be nobody to notice the crimson cape, nobody to make blue neckties for; none for whom to save the Bonnes de Jersey, or to take sweet, tired steps, or make dear, dreamy plans. To be sure, there was her father; but fathers do not count for much in a time like this on which Sene had fallen.

That Del Ivory was—Del Ivory, added intricacies to the question. It was a very unpoetic but undoubted fact that Asenath could in no way so insure Dick's unhappiness as to pave the way to his marriage with the woman whom he loved. There would be a few merry months, then slow worry and disappointment; pretty Del accepted at last, not as the crown of his young life, but as its silent burden and misery. Poor Dick! good Dick! Who deserved more wealth of wifely sacrifice? Asenath, thinking this, crimsoned with pain and shame. A streak of good common sense in the girl told her—though she half scorned herself for the conviction—that even a crippled woman who should bear all things and hope all things for his sake might blot out the memory of this rounded Del;[15] that, no matter what the motive with which he married her, he would end by loving his wife like other people.

She watched him sometimes in the evenings, as he turned his kind eyes after her over the library book which he was reading.

"I know I could make him happy! I *know* I could!" she muttered fiercely to herself.

November blew into December, December congealed into January, while she kept her silence. Dick, in his honorable heart, seeing that she suffered, wearied himself with plans to make her eyes shine; brought her two pails of water instead of one, never forgot the fire, helped her home from the mill. She saw him meet Del Ivory once upon Essex Street with a grave and silent bow; he never spoke with her now. He meant to pay the debt he owed her down to the uttermost farthing; that grew plain. Did she try to speak her wretched secret, he suffocated her with kindness, struck her dumb with tender words.

She used to analyze her life in those days, considering what it would be without him. To be up by half past five o'clock in the chill of all the winter mornings, to build the fire and cook the breakfast and sweep the floor, to hurry away, faint and weak, over the raw, slippery streets, to climb at half past six the endless stairs and stand at the endless loom, and hear the endless wheels go buzzing round, to sicken in the oily smells, and deafen at the remorseless noise, and weary of the rough girl swearing at the other end of the pass; to eat her cold dinner from a little cold tin pail out on the stairs in the three-quarters-of-an-hour recess; to come exhausted home at half past six at night, and get the supper, and brush up about the shoemaker's bench, and be too weak to eat; to sit with aching shoulders and make the button-holes of her best dress, or darn her father's stockings, till nine o'clock; to hear no bounding step or cheery whistle about the house; to creep into bed and lie there trying not to think, and wishing that so she might creep into her grave,—this not for one winter, but for all the winters,—how should *you* like it, you young girls, with whom time runs like a story?

The very fact that her employers dealt honorably by her; that she was fairly paid, and promptly, for her wearing toil; that the limit of endurance was consulted in the temperature of the room, and her need to rest in an occasional holiday,—perhaps, after all, in the mood she was in, did not make this factory life more easy. She would have found it rather a relief to have somebody to complain of,—wherein she was like the rest of us, I fancy.

But at last there came a day—it chanced to be the ninth of January— when Asenath went away alone at noon, and sat where Merrimack sung his songs to her.[16] She hid her face upon her knees, and listened and thought her own thoughts, till they and the slow torment of the winter seemed greater than she could bear. So, passing her hands confusedly over her forehead, she said at last aloud, "That's what God means, Asenath Martyn!" and went back to work with a purpose in her eyes.

She "asked out" a little earlier than usual, and went slowly home. Dick was there before her; he had been taking a half-holiday. He had made the tea and toasted the bread for a little surprise. He came up and said, "Why, Sene, your hands are cold!" and warmed them for her in his own.

After tea she asked him, would he walk out with her for a little while? and he in wonder went.

The streets were brightly lighted, and the moon was up. The ice cracked crisp under their feet. Sleighs, with two riders in each, shot merrily by. People were laughing in groups before the shop-windows. In the glare of a jeweler's counter somebody was buying a wedding-ring, and a girl with red cheeks was looking hard the other way.

"Let's get away," said Asenath,—"get away from here!"

They chose by tacit consent that favorite road of hers over the eastern bridge. Their steps had a hollow, lonely ring on the frosted wood; she was glad when the softness of the snow in the road received them. She looked back once at the water, wrinkled into thin ice on the edge for a foot or two, then open and black and still.

"What are you doing?" asked Dick. She said that she was wondering how cold it was, and Dick laughed at her.

They strolled on in silence for perhaps a mile of the desolate road.

"Well, this is social!" said Dick at length; "how much farther do you want to go? I believe you'd walk to Reading if nobody stopped you!"[17]

She was taking slow, regular steps like an automaton, and looking straight before her.

"How much farther? Oh!" She stopped and looked about her.

A wide young forest spread away at their feet, to the right and to the left. There was ice on the tiny oaks and miniature pines; it glittered sharply under the moon; the light upon the snow was blue; cold roads wound away through it, deserted; little piles of dead leaves shivered; a fine keen spray ran along the tops of the drifts; inky shadows lurked and dodged about the undergrowth; in the broad spaces the snow glared; the lighted mills, a zone of fire, blazed from east to west; the skies were bare, and the wind was up, and Merrimack in the distance chanted solemnly.

"Dick," said Asenath, "this is a dreadful place! Take me home."

But when he would have turned, she held him back with a sudden cry, and stood still.

"I meant to tell you—I meant to say—Dick! I was going to say—"

But she did not say it. She opened her lips to speak once and again, but no sound came from them.

"Sene! why, Sene, what ails you?"

He turned, and took her in his arms.

"Poor Sene!"

He kissed her, feeling sorry for her unknown trouble. He wondered why she sobbed. He kissed her again. She broke from him, and away with a great bound upon the snow.

"You make it so hard! You've no right to make it so hard! It ain't as if you loved me, Dick! I know I'm not like other girls! Go home and let me be!"

But Dick drew her arm through his, and led her gravely away. "I like you well enough, Asenath," he said, with that motherly pity in his eyes; "I've always liked you. So don't let us have any more of this."

So Asenath said nothing more.

The sleek black river beckoned to her across the snow as they went home. A thought came to her as she passed the bridge,—it is a curious study what wicked thoughts will come to good people!—she found herself considering the advisability of leaping the low brown parapet; and if it would not be like Dick to go over after her; if there would be a chance for them, even should he swim from the banks; how soon the icy current would paralyze him; how sweet it would be to chill to death there in his arms; how all this wavering and pain would be over; how Del would look when they dragged them out down below the machine-shop!

"Sene, are you cold?" asked puzzled Dick. She was warmly wrapped in her little squirrel furs; but he felt her quivering upon his arm, like one in an ague, all the way home.

About eleven o'clock that night her father waked from an exciting dream concerning the best method of blacking patent-leather; Sene stood beside his bed with her gray shawl thrown over her night-dress.

"Father, suppose some time there should be only you and me—"

"Well, well, Sene," said the old man sleepily,—"very well."

"I'd try to be a good girl! Could you love me enough to make up?"

He told her indistinctly that she always was a good girl; she never had a whipping from the day her mother died. She turned away impatiently; then cried out and fell upon her knees.

"Father, father! I'm in a great trouble. I have n't got any mother, any friend, anybody. Nobody helps me! Nobody knows. I've been thinking such things—O, such wicked things—up in my room! Then I got afraid of myself. You're good. You love me. I want you to put your hand on my head and say, 'God bless you, child, and show you how.'"

Bewildered, he put his hand upon her unbound hair, and said: "God bless you, child, and show you how!"

Asenath looked at the old withered hand a moment, as it lay beside her on the bed, kissed it, and went away.

There was a scarlet sunrise the next morning. A pale pink flush stole through a hole in the curtain, and fell across Asenath's sleeping face, and lay there like a crown. It woke her, and she threw on her dress, and sat down for a while on the window-sill, to watch the coming-on of the day.

The silent city steeped and bathed itself in rose-tints; the river ran red, and the snow crimsoned on the distant New Hampshire hills; Pemberton, mute and cold, frowned across the disk of the climbing sun, and dripped, as she had seen it drip before, with blood.

The day broke softly, the snow melted, the wind blew warm from the river. The factory-bell chimed cheerily, and a few sleepers, in safe, luxurious beds, were wakened by hearing the girls sing on their way to work.

Asenath came down with a quiet face. In her communing with the sunrise helpful things had been spoken to her. Somehow, she knew not how, the peace of the day was creeping into her heart. For some reason, she knew not why, the torment and unrest of the night were gone. There was a future to be settled, but she would not trouble herself about that just now. There was breakfast to get; and the sun shone, and a snow-bird was chirping outside of the door. She noticed how the tea-kettle hummed, and how well the new curtain, with the castle and waterfall on it, fitted the window. She thought that she would scour the closet at night, and surprise her father by finishing those list slippers.[18] She kissed him when she had tied on the red hood, and said good-by to Dick, and told them just where to find the squash-pie for dinner.

When she had closed the twisted gate, and taken a step or two upon the snow, she came thoughtfully back. Her father was on his bench, mending one of Meg Match's shoes. She pushed it gently out of his hands, sat down upon his lap, and stroked the shaggy hair away from his forehead.

"Father!"

"Well, what now, Sene?—what now?"

"Sometimes I believe I've forgotten you a bit, you know. I think we 're going to be happier after this. That's all."

She went out singing, and he heard the gate shut again with a click.

Sene was a little dizzy that morning,—the constant palpitation of the floors always made her dizzy after a wakeful night,—and so her colored cotton threads danced out of place, and troubled her.

Del Ivory, working beside her, said, "How the mill shakes! What's going on?"

"It's the new machinery they 're h'isting in," observed the overseer, carelessly. "Great improvement, but heavy, very heavy; they calc'late on getting it all into place to-day; you 'd better be tending to your frame, Miss Ivory."

As the day wore on, the quiet of Asenath's morning deepened. Round and round with the pulleys over her head she wound her thoughts of Dick. In and out with her black and dun-colored threads she spun her future. Pretty Del, just behind her, was twisting a pattern like a rainbow. She noticed this, and smiled.

"Never mind!" she thought, "I guess God knows."

Was He ready "to bless her, and show her how"? She wondered. If, indeed, it were best that she should never be Dick's wife, it seemed to her that He would help her about it. She had been a coward last night; her blood leaped in her veins with shame at the memory of it. Did He understand? Did He not know how she loved Dick, and how hard it was to lose him?

However that might be, she began to feel at rest about herself. A curious apathy about means and ways and decisions took possession of her. A bounding sense that a way of escape was provided from all her troubles, such as she had when her mother died, came upon her.

Years before, an unknown workman in South Boston, casting an iron pillar upon its core, had suffered it to "float" a little, a very little more, till the thin, unequal side cooled to the measure of an eighth of an inch.[19] That man had provided Asenath's way of escape.

She went out at noon with her luncheon, and found a place upon the stairs, away from the rest, and sat there awhile, with her eyes upon the river, thinking. She could not help wondering a little, after all, why God need to have made her so unlike the rest of his fair handiwork. Del came bounding by, and nodded at her carelessly. Two young Irish girls, sisters,—the beauties of the mill,—magnificently colored creatures,—were singing a little love-song together, while they tied on their hats to go home.

"There *are* such pretty things in the world!" thought poor Sene.

Did anybody speak to her after the girls were gone? Into her heart these words fell suddenly, "*He* hath no form nor comeliness. *His* visage was so marred more than any man."[20]

They clung to her fancy all the afternoon. She liked the sound of them. She wove them in with her black and dun colored threads.

The wind began at last to blow chilly up the staircases, and in at the cracks; the melted drifts out under the walls to harden; the sun dipped above the dam; the mill dimmed slowly; shadows crept down between the frames.

"It's time for lights," said Meg Match, and swore a little at her spools.

Sene, in the pauses of her thinking, heard snatches of the girls' talk.

"Going to ask out to-morrow, Meg?"

"Guess so, yes; me and Bob Smith we thought we'd go to Boston, and come up in the theatre train."

"Del Ivory, I want the pattern of your zouave."[21]

"Did I go to church? No, you don't catch me! If I slave all the week, I'll do what I please on Sunday."

"Hush-sh! There's the boss looking over here!"

"Kathleen Donnavon, be still with your ghost-stories. There's one thing in the world I never will hear about, and that's dead people."

"Del," said Sene, "I think to-morrow—"

She stopped. Something strange had happened to her frame; it jarred, buzzed, snapped; the threads untwisted and flew out of place.

"Curious!" she said, and looked up.

Looked up to see her overseer turn wildly, clap his hands to his head, and fall; to hear a shriek from Del that froze her blood; to see the solid ceiling gape above her; to see the walls and windows stagger; to see iron pillars reel, and vast machinery throw up its helpless, giant arms, and a tangle of human faces blanch and writhe!

She sprang as the floor sunk. As pillar after pillar gave way, she bounded up an inclined plane, with the gulf yawning after her. It gained upon her, leaped at her, caught her; beyond were the stairs and an open door; she threw out her arms, and struggled on with hands and knees, tripped in the gearing, and saw, as she fell, a square, oaken beam above her yield and crash; it was of a fresh red color; she dimly wondered why,—as she felt her hands slip, her knees slide, support, time, place, and reason, go utterly out.

"At ten minutes before five, on Tuesday, the tenth of January, the Pemberton Mill, all hands being at the time on duty, fell to the ground."

So the record flashed over the telegraph wires, sprang into large type in the newspapers, passed from lip to lip, a nine days' wonder, gave place to the successful candidate, and the muttering South, and was forgotten.[22]

Who shall say what it was to the seven hundred and fifty souls who were buried in the ruins? What to the eighty-eight who died that death of exquisite agony? What to the wrecks of men and women who endure until this day a life that is worse than death? What to that architect and engineer who, when the fatal pillars were first delivered to them for inspection, had found one broken under their eyes, yet accepted the contract, and built with them a mill whose thin walls and wide, unsupported stretches might have tottered over massive columns and on flawless ore?[23]

One that we love may go upon battle-ground, and we are ready for the worst: we have said our good-bys; our hearts wait and pray: it is his life, not his death, which is the surprise. But that he should go out to his safe, daily, commonplace occupations, unnoticed and uncaressed,—scolded a little, perhaps, because he leaves the door open, and tells us how cross we are this morning; and they bring him up the steps by and by, a mangled mass of death and horror,—that is hard.

Old Martyn, working at Meg Match's shoes,—she was never to wear those shoes, poor Meg!—heard, at ten minutes before five, what he thought to be the rumble of an earthquake under his very feet, and stood with bated breath, waiting for the crash. As nothing further appeared to happen, he took his stick and limped out into the street.

A vast crowd surged through it from end to end. Women with white lips were counting the mills,—Pacific, Atlantic, Washington,—Pemberton? Where was Pemberton?

Where Pemberton had winked its many eyes last night, and hummed with its iron lips this noon, a cloud of dust, black, silent, horrible, puffed a hundred feet into the air.

Asenath opened her eyes after a time. Beautiful green and purple lights had been dancing about her, but she had had no thoughts. It occurred to her now that she must have been struck upon the head. The church-clocks were striking eight. A bonfire which had been built at a distance, to light the citizens in the work of rescue, cast a little gleam in through the *débris* across her two hands, which lay clasped together at her side. One of her fingers, she saw, was gone; it was the finger which held Dick's little engagement ring. The red beam lay across her forehead, and drops dripped from it upon her eyes. Her feet, still tangled in the gearing which had tripped her, were buried beneath a pile of bricks.

A broad piece of flooring, that had fallen slantwise, roofed her in, and saved her from the mass of iron-work overhead, which would have crushed the breath out of Titans.[24] Fragments of looms, shafts, and pillars were in heaps about. Some one whom she could not see was dying just behind her. A little girl who worked in her room—a mere child—was crying, between her groans, for her mother. Del Ivory sat in a little open space, cushioned about with reels of cotton; she had a shallow gash upon her cheek; she was wringing her hands. They were at work from the outside, sawing entrances through the labyrinth of planks. A dead woman lay close by, and Sene saw them draw her out. It was Meg Match. One of the pretty Irish girls was crushed quite out of sight; only one hand was free; she moved it feebly. They could hear her calling for Jimmy Mahoney, Jimmy Mahoney! and would they be sure and give him back the handkerchief? Poor Jimmy Mahoney! By and by she called no more; and in a little while the hand was still. On the other side of the slanted flooring some one prayed aloud. She had a little baby at home. She was asking God to take care of it for her. "For Christ's sake," she said. Sene listened long for the Amen, but it was never spoken. Beyond, they dug a man out from under a dead body, unhurt. He crawled to his feet, and broke into furious blasphemies.

As consciousness came fully, agony grew. Sene shut her lips and folded her bleeding hands together, and uttered no cry. Del did screaming enough for two, she thought. She pondered things calmly as the night deepened, and the words that the workers outside were saying came brokenly to her. Her hurt, she knew, was not unto death; but it must be cared for before very long; how far could she support this slow bleeding away? And what were the chances that they could hew their way to her without crushing her?

She thought of her father, of Dick; of the bright little kitchen and supper-table set for three; of the song that she had sung in the flush of the morning. Life—even her life—grew sweet, now that it was slipping from her.

Del cried presently, that they were cutting them out. The glare of the bonfires struck through an opening; saws and axes flashed; voices grew distinct.

"They never can get at me," said Sene. "I must be able to crawl. If you could get some of those bricks off of my feet, Del!"

Del took off two or three in a frightened way; then, seeing the blood on them, sat down and cried.

A Scotch girl, with one arm shattered, crept up and removed the pile, then fainted.

The opening broadened, brightened; the sweet night-wind blew in; the safe night-sky shone through. Sene's heart leaped within her. Out in the wind and under the sky she should stand again, after all! Back in the little kitchen, where the sun shone, and she could sing a song, there would yet be a place for her. She worked her head from under the beam, and raised herself upon her elbow.

At that moment she heard a cry:

"Fire! *fire!* GOD ALMIGHTY HELP THEM,—THE RUINS ARE ON FIRE!"

A man working over the *débris* from the outside had taken the notion— it being rather dark just there—to carry a lantern with him.

"For God's sake," a voice cried from the crowd, "don't stay there with that light!"

But before the words had died upon the air, it was the dreadful fate of the man with the lantern to let it fall,—and it broke upon the ruined mass.

That was at nine o'clock. What there was to see from then till morning could never be told or forgotten.

A network twenty feet high, of rods and girders, of beams, pillars, stairways, gearing, roofing, ceiling, walling; wrecks of looms, shafts, twisters, pulleys, bobbins, mules, locked and interwoven; wrecks of human creatures wedged in; a face that you know turned up at you from some pit which twenty-four hours' hewing could not open; a voice that you know crying after you from God knows where; a mass of long, fair hair visible here, a foot there, three fingers of a hand over there; the snow bright-red under foot; charred limbs and headless trunks tossed about; strong men carrying covered things by you, at sight of which other strong men have fainted; the little yellow jet that flared up, and died in smoke, and flared again, leaped out, licked the cotton-bales, tasted the oiled machinery, crunched the netted wood, danced on the heaped-up stone, threw its cruel arms high into the night, roared for joy at helpless firemen, and swallowed wreck, death, and life together out of your sight,—the lurid thing stands alone in the gallery of tragedy.

"Del," said Sene, presently, "I smell the smoke." And in a little while, "How red it is growing away over there at the left!"

To lie here and watch the hideous redness crawling after her, springing at her!—it had seemed greater than reason could bear, at first.

Now it did not trouble her. She grew a little faint, and her thoughts wandered. She put her head down upon her arm, and shut her eyes. Dreamily she heard them saying a dreadful thing outside, about one of the overseers; at the alarm of fire he had cut his throat, and before the flames touched him he was taken out. Dreamily she heard Del cry that the shaft behind the heap of reels was growing hot. Dreamily she saw a tiny puff of smoke struggle through the cracks of a broken fly-frame.

They were working to save her, with rigid, stern faces. A plank snapped, a rod yielded; they drew out the Scotch girl; her hair was singed; then a man with blood upon his face and wrists held down his arms.

"There's time for one more! God save the rest of ye,—I can't!"

Del sprang; then stopped,—even Del,—stopped ashamed, and looked back at the cripple.

Asenath at this sat up erect. The latent heroism in her awoke. All her thoughts grew clear and bright. The tangled skein of her perplexed and troubled winter unwound suddenly. This, then, was the way. It was better so. God had provided himself a lamb for the burnt-offering.[25]

So she said, "Go, Del, and tell him I sent you with my dear love, and that it's all right."

And Del at the first word went.

Sene sat and watched them draw her out; it was a slow process; the loose sleeve of her factory sack was scorched.

Somebody at work outside turned suddenly and caught her. It was Dick. The love which he had fought so long broke free of barrier in that hour. He kissed her pink arm where the burnt sleeve fell off. He uttered a cry at the blood upon her face. She turned faint with the sense of safety; and, with a face as white as her own, he bore her away in his arms to the hospital, over the crimson snow.

Asenath looked out through the glare and smoke with parched lips. For a scratch upon the girl's smooth cheek, he had quite forgotten her. They had left her, tombed alive here in this furnace, and gone their happy way. Yet it gave her a curious sense of relief and triumph. If this were all that she could be to him, the thing which she had done was right, quite right. God must have known. She turned away, and shut her eyes again.

When she opened them, neither Dick, nor Del, nor crimsoned snow, nor sky, were there; only the smoke writhing up a pillar of blood-red flame.

The child who had called for her mother began to sob out that she was afraid to die alone.

"Come here, Molly," said Sene. "Can you crawl around?"

Molly crawled around.

"Put your head in my lap, and your arms about my waist, and I will put my hands in yours,—so. There! I guess that 's better."

But they had not given them up yet. In the still unburnt rubbish at the right, some one had wrenched an opening within a foot of Sene's face. They clawed at the solid iron pintles like savage things.[26] A fireman fainted in the glow.

"Give it up!" cried the crowd from behind. "It can't be done! Fall back!"—then hushed, awe-struck.

An old man was crawling along upon his hands and knees over the heated bricks. He was a very old man. His gray hair blew about in the wind.

"I want my little gal!" he said. "Can't anybody tell me where to find my little gal?"

A rough-looking young fellow pointed in perfect silence through the smoke.

"I 'll have her out yet. I 'm an old man, but I can help. She 's my little gal, ye see. Hand me that there dipper of water; it 'll keep her from choking, may be. Now! Keep cheery, Sene! Your old father 'll get ye out. Keep up good heart, child! That 's it!"

"It 's no use, father. Don't feel bad, father. I don't mind it very much."

30

He hacked at the timber; he tried to laugh; he bewildered himself with cheerful words.

"No more ye need n't, Senath, for it 'll be over in a minute. Don't be downcast yet! We'll have ye safe at home before ye know it. Drink a little more water,—do now! They 'll get at ye now, sure!"

But out above the crackle and the roar a woman's voice rang like a bell:—

"We 're going home, to die no more."[27]

A child's notes quavered in the chorus. From sealed and unseen graves, white young lips swelled the glad refrain,—

"We 're going, going home."

The crawling smoke turned yellow, turned red. Voice after voice broke and hushed utterly. One only sang on like silver. It flung defiance down at death. It chimed into the lurid sky without a tremor. For one stood beside her in the furnace, and his form was like unto the form of the Son of God.[28] Their eyes met. Why should not Asenath sing?

"Senath!" cried the old man out upon the burning bricks; he was scorched now, from his gray hair to his patched boots.

The answer came triumphantly,—

"To die no more, no more, no more!"

"Sene! little Sene!"
But some one pulled him back.[29]

First appeared in *Atlantic Monthly* (March 1868): 345–62. Collected in *Men, Women, and Ghosts* (Boston: Fields, Osgood, 1869). In recent years the story has attracted some critical attention and has been reprinted in Mari Jo Buhle and Florence Howe, eds., *The Silent Partner and "The Tenth of January"* (New York: Feminist Press, 1983); Karen L. Kilcup, ed., *Nineteenth-century American Women Writers: An Anthology* (Cambridge, U.K.: Blackwell, 1997); and Elaine Showalter, ed., *The Vintage Book of American Women Writers* (New York: Vintage, 2011).

Dr. Trotty

"I don't think I like the looks of it," said Trotty, very distinctly.

He meant the baby. It was Aunt Matthews's baby. Aunt Matthews, and Cousin Ginevra, and the baby's nurse, and the baby's trunks, and the baby's carriage, and the baby's crib, *and* the baby, were making a visit at Trotty's house.

They had just gone into the spare chamber to take off their things, and Trotty had hopped up stairs on one foot after them, with an interested air. It struck him that people were making a great fuss over that pink bundle in that freckled woman's lap,—kissing it, and squeezing it, and feeling of its fingers, and chucking it under the chin; saying how it had grown! and how much it looked like papa! and what a little dear it was! and *see* it laughing at you! He wondered whether, if he were a pink bundle in a freckled woman's lap, they would pay so much attention to him.

"I'm four years old, and I'm going to be five, bime by," he said, feeling that he had been neglected long enough. But nobody listened.

"I'm four years old. I've got a tip-cart, and some rubber boots," he continued, severely. "I have free griddle-cakes for breakfast, and I eat my supper down stairs."

But nobody heard that, either. However painful it may be to inflict a gentle reproof upon one's inferiors, it is undoubtedly sometimes a necessity. Trotty, with quiet dignity, crept up behind Aunt Matthews, and jerked her by the waterfall.[1]

"Oh!" said everybody, talking at once, "do let Trotty see the baby. I don't believe he ever saw a baby near enough to touch it in his life."

So they made room for Trotty beside the freckled woman, and he examined the pink bundle with attention. It was a very pink bundle. Its flannel cloak was pink; its crocheted sack was pink; its little knit shoes were pink; its ribbons were pink; its hands were pink; and its face was very pink. It had two great black eyes, a funny little flat nose, no hair to speak of, and no teeth, whether you spoke of them or not. It stared at Trotty for a minute doubtfully; then scowled a little, scowled a little more, scowled very much, wrinkled, writhed, twisted, grew red, grew purple, opened its mouth wide, and screamed at him, then doubled its fists close, and punched him in the face.

"You frighten her, the blessed little dear!" said Aunt Matthews.

"I don't wonder," said Lill;[2] "you 've been to the sirup-pitcher, and the quince-jar, and the sugar-bowl, and the apple-barrel, since you washed your face last, to say nothing of the red crayon mark on your neck, and the black one on your nose. You 've been at my paint-box, too, I know from the gamboge streak on your forehead,[3] and the pea-green on that front curl."

"No," repeated Trotty, with decision, as he was marched off to the washbowl, "I don't like the looks of it, and if God can't find a better-looking baby than that for me, when I 'm a man, he need n't throw me down any!"

But by and by the baby had had a nap, and felt better, and Trotty had been washed, and looked better. So they cultivated each other's acquaintance a little further. He sat on a cricket, and looked at the baby, and the baby sat on the floor, and looked at him.

"She makes faces at me," he said, after some thought. "She puts her shoes in her mouth. She eats up all her fingers. I guess they made her of injun-rubber; I pinched her a little to see. She squealed. But then she 'll just fit into the tip-cart, and when she cries, why don't they fill her mouth all up with sawdust? It 'll go in just as easy! You le' me get some and try."

In the course of a day or two they were the best of friends. He did take her to ride in the tip-cart, and he did fill her mouth with sawdust, and it did go in "just as easy," though it was another matter to get it out. Nobody has ever dared to inquire how fully he experimented on that baby. It is known that he managed to share all his raw apples and hot cookies with her at luncheon-time; that she cried two nights with colic, in consequence of his feeding her with pickled grapes; that he tied her feet together with a tippet and made a little face with pen and ink upon every one of her ten fingernails;[4] that when she was undressed at night she rattled and rolled with cold pennies and marbles, that he had dropped down her neck; and that once, when the nurse was looking the other way, he contrived to lift her into the bath-tub, and turn the faucet on her.

But still no serious harm had happened to the child. Trotty had promised never to give her pickles again; he was very gentle, and did not tease her, or make her cry, so the grown people, with a little watching, let them play together when they would, and so that Saturday afternoon came when they took the drive to Pomp's Pond.[5]

They all went,—Aunt Matthews, and Ginevra, and Lill, and Lill's mother, and Max. Grandmother was making calls. Trotty delicately hinted that he would like to go to ride too; but there was no room for Trotty. His mother gave him a kiss, and Max gave him a penny, (as if kisses and pennies could make up, O you stupid grown-up men and women! for a ride in mamma's lap, on the front seat, away five miles through the sweet pine woods, and by the dimpled water!) and they drove merrily off and left him.

Trotty stood still for a minute, and looked after them with a crimson flush all over his little face. But he did not cry,—no, little boys, he did not cry one bit, and I think that was better than half a dozen rides. *You* don't think so? No, I know it; but it is true for all that.

Trotty turned round and went slowly up stairs. Biddy was in the kitchen, and the baby and Kathleen—that was the freckled woman's pleasant name, and she was a pleasant-looking freckled woman, too—were in the nursery. Trotty came in, dragging his toes on the carpet in a melancholy manner, sat down in the corner on top of Jerusalem,[6] and, for about five minutes, refused to be comforted. Then the baby crept up and pulled his longest curl,—it was precisely in the middle behind, and she could just reach it,—and pulled his fingers, and pulled his shoe-strings, and gurgled at him, and giggled at him, and crowed at him, and coughed at him,—and in five minutes more he was shoving her under the bed, in a rather tight-fitting mending-basket, as vigorously and as happily as if he had never heard of Pomp's Pond in his life.

By and by the grocer's boy drove into the back yard. Kathleen was sitting by the window, looking out.

"Trotty," said she, laying down her work, "I've got a dress of me own that wants ironin' for the Sunday. You be a good boy, now, and don't let nothing happen to the baby, till I come back."

So Kathleen took a pretty light calico of hers from the closet, threw it jauntily over one arm, tied a blue ribbon around her waterfall, and went down stairs singing.

Presently Trotty was tired of shoving the baby under the bed.

"O, I tell you," said he, "le''s play Dr. Trotty. You stay in mending-basket till I get ready, and ven you be a ninfidel, and I'll come to see you."

The baby, not being very well able to offer a contrary opinion, stayed in the mending-basket, and Trotty went away to make a doctor of himself. Up garret in the first place. He knew something about a long dressing-gown, folded away carefully in the blue trunk; he had watched his mother through the crack of the door, when she put the camphor in it at house-cleaning time.

It had been his father's, that soft merino dressing-gown, but Trotty saw in that no reason why he should not play Dr. Trotty in it. Of course his pretty dead papa would let him! In fact, Trotty had a vague idea that he must have died before it was worn out on purpose that his little boy might have it that bright spring afternoon. So he pulled it out of the blue trunk (catching it on the lock, and tearing it in three separate and very large places), and crept into it. It dragged a half-yard on the dusty floor behind, and it took him the rest of the afternoon to find his arms; but he managed to make his way down stairs, a step at a time, and into the medicine-closet.

Ugh! that medicine-closet! What ghosts of croup, and measles, and green apples, and mince-pie, and "'lixy Pro," stalked through its dark shelves![7] Trotty looked about with great eyes. He thought what fun it would be to take all those bottles away in a bushel-basket that he knew of, and jump up and down on them with his leather boots. He laid the brilliant idea aside, however, for future use, and climbed up on the drawers, to take down the homeopathic box that stood on the lower shelf.[8] It was a neat little well-worn homeopathic box, with a great many bits of bottles in it. Most of these were empty, but two of them held a white powder, and one of them some dark yellow liquid. Trotty took the box to the great silver pitcher on the dining-room sideboard, and filled the empty bottles with water, and corked them tightly.

He put on Max's rubber boots after that; they came nearly up to his neck. Then he put on Max's tall hat, and that came just about to the tops of the boots. Then he put his box under his arm, and started for the nursery. He stopped a moment, and looked at that box. He wondered, with some interest precisely what his mother was going to say when she came home.

He forgot all about that, though, when he came to go up the stairs. Such a time as he had climbing those stairs! First he trod on the dressing-gown with one foot, and fell flat, and bumped his nose; then he trod on it with the other foot, and fell down and bumped his nose again; then he trod on it with both feet, and tripped up, and sat down hard. Then Max's hat slipped down to his neck,—O, how dark it was inside that hat!—and he pushed it up, and it slipped down again, and he jerked it up, and it jerked down; then the long sleeves of the dressing-gown folded up on the outside so that he lost his fingers altogether, and while he was trying to find them, down went the hat again; then he dropped the medicine-box, and tipped out all the bottles, and when he stooped to pick them up, down came the hat; then he tried to climb up on "all fours," and his rubber boots fell off behind and flopped from stair to stair. He sat down in despair to watch them hopping down, when darkness fell, and there was that hat.

However, he managed, with a patience worthy of a better cause, to gain the nursery door at last. The baby, in her mending-basket, lay with her face all puckered into a red knot, crying.

"Good afternoon, mum," said Dr. Trotty. "I'm sorry to find you so sick, mum. You should say, 'How do you do, Dr. Trotty?' and let me see your tongue."

This, by the way, was a most unnecessary remark, for one could see, not only the baby's tongue, but three quarters of the way down the baby's screaming throat. Trotty lifted her out of the basket, and gravely put one of Lill's dolls' pewter spoons into her mouth. He had n't the shadow of an idea what for, you know; but he had seen Dr. Bryonia use a spoon when Max had the diphtheria, and he supposed that it was the proper thing to do. The baby did n't like the taste of the spoon, and sputtered and wriggled and screamed harder than ever.

"Your tongue is quite serious, mum," said Dr. Trotty,—"quite serious. And your pulps,"—he pinched her right elbow several times,— "your pulps, mum, is *horrid!* You 'll have to be a good boy, and take this medicine,—I mean girl,—and not kick the tumbler over, like I did the day after I got at the sardine-box,—and so you 'll get well, you see, and have some candy."

He filled the pewter spoon from the bottles of water, and gave the baby a dose. This was very easy, you see, because her mouth was open so wide, that all he had to do was to put the spoon in and tip it over; she was crying so hard, that she must either swallow it, or choke. Trotty found the process quite entertaining.

By and by he did not care about feeding her with a spoon any more; she had stopped crying, and the fun was gone.

"I s'pose you 'll have to take a whole bottleful this time," he said hopefully. "You might die, if you did n't, 'n' when I tip it bottom up'ards, it comes out just as cunning!—you see, now!"

Just as he put his hand into the box to take out one of the bottles of water, that hat went down to his shoulders. In the dark he emptied the bottle down the baby's throat. In the dark he heard her gasp and cry out. When he pushed up the hat—O the poor baby! the poor baby!—it was not the bottle of water that he had given her, but the bottle—nearly empty now—of yellow medicine. Across the yellow bottle a yellow label was pasted, and on it in distinct, black letters was a word which Trotty could not read,—Aconite.[9]

Kathleen was just telling the grocer's boy what a saucy fellow he was, when the kitchen door opened slowly, and a very white little face peeped in, under a great hat.

"You 'd better come up to the baby," it said faintly; "she 's squealin' and kickin' all in a heap on the floor. We were playing Dr. Trotty, and—"

"O my good gracious!" Kathleen ran up stairs, three steps at a time, and her face was as white as the baby's little doctor's when she came to where the baby lay.

The carryall drove into the yard just as the grocer's boy was driving out. Kathleen's sobs came down through the open window, and the baby's gasping scream. Aunt Matthews was up stairs in less time than it takes to say so. Kathleen was wringing her helpless hands. Trotty, extinguished by his hat, sat behind the bed, and the baby, in convulsions, was writhing on the floor. The cry ran through the house: "Poisoned! Poisoned! Oh! the baby's poisoned!"

Then there was the sound of Max galloping for Dr. Bryonia,—of Dr. Bryonia galloping back,—of quick orders, and sobs, and cries, and steps running to and fro. By and by, silence, and Dr. Bryonia coming slowly down stairs, and driving slowly away.

They hunted all over the house for poor little Dr. Trotty. His mother found at last, in a corner, a queer little figure, all hat and boots, sitting with its face to the wall.

"Trotty," said she.

He made no answer.

"Trotty, the baby—"

Trotty tumbled into her lap, hat, and boots, and all, and buried his face under her arm.

"O, I did n't mean to kill her, I did n't *mean* to kill her! O mamma, mamma, mamma! I was only going to be Dr. Trotty, and ve homeopoptic box got tipped about, and ve old hat fell down, and ven sumfin was 'e matter to her all to once, and—"

"Why, Trotty, hush! the baby is n't dead. There, don't cry so! Dr. Bryonia has given her some medicine, and he thinks God won't let her die now. Come! put both your hands in mother's, and we'll kneel right down here and thank Him."

Originally appeared in *Our Young Folk: An Illustrated Magazine for Boys and Girls*, May 1869, 5. The story was also published in *The Trotty Book* (Boston: Fields, Osgood, 1869), 26–36, and *That Dreadful Boy Trotty: What He Did and What He Said* (London: Ward, Lock, 1877), 29–40. Phelps wrote six stories about Trotty's various adventures; this is the third in the series. Phelps's brother, Edward Johnson Phelps, served as her inspiration for Trotty.

A Woman's Pulpit

I fell to regretting to-day, for the first time in my life, that I am an old maid; for this reason: I have a very serious, long, religious story to tell, and a brisk matrimonial quarrel would have been such a vivacious, succinct, and secular means of introducing it.

But when I said, one day last winter, "I want some change," it was only Mädchen who suggested, "Wait for specie payment."[1]

And when I said, for I felt sentimental, and it was Sunday too, "I will offer myself as a missionary in Boston," I received no more discouraging reply than, "I think I see you! You'd walk in and ask if anything could be done for their souls to-day? And if they said No, you'd turn around and come out!"

And when I urged, "The country heathen requires less courage; I will offer myself in New Vealshire,"[2] I was met by no louder lion than the insinuation, "Perhaps I meant to turn Universalist, then?"[3]

"Mädchen!" said I, "you know better!"

"Yes," said Mädchen.

"And you know I could preach as well as anybody!"

"Yes," said Mädchen.

"Well!" said I.

"Well!" said Mädchen.

So that was all that was said about it. For Mädchen is a woman and minds her own business.

It should be borne in mind, that I am a woman "myself, Mr. Copperfull," and that the following correspondence, now for the first time given to the public, was accordingly finished and filed, before Mädchen ever saw or thought of it.[4]

This statement is not at all to the point of my purpose, further than that it may have, as I suppose, some near or remote bearings upon the business abilities—by which, as nearly as I can make out, is meant the power of holding one's tongue—of the coming woman, and that I am under stress of oath never to allow an opportunity to escape me, of strewing my garments in the way of her distant, royal feet.

"To be sparing," as has been said, "of prefatory, that is to say, of condemnatory remarking," I append at once an accurate vellum copy of the valuable correspondence in question.[5]

HERCULES, *February 28, 18–.*

SECRETARY OF THE NEW VEALSHIRE HOME MISSIONARY SOCIETY:

REVEREND AND DEAR SIR,—I am desirous of occupying one of your vacant posts of ministerial service: place and time entirely at your disposal. I am not a college graduate, nor have I yet applied for license to preach. I am, however, I believe, the possessor of a fair education, and of some slight experience in usefulness of a kind akin to that which I seek under your auspices, as well as of an interest in the neglected portions of New England, which *ought* to warrant me success in an attempt to serve their religious welfare.

For confirmation of these statements I will refer you, if you like, to the Rev. Dr. Dagon of Dagonsville, and to Professor Tacitus of Sparta.[6]

An answer at your earliest convenience, informing me if you are disposed to accept my services, and giving me details of terms and times, will oblige,

Yours respectfully,

J. W. BANGS.

HARMONY, N. V., *March 5, 18–.*

J. W. BANGS, ESQ.:

MY DEAR SIR,—Your lack of collegiate education is an objection to your filling one of our stations, but not an insurmountable one. I like your letter, and am inclined to think favorably of the question of accepting your services. I should probably send you among the Gray

Hills, and in March. We pay six dollars a week and "found."[7] Will this be satisfactory? Let me hear from you again.

> Truly yours,
> Z. Z. ZANGROW,
> Sect. N. V. H. M. S.

P. S. I have been too busy as yet to pursue your recommendations, but have no doubt that they are satisfactory.

> HERCULES, *March 9, 18–.*

REV. DR. ZANGROW:

DEAR SIR,—Yours of the 5th is at hand. Terms are satisfactory. I neglected to mention in my last that I am a woman.

> Yours truly,
> JERUSHA W. BANGS.

> HARMONY, *N.V., March 9, 18–.*

JERUSHA W. BANGS

DEAR MADAM,—You have played me an admirable joke. Regret that I have no time to return it.

> Yours very sincerely,
> Z. Z. ZANGROW, *Sect.*

> HERCULES, *March 11th.*

DEAR SIR,—I was never more in earnest in my life.

> Yours,
> J. W. BANGS.

> HARMONY, *March 14th.*

DEAR MADAM,—I am sorry to hear it.

> Yours,
> Z. Z. ZANGROW.

HERCULES, *March 15, 18–.*

REV. DR. ZANGROW:

MY DEAR SIR,—After begging your pardon for encroaching again upon your time and patience, permit me to inquire if you are not conscious of some slight inconsistency in your recent correspondence with me? By your own showing, I am individually and concretely qualified for the business in question; I am generally and abstractly beyond its serious recognition. As an educated American Christian, I am capable, by the word that goeth forth out of my mouth, of ministering to the Vealshire Mountain soul.[8] As an educated American Christian woman, I am remanded by the piano and the crochet-needle to the Hercules parlor soul.

You will—or you would, if it fell to your lot—send me under the feminine truce flag of "teacher" into Virginia, to speak on Sabbath mornings to a promiscuous audience of a thousand negroes: you forbid me to manage a score of mountaineers. Mr. Spurgeon's famous lady parishioner may preach to a "Sabbath-school class" of seven hundred men:[9] you would deny her the scanty hearing of your mission pulpits.

My dear sir, to crack a hard argument, you have, in the words of Sir William the logical, "mistaken the associations of thought for the connections of existence."[10] If you will appoint me a brief meeting at your own convenience in your own office in Harmony, I shall not only be very much in debt to your courtesy, but I shall convince you that you ought to send me into New Vealshire. Meantime

I am sincerely yours,

J. W. BANGS.

HARMONY, *March 18, 18–.*

MY DEAR MISS BANGS,—You are probably aware that, while it is not uncommon in the Universalist pulpit to find the female preacher, she is a specimen of humanity quite foreign to Orthodox ecclesiastical society.

I will confess to you, however (since you are determined to have your own way), that I have expressed in our hurried correspondence rather a denominational and professional than an individual opinion.

I can give you fifteen minutes on Tuesday next at twelve o'clock in my office, No. 41 Columbia Street.

It will at least give me the pleasure to make your personal acquaintance, whether I am able or not to gratify your enthusiastic and somewhat eccentric request. I am, my dear madam, cordially yours,

Z. Z. ZANGROW, Sect.

I went, I saw, I conquered. I stayed fifteen minutes, just. I talked twelve of them. The secretary sat and drummed meditatively upon the table for the other three. He was a thin man in a white cravat. Two or three other thin men in white cravats came in as I was about to leave. The secretary whispered to them; they whispered to the secretary: they and the secretary looked at me. Somebody shook his head: somebody else shook his head. The secretary, drumming, smiled. Drumming and smiling, he bowed me out, merely remarking that I should hear from him in the course of a few days.

I have since acquired a vague suspicion, which did not dawn at the time upon my broadest imagination, that the secretary sent me into New Vealshire as a private, metaphysical speculation upon the woman question, and that the New Vealshire Home Missionary Society would sooner have sent me to heaven.

However that may be, I received from the secretary the following:—

HARMONY, N. V., March 23, 18–.

DEAR MISS BANGS,—I propose to send you as soon as possible to the town of Storm, New Vealshire, to occupy on trial, for a few weeks, a small church long unministered to, nearly extinct. You will be met at the station by a person of the name of Dobbins, with whom I shall make all necessary arrangements for your board and introduction.

When can you go?

Yours, etc., Z. Z. ZANGROW, Sect.

HERCULES, *March 24, 18–.*

MY DEAR DR. ZANGROW,—I can go to-morrow.
Yours, etc.,   Z. Z. ZANGROW, *Sect.*

A telegram from the secretary, however, generously allowed me three days "to pack." If I had been less kindly entreated at his hands, I should have had nothing to pack but my wounded dignity. I *always* travel in a bag. Did he expect me to preach out a Saratoga trunkful of flounces? I explosively demanded of Mädchen?

"He is a man," said Mädchen, soothingly, "and he has n't behaved in the least like one. Don't be hard upon him."

I relented so far as to pack a lace collar and an extra paper of hairpins. Mädchen suggested my best bonnet. I am sorry to say that I locked her out of the room.

For the benefit of any of my sex who may feel induced to follow in my footsteps, I will here remark that I packed one dress, Barnes on Matthew, Olshausen on something else, a Tischendorff Testament, Mädchen's little English Bible, Jeremy Taylor (Selections), and my rubber boots.[11] Also, that my bag was of the large, square species, which gapes from ear to ear.

"It is n't here," said Mädchen, patiently, as I locked the valise.

"Mädchen," said I, severely, "if you mean my Florentine, I am perfectly aware of it. I am going to preach in black ties,—always!"

"Storm!" said Mädchen, concisely. As that was precisely what I was doing, to the best of my abilities, I regarded Mädchen confusedly, till I saw the Pathfinder on her knees, her elbows on the Pathfinder, and her chin in her hands.

"It is n't here," repeated Mädchen, "nor anything nearer to it than Whirlwind. That's in the eastern part of Connecticut."

I think the essentially feminine fancy will before this have dwelt upon the fact that the secretary's letter was not, to say the least of it, opulent in directions for reaching the village of Storm. I do not think mine is an essentially feminine fancy. I am sure this never had occurred to me.

When it comes to Railway Guides, I am not, nor did I ever profess to be, strong-minded. When I trace, never so patiently, the express to Kamtschatka,[12] I am let out of the Himalaya, Saturday-night accommodation. If I aim at a morning call in the Himalayas, I am morally sure to be landed on the southern peak of Patagonia. Mädchen, you understand, would leave her card in the Himalayas, if she had to make the mountains when she got there.

So, when Mädchen closed the Pathfinder with a snap of despair, I accepted her fiat without the wildest dream of disputing it, simply remarking that perhaps the conductor would know.

"Undoubtedly," said Mädchen, with her scientific smile. "Tell him you are going to see Mr. Bobbin of New Vealshire. He cannot fail to set you down at his backdoor."

He did, or nearly. If I cannot travel on paper, I can on iron. Although in the Pathfinder's index I am bewildered, routed, *non est inventus*, "a woman and an idiot," I can master the *patois* of brakemen and the hearts of conductors with unerring ease.[13] I am sure I don't know how I got to Storm, and when I got there I was sure I did n't know how I was to get back again; but the fact remains that I got there. I repeat it with emphasis. I beg especially to call the masculine attention to it. I desire the future historian of "Woman in the Sacred Desk," as he playfully skims the surface of antiquated opposition to this then long-established phase of civilization, to make a note of it, that there *was* a woman, and she at the disadvantage of a pioneer, who got there.

Before proceeding to a minute account of my clerical history, I should like to observe, for the edification of the curious as well as for the instruction of the imitative, that I labored under the disadvantage of ministering to two separate and distinct parishes, which it was as impossible to reconcile as hot coals and parched corn. These were the Parish Real and the Parish Ideal. At their first proximity to each other, my ideal parish hopped in the corn-popper of my startled imagination, and, as nearly as I can testify, continued in active motion till the popper was full.

Let us, then, in the first place, briefly consider (you will bear, I am sure, under the circumstances, with my "porochial" style)

The Parish Ideal.

It was "in the wilderness astray," but it abounded in fresh meat and canned vegetables. Its inhabitants were heathen, of a cultivated turn of mind. Its opportunities were infinite, its demands delicately considerate; its temper was amiable, its experience infantine. It numbered a score or so of souls, women and children for the most part; with a few delightful old men, whose white hairs would go down in sorrow to the grave, should they miss, in the afternoon of life, the protecting shade of my ministrations. I collected my flock in some rude tenement,—a barn perhaps, or antiquated school-house,—half exposed to the fury of the elements, wholly picturesque and poetical. Among them, but not of them, at a little table, probably, with a tallow candle, I sat and talked, as the brooks run, as the clouds fly, as waves break; smoothly, as befitted a kind of New Vealshire *conversazione*; eloquently, as would Wesley, as would Whitfield, as would Chalmers, Spurgeon, Beecher.[14]

Royally, but modestly, I ruled their stormy hearts. (N.B.—No pun intended.) Their rude lives opened, paved with golden glories, to my magic touch. Hearts, which masculine wooing would but have intrenched in their shells of ignorance and sin, bowed, conquered, and chained to their own well-being and the glory of God—or their minister—by my woman's fingers. I lived among them as their idol, and died—for I would die in their service—as their saint. Mädchen might stay at home and make calls. For me, I had found the arena worthy of my possibilities, and solely created for my happiness.

I wish to say just here, that, according to the best information which I can command, there was nothing particularly uncommon, certainly nothing particularly characteristic of my sex, in this mental *pas seul* through which I tripped.[15] I suspect that I was no more interested in myself than and as much interested in my parishioners, as most young clergymen. The Gospel ministry is a very poor business investment, but an excellent intellectual one. Your average pastor must take care of his own horse, dress his daughter in her rich relations' cast-off clothing, and never be able to buy the new Encyclopædia, and this as well at the end of twenty years as of two. But he bounds from his recitation-room into a position of unquestioned and unquestionable official authority and public importance in two months. No other profession offers him this advantage. To be sure, no other profession enfolds the tremendous struggles and triumphs, serving and crowning, of the Christian minister,—a struggle and service which no patent business motive can touch at arm's length; a triumph and crown which it is impossible to estimate by the tests of the bar, the bench, the lecture-room. But as it is perfectly well known that this book is never read on Sundays, and that the introduction of any but "week-day holiness" into it would be the ruin of it, I refrain from pursuing my subject in any of its finer, inner lights, such as you can bear, you know, after church, very comfortably;[16] and have only to bespeak your patience for my delay in introducing you to

The Parish Real.

I arrived there on Saturday night, at the end of the day, a ten miles' stage-ride, and a final patch of crooked railway, in a snow-storm. Somebody who lectures has somewhere described the unique sensations of hunting in a railway station for a "committee" who never saw you, and whom you never saw.[17] He should tell you how I found Mr. Dobbins, for I am sure I cannot. I found myself landed in a snow-drift—I suppose there was a platform under it, but I never got so far—with three other women. The three women had on waterproofs; I had on a waterproof. There were four men and a half, as nearly as I could judge, in slouched hats, to be seen in or about the little crazy station. One man, one of the whole ones, was a ticketed official of some kind; the other two were lounging against the station walls, making a spittoon of my snow-drift; the half-man was standing with his hands in his pockets.

"Was you lookin' for anybody in partikkelar?" said one of the waterproofs, thoughtfully, or curiously, as I stood dismally regarding the prospect.

"Thank you. Yes. Can you tell me if Mr. Do"—

"obbins," said the half-man at this juncture. "Bangs?"

"Yes, sir."

"New parson?"

"Yes, sir."

"That's the talk!" said Mr. Dobbins. "Step right round here, ma'am!"

"Right round here," brought us up against an old buggy sleigh, and an old horse with patient ears. "Hold on a spell," said Mr. Dobbins, "I'll put ye in."

Now Mr. Dobbins was not, as I have intimated, a large man. Whether he were actually a dwarf, or whether he only got so far and stopped, I never satisfactorily discovered. But at all events, I could have "put" Mr. Dobbins into anything twice as comfortably as I could support the reversal of the process; to say nothing of the fact that the ascent of a sleigh is not at most a superhuman undertaking. However not wishing to wound his feelings, I submitted to the situation, and Mr. Dobbins handed me in and tucked me up with consummate gallantry. I mention this circumstance, not because I was prepared for, or expected, or demanded, in my ministerial capacity, any peculiar deference to my sex, but because it is indicative of the treatment which, throughout my ministerial experience, I received.

"Comfortable?" asked Mr. Dobbins after a pause, as we turned our faces eastward, towards a lonely landscape of billowy gray and white, and in the jaws of the storm; "cause there's four miles and three quarters of this. Tough for a lady."

I assured him that I was quite comfortable and that if the weather were tough for a lady, I was too.

"You don't!" said Mr. Dobbins.

Another pause followed, after which Mr. Dobbins delivered himself of the following:—

"Been at the trade long?"

"Of preaching? Not long."

"Did n't expect it, you know" (confidentially). "Not such a young un. Never thought on 't."

Not feeling called upon to make any reply to this, I made none, and we braved in silence the great gulps of mountain wind that well-nigh swept the buggy sleigh over.

"Nor so good lookin', neither," said Mr. Dobbins, when we had ridden perhaps half a mile.

This was discouraging. A vision of Mädchen scientifically smiling, of the Rev. Dr. Z. Z. Zangrow dubiously drumming, of the New Vealshire Home Missionary Society shaking its head, drifted distinctly by me, in the wild white whirlpool over Mr. Dobbins's hat.

Were my professional prospects to be gnawed at the roots by a dispensation of Providence for which I was, it would be admitted by the most prejudiced, not in the least accountable? Were the Universalist clergywomen never young and "good lookin'?"

I did not ask Mr. Dobbins the question, but his next burst of eloquence struck athwart it thus:—

"Had 'em here in spots, ye see; Spiritooalist and sech. There's them as thinks 't ain't scriptooral in women folks to hev a hand in the business, noway.[18] Then ag'in there's them as feels very like the chap whose wife took to beatin' of him; 'It amuses her, and it don't hurt me.' Howsomever, there's them as jest as lieves go to meetin' as not when there's nothin' else goin' on. Last one brought her baby, and her husband he sat with his head ag'in the door, and held it."

To these consoling observations Mr. Dobbins added, I believe, but two others in the course of our four miles and three quarters drive; these were equally cheering:—

"S'pose you know you're ticketed to Samphiry's?"

I was obliged to admit that I had never so much as heard a rumor of the existence of Samphiry.

"Cousin of mine," explained Mr. Dobbins, "on the mother's side. Children got the mumps down to her place. Six on 'em."

It will be readily inferred that Mr. Dobbins dropped me in the drifts about Samphiry's front door in a subdued state of mind. Samphiry greeted me with a sad smile. She was a little yellow woman in a red calico apron. Six children, in various picturesque stages of the disease which Mr. Dobbins had specified, hung about her.

"Law me, child!" said Samphiry, when she had got me in by the fire, taken my dripping hat and cloak, and turned me full in the dying daylight and living firelight. "Why, I don't believe you're two year older than Mary Ann!"

Mary Ann, an overgrown child of perhaps seventeen, in short dresses buttoned up behind, sat with her mouth open, and looked at me during the expression of this encouraging comparison.

I assumed my severest ministerial gravity and silence, but my heart was sinking.

I had salt pork and barley bread for supper, and went to bed in a room where the ice stood on my hair all night, where I wrapped it around my throat as a preventive of diphtheria.[19] I was prepared for hardship, however, and bore these little physical inconveniences bravely; but when one of Mary Ann's brothers, somewhere in the extremely small editions, cried aloud from midnight to five A.M., and Samphiry apologized for the disturbance the next morning on this wise,—"Hope you was n't kept awake last night, I 'm sure. They generally cry for a night or two before they get through with it. If you 'd been a man-minister now, I don't s'pose I should have dared to undertake the keep of you, with mumps in the house; but it 's so different with a woman; she 's got so much more fellow-feeling for babies; I thought you would n't mind!"—I confess that my heart dropped "deeper than did ever plummet sound."[20] For about ten minutes I would rather have been in Hercules making calls than in New Vealshire preaching the Gospel.

I was aroused from this brief state of despair, however, by the remembrance of my now near-approaching professional duties; and after a hot breakfast (of salt pork and barley bread) I retired to my icy room to prepare my mind appropriately for my morning's discourse.

The storm had bent and broken since early dawn. The sun and the snow winked blindly at each other. The great hills lifted haughty heads out of wraps of ermine and gold. Outlines in black and gray of awful fissures and caverns gaped through the mass of wealthy color which they held. Little, shy, soft clouds fled over these, frightened, one thought; now and then a row of ragged black teeth snapped them up; I could see them struggle and sink. Which was the more relentless, the beauty or the power of the sight, it were difficult choosing. But I, preparing to preach my first sermon, and feeling in myself (I hope) the stillness and smallness of the very valley of humiliation, did not try to choose. I could only stand at my window and softly say, "Before the mountains were brought forth, THOU art."[21]

I do not know whether Mary Ann heard me, but when she appeared at that crisis with my "shaving-water," and blushed scarlet, transfixed in the middle of the room, with her mouth open, to beg pardon for the mistake, but "she'd got kinder used to it with the last minister, and never thought till she opened the door and see my crinoline on the chair!" I continued, with a gentle enthusiasm:—

"That is a grand sight, my dear, over there. It ought to make one very good, I think, to live in the face of such hills as those."

"I want to know!" said Mary Ann, coming and gaping over my shoulder. "Why, I get as used to 'em as I do to washing-day!"

I had decided upon extempore preaching as best adapted to the needs of my probable audience, and, with my icy hands in the warm "shaving-water" and my eyes on the icy hills, was doing some rambling thinking about the Lord's messages and messengers; but wondering, through my slicing of introduction, firstly, secondly, a, b, c, d, and conclusion, if the rural tenement in which we should worship possessed a dinner-bell, or a gong, or anything of that sort, which could be used as summons to assemble, and if it were not quite time to hear the sound, when Mary Ann introduced herself upon the scene again, to signify that Mr. Dobbins awaited my pleasure down-stairs. Somewhat confused by this sudden announcement, I seized my Bible and my hat, and presented myself promptly but palpitating.

"Morning," said Mr. Dobbins, with a pleasant smile. "Rested yet?"

I thanked him, and was quite rested.

"You don't!" said Mr. Dobbins. "Wal, you see I come over to say that meetin's gin up for to-day."

"Given up!"

"Wal, yes. Ye see there's such a heft of snow, and no paths broke, and seein' it was a gal as was goin' to preach, me and the other deacon we thought she'd get her feet wet, or suthin', and so we 'greed we would n't ring the bell! Thought ye'd be glad to be let off, after travellin' all day yesterday, too!"

I looked at Mr. Dobbins. Mr. Dobbins looked at me. There was a pause.

"Will your paths be broken out by night?" I asked, with a terrible effort at self-control.

"Wal, yes. In spots; yes; middlin' well."

"Will my audience be afraid of wetting their feet, after the paths are broken?"

"Bless you, no!" said Mr. Dobbins, staring, "they 're used to 't."

"Then you will please to appoint an evening service, and ring your bell at half past six precisely. I shall be there, and shall preach, if there is no one but the sexton to hear me. And next Sabbath you will oblige me by proceeding with the regular services, whatever the weather, without the least anxiety for my feet."

"If you was n't a minister, I should say you was spunky," said Mr. Dobbins, thoughtfully. He regarded me for some moments with disturbed interest, blindly suspicious that somebody was offended, but whether pastor or parishioner he could not make out. He was still undecided, when he took to his hat, and I to my own reflections.

This incident vitally affected my programme for the day. It was harrowing, but it was stimulative. There was the inspiration of the rack about it. The *animus* of the stake was upon me.[22] I could die, but I would not surrender. I would gain the respect of my parishioners, whether—well, yes—whether I gained their souls or not; I am not ashamed to say it now, partly because of the gnawing hunger for usefulness for usefulness' sake, and for higher than usefulness' sake, which came to me afterwards, and which, you remember, is all left out for the Sunday books, partly because the acquisition of my people's respect was a necessary antecedent to that of their salvation.

So by help of a fire which I cajoled from Samphiry, and the shaving-water which was warmer than the fire, I contrived to employ the remainder of the Sabbath in putting my first sermon upon paper.

The bell rang, as I had directed, at half past six. It did not occur to me at the time that it sounded less like a dinner-gong than a church-bell of average size and respectability. I and my sermon were both quite ready for it, and I tramped off bravely (in my rubber boots), with Mary Ann as my guide, through the drifted and drifting paths. Once more, for the benefit of my sex, I may be permitted to mention that I wore a very plain street suit of black, *no crimps*, a white collar of linen, and a black tie; and that I retained my outside garment—a loose sack—in the pulpit.

"Here we are," said Mary Ann, as I floundered up half blinded from the depths of a three-feet drift. Here we were indeed. If Mary Ann had not been with me I should have sat down in the drift, and—no, I do not think I should have cried, but I should have gasped a little. *Why* I should have been horribly unprepared for the sight of a commodious white church, with a steeple, and a belfry and stone steps, and people going up the steps in the latest frill and the stove-pipe hat, the reader who has ever tried to patronize an American seamstress, or give orders to an American servant, or asked an American mechanic if he sees a newspaper, must explain. The citizens of Storm might be heathen, but they were Yankees; what more could be said? Sentence a Yankee into the Desert of Sahara for life, and he would contrive means to live like "other folks."

However, I did not sit down in the drift, but went on, with meeting-house and worshipers all in an unnatural light like stereoscopic figures, and sat down in the pulpit; a course of conduct which had at least one advantage,—it saved me a cold.

Mr. Dobbins, it should be noted, met me at the church door, and conducted me, with much respect, up the pulpit stairs. When he left me, I removed my hat and intrenched my beating heart behind a hymn-book.

It will be understood that, while I was not unpracticed in Sabbath-school teaching, mission prayer-meeting exhortation, "remarks" at sewing-schools, and other like avenues of religious influence, of the kind considered suitable for my sex, I had never engaged in anything which could be denominated public speech; and that, when the clear clang of the bell hushed suddenly, and the pause on the faces of my audience—there may have been forty of them—warned me that my hour had come, I was in no wise more ready to meet it than any Miss A, B, or C, who would be content to employ life in making sofa-pillows, but would be quite safe from putting it to the *outré* purpose of making sermons.[23]

So I got through my introductory exercises with a grim desperation, and made haste to my sermon. Once with the manuscript in my hands, I drew breath. Once having looked my audience fairly in the eye, I was prepared to conquer or be conquered by it. There should be no half-way work between us. So I held up my head and did my best.

The criticism of that sermon would be, I suspect, a choice morning's work for any professor of homiletics in the country. Its divisions were numerous and startling; its introduction occurred just where I thought it would sound best, and its conclusion was adjusted to the clock. I reasoned of righteousness and judgment to come, in learned phrase. Theology and metaphysics, exegesis and zoölogy, poetry and botany, were impressed liberally into its pages.[24] I quoted Sir William Hamilton, Strauss, Aristotle, in liberal allowance.[25] I toyed with the names of Schleiermacher and Copernicus.[26] I played battledoor and shuttlecock with "views" of Hegel and Hobbes.[27] As nearly as I can recollect, that sermon was a hash of literature in five syllables, with a seasoning of astronomy and Adam.

I had the satisfaction of knowing, when I read as modestly, reverently, and as much like an unanointed church-member as I knew how, a biblical benediction, and sat down again on the pulpit cushions, that if I had not preached the Gospel, I had at least subdued the church-going population of Storm.

Certain rough-looking fellows, upon whom I had had my eye since they came in,—there were several of them, grimy and glum, with keen eyes; men who read Tom Paine,[28] you would say, and had come in "to see the fun,"—while I must admit that they neither wept nor prayed, left the house in a respectful, stupid way that was encouraging.

"You gin it to us!" said Mr. Dobbins, enthusiastically. "Folks is all up-sot about ye. That there was an eloquent discourse, marm. Why, they don't see but ye know jest as much as if ye was n't a woman!"

And when I touched Mary Ann upon the shoulder to bring her home, I found her sitting motionless, not quite strangled stiff. She had made such a cavern of her mouth, during my impassioned peroration, that an irreligious boy somewhere within good aim had snapped an India-rubber ball into it, which had unfortunately stuck.

Before night, I had reason to feel assured from many sources that I had "made a hit" in my corner of New Vealshire. But before night I had locked myself into the cool and dark, and said, as was said of the Charge of the Six Hundred: "It is magnificent; but it is not war!"[29]

But this is where the Sunday part of my story comes in again, so it is of no consequence to us. Suffice it to say that I immediately appointed a little prayer-meeting, very much after the manner of the ideal service, for the following Wednesday night, in the school-house, with a table, and a tallow candle, too. The night was clear, and the room packed. The men who read Tom Paine were there. There were some old people present who lived out of walking distance of the church. There were a few young mothers with very quiet children. I succeeded in partially ventilating the room, and chanced on a couple of familiar hymns. It needed only a quiet voice to fill and command the quiet place. I felt very much like a woman, quite enough like a lady, a little, I hope, like a Christian, too. Like the old Greek sages, I "was not in haste to speak; I said only that which I had resolved to say."[30] The people listened to me, and prayed as if they felt the better for it. My meeting was full of success and my heart of hope.

Arrived at this point in my narrative, I feel myself in strong sympathy with the famous historian of Old Mother Morey. For, when "my story's just begun," why, "now, my story's done."[31]

"Ce n'est pas la victoire, mais le combat," which is as sure to make the best autobiography as to "make the happiness of noble hearts."[32]

From the time of that little Wednesday-evening meeting my life in Storm was a triumph and a joy, in all the better meanings of these words. My people respected me first and loved me afterwards. I taught them a little, and they taught me a great deal. I brightened a few weeks of their dulled, drowsy, dejected life: they will gild years of mine.

I desire especially to record that all sense of personal embarrassment and incongruity to the work rapidly left me. My people at once never remembered and never forgot that I was a woman. The rudest of the readers of the "Age of Reason" tipped his hat to me, and read "Ecce Homo" to gratify me, and after that the Gospel of John to gratify himself.[33]

Every Sabbath morning I read a plain-spoken but carefully written sermon, which cost me perhaps three days of brain-labor. Every Sabbath afternoon I talked of this and that, according to the weather and the audience. Every Wednesday night I sat in the school-house, behind the little table and the tallow candle, with the old people and the young mothers, and the hush, and the familiar hymns, and lines of hungry faces down before me that made my heart ache at one look and bound at the next. It used to seem to me that the mountains had rather starved than fed them. They were pinched, compressed, shut-down faces. All their possibilities and developments of evil were those of the dwarf, not of the giant. They were like the poor little Chinese monsters, molded from birth in pitchers and vases; all the crevices and contortions of life they filled stupidly. Whether it was because, as Mary Ann said, they "got as used to the mountains as they did to washing-day," and the process of blunting to one grandeur dulled them to all others, I can only conjecture; but of this my New Vealshire experience convinced me: the temptations to evil of the city of Paris will bear no comparison to those of the grandest solitude that God ever made. It is in repression, not in extension, that the danger of disease lies to an immortal life. No risks equal those of ignorance. Daniel Webster may or may not escape the moral shipwrecks of life, but what chance has an idiot beside him?[34]

"It's enough to make a man wish he'd been born a horse in a treadmill and done with it!" said Happen to me one day. Happen was a poor fellow on whom I made my first "parish call"; and I made a great many between Sunday and Sunday. He lived five miles out of the village, at the end of an inexpressible mountain road, in a gully which lifted a pinched, purple face to the great Harmonia Range. I made, with difficulty, a riding-skirt out of my waterproof, and three miles an hour out of Mr. Dobbins's horse, and got to him.

The road crawled up a hill into his little, low, brown shanty, and there stopped. Here he had "farmed it, man and boy," till the smoke of Virginia battles puffed over the hills into his straightforward brown, young eyes.

"So I up and into it, marm, two years on 't tough; then back again to my hoe and my wife and my baby, to say nothing of the old lady,—you see her through the door there, bedridden this dozen year,—and never a grain of salt too much for our porridge, I can tell ye, when one day I 'm out to cut and chop, ten mile deep in the furrest,—alon' too,—and first I know I 'm hit and down with the trunk of a great hickory lyin' smash! along this here leg.

"A day and a half before folks found me; and another half day before the nighest doctor could get over to East Storm. Well; I s'pose he done his best by me, but mebbe he did n't know no more how to set a leg nor you do. He vowed there war n't no fracture there. Fracture! It was a jelly afore his eyes. So he ties it up and leaves a tumbler of suthin and goes off. So it mortified. So I 've ben here ever sence, on this sofy. Likely to be here—bless you, yes. My wife she tends the farm and the baby and the old lady and me. Sometimes we have two meals a day and ag'in we don't. When you come to think as your nighest neighbor is five mile off, and that in winter-time—why, I can see, a lookin from my sofy, six feet of snow drifted across that there road to town—and nought but one woman in gunshot of you able to stir for you if you starve—why, I feel sometimes, beggin' your pardon, marm, I feel like Hell! There's summer-folks in their kerridges comes riding by, to see them hills— and kind enough some of 'em is, I 'll say that for 'em—and I hear 'em chatterin' among themselves.

"'The grand sight!' says they. 'The damned sight!' says I; "for I lie on my sofy marm, and look over their heads at things they never see—lines and bars like over Harmonia red-hot and criss-cross like prison grates. Which comes mebbe of layin' and lookin' so long, and fanciful. They say I'd stand a chance to the hospital to New York or Boston, mebbe. I hain't gin it up yet. I 've hopes to go and try my luck some day. But I suppose it costs a sight. And my wife, she 's set her heart on the leg's coming to of itself, and so we hang along. Sometimes folks send me down books and magazines and such like. I got short o' reading this winter and read the Bible through; every word, from 'In the beginning' to 'Amen.' It 's quite a pretty little story-book, too. True? I don't know about that. Most stories set up to be true. I s'pose if I was a parson, and a woman into the bargain, I should think so."

Among my other parochial discoveries I learned one day, to my exceeding surprise, that Samphiry—who had been reticent on her family affairs—was the widow of one of my predecessors. She had married him when she was young and pretty, and he was young and ambitious,— "Fond of his book, my dear," she said, as if she had been talking of some dead child, "but slow in speech, like Moses of old. And three hundred and fifty dollars was tight living for a family like ours. And his heart ran out, and his people, and maybe his sermons, too. So the salary kept a-dropping off, twenty-five dollars at a time, and he could n't take a newspaper, besides selling the library mostly for doctor's bills. And so he grew old and sick and took to farming here, without the salary, and baptized babies and prayed with sick folks free and willing, and never bore anybody a grudge. So he died year before last, and half the valley turned out to bury him. But that did n't help it any, and I know you 'd never guess me to be a minister's widow, as well as you do, my dear. I 'm all washed out and flattened in. And I can't educate my children, one of them. If you 'll believe it, I don't know enough to tell when they talk bad grammar half the time, and I 'd about as lieves they 'd eat with their knives as not. If they get anything to eat, it 's all I 've got heart to care. I 've got an aunt down in Massachusetts, but it 's such a piece of work to get there. So I suppose we shall live and die here, and I don't know but it 's just as well."

What a life it was! I felt so young, so crude, so blessed and bewildered beside it, that I gave out that night, at evening prayers, and asked Samphiry to "lead" for herself and me. But I felt no older when she had done so.

I should not neglect to mention that I conducted several funerals while I was in Storm. I did not know how, but I knew how to be sorry, which seemed to answer the same purpose; at least they sought me out for the object from far and near. On one occasion I was visited by a distant neighbor, with the request that I would bury his wife. I happened to know that the dead woman had been once a member of the Methodist church in East Storm, whose pastor was alive, active, and a man.

"Would it not be more suitable," I therefore suggested, "at least more agreeable to the feelings of Brother Hand, if you were to ask him to conduct either the whole or a part of the service?"

"Waal, ye see, marm," urged the widower, "the cops was partikelar sot on hevin' you, and as long as I promised her afore she drawed her last that you should conduct the business, I think we 'd better perceed without any reference to Brother Hand. I 've been thinking of it over, and I come to the conclusion that he could n't take offence *on so slight an occasion!*"

I had ministered "on trial" to the people of Storm, undisturbed by

Rev. Dr. Zangrow, who, I suspect, was in private communication of some sort with Mr. Dobbins, for a month,—a month of pouting, spring weather, and long, lazy walks for thinking, and brisk ones for doing; of growing quite fond of salt pork and barley bread; of calling on old bedridden women, and hunting up neglected girls, and keeping one eye on my Tom Paine friends; of preaching and practicing, of hoping and doubting, of struggling and succeeding, of finding my heart and hands and head as full as life could hold; of feeling that there was a place for me in the earnest world, and that I was in my place; of feeling thankful that my womanhood and my work, like "righteousness and peace," had "kissed each other;" of many other things which I have agreed not to mention here,—[35] when, one day the stage brought me a letter which ran:—

HERCULES, *April 28, 18–.*

MY DEAR,—I have the measles. MÄDCHEN.

Did ever a woman try to do anything, that some of the children did not have the measles?

I felt that fate was stronger than I. I bowed my head submissively, and packed my valise shockingly. Some of the people came in a little knot that night to say good by. The women cried and the men shook hands hard. It was very pleasant and very heartbreaking. I felt a dismal foreboding that, once in the clutches of Hercules and Mädchen, I should never see their dull, dear faces again. I left my sorrow and my Jeremy Taylor for Happen, and my rubber boots for Samphiry; I tucked the lace collar and the spare paper of hairpins into Mary Ann's upper drawer. I begged Mr. Dobbins's acceptance of Barnes on Matthew, with the request that he would start a Sunday-school.

In the gray of the early morning the patient horse trotted me over, with lightened valise and heavy heart, to the crazy station. When I turned my head for a farewell look at my parish, the awful hills were crossed with Happen's red-hot bars, and Mary Ann, with her mouth open, stood in her mother's crumbling door.

Originally appeared in the *Atlantic Monthly*, July 1870, 11–22, then reprinted in *American and Continental Monthly: A Magazine of Choice Selections from the Best American and Continental Literature*, August 1870; *Christian World Magazine and Family Visitor*, August 1870; and as a small book by the Boston publishers Fields, Osgood. Phelps later included the story in the 1879 collection *Sealed Orders* (Boston: Houghton, Osgood).

Since I Died

How very still you sit!

If the shadow of an eyelash stirred upon your cheek; if that gray line about your mouth should snap its tension at this quivering end; if the pallor of your profile warmed a little; if that tiny muscle on your forehead, just at the left eyebrow's curve, should start and twitch; if you would but grow a trifle restless, sitting there beneath my steady gaze; if you moved a finger of your folded hands; if you should turn and look behind your chair, or lift your face, half lingering and half longing, half loving and half loth, to ponder on the annoyed and thwarted cry which the wind is making, where I stand between it and yourself, against the half-closed window—Ah, there! You sigh and stir, I think. You lift your head. The little muscle is a captive still; the line about your mouth is tense and hard; the deepening hollow in your cheek has no warmer tint, I see, than the great Doric column which the moonlight builds against the wall.[1] I lean against it; I hold out my arms.

You lift your head and look me in the eye.

If a shudder crept across your figure; if your arms, laid out upon the table, leaped but once above your head; if you named my name; if you held your breath with terror, or sobbed aloud for love, or sprang, or cried—

But you only lift your head and look me in the eye.

If I dared step near, or nearer; if it were Permitted that I should cross the current of your living breath; if it were Willed that I should feel the leap of human blood within your veins; if I should touch your hands, your cheeks, your lips; if I dropped an arm as lightly as a snow-flake round your shoulder—

The fear which no heart has fathomed, the fate which no fancy has faced, the riddle which no soul has read, steps between your substance and my soul.

I drop my arms. I sink into the heart of the pillared light upon the wall. I will not wonder what would happen if my outlines defined upon it to your view. I will not think of that which could be, would be, if I struck across your vision, face to face.

Ah me, how still she sits! With what a fixed, incurious stare she looks me in the eye!

The wind, now that I stand no longer between it and yourself, comes enviously in. It lifts the curtain, and whirls about the room. It bruises the surface of the great pearled pillar where I lean. I am caught within it. Speech and language struggle over me. Mute articulations fill the air. Tears and laughter, and the sounding of soft lips, and the falling of low cries, possess me. Will she listen? Will she bend her head? Will her lips part in recognition? Is there an alphabet between us? Or have the winds of night a vocabulary to lift before her holden eyes?

We sat many times together, and talked of this. Do you remember, dear? You held my hand. Tears that I could not see, fell on it; we sat by the great hall-window up-stairs, where the maple shadow goes to sleep, face down across the floor upon a lighted night; the old green curtain waved its hands upon us like a mesmerist, I thought; like a priest, you said.

"When we are parted, you shall go," you said; and when I shook my head you smiled—you always smiled when you said that, but you said it always quite the same.

I think I hardly understood you then. Now that I hold your eyes in mine, and you see me not; now when I stretch my hand and you touch me not; now that I cry your name, and you hear it not,—I comprehend you, tender one! A wisdom not of earth was in your words. "To live, is dying; I will die. To die is life, and you shall live."

Now when the fever turned, I thought of this.

That must have been—ah! how long ago? I miss the conception of that for which *how long* stands index.

Yet I perfectly remember that I perfectly understood it to be at three o'clock on a rainy Sunday morning that I died. Your little watch stood in its case of olive-wood upon the table, and drops were on the window. I noticed both, though you did not know it. I see the watch now, in your pocket; I cannot tell if the hands move, or only pulsate like a heart-throb, to and fro; they stand and point, mute golden fingers, paralyzed and pleading, forever at the hour of three. At this I wonder.

When first you said I "was sinking fast," the words sounded as old and familiar as a nursery tale. I heard you in the hall. The doctor had just left, and you went to mother and took her face in your two arms, and laid your hand across her mouth, as if it were she who had spoken. She cried out and threw up her thin old hands; but you stood as still as Eternity. Then I thought again: "It is she who dies; I shall live."

So often and so anxiously we have talked of this thing called death, that now that it is all over between us, I cannot understand why we found in it such a source of distress. It bewilders me. I am often bewildered here. Things and the fancies of things possess a relation which as yet is new and strange to me. Here is a mystery.

Now, in truth, it seems a simple matter for me to tell you how it has been with me since your lips last touched me, and your arms held me to the vanishing air.

Oh, drawn, pale lips! Nerveless, dropping arms! I told you I would come. Did ever promise fail I spoke to you? "Come and show me Death," you said. I have come to show you Death. I could show you the fairest sight and sweetest, that ever blessed your eyes. Why, look! Is it not fair? Am I terrible? Do you shrink or shiver? Would you turn from me, or hide your strained, expectant face?

Would she? Does she? Will she?—

Ah, how the room widened! I could tell you that. It grew great and luminous day by day. At night the walls throbbed; lights of rose ran round them, and blue fire, and a tracery as of the shadows of little leaves. As the walls expanded, the air fled. But I tried to tell you how little pain I knew or feared. Your haggard face bent over me. I could not speak; when I would I struggled, and you said "She suffers!" Dear, it was so very little!

Listen, till I tell you how that night came on. The sun fell, and the dew slid down. It seemed to me that it slid into my heart, but still I felt no pain. Where the walls pulsed and receded, the hills came in. Where the old bureau stood, above the glass, I saw a single mountain with a face of fire, and purple hair. I tried to tell you this, but you said: "She wanders." I laughed in my heart at that, for it was such a blessed wandering! As the night locked the sun below the mountain's solemn, watching face, the Gates of Space were lifted up before me; the everlasting doors of Matter swung for me upon their rusty hinges, and the King of Glories entered in and out.[2] All the kingdoms of the earth, and the power of them, beckoned to me, across the mist my failing senses made,—ruins and roses, and the brows of Jura and the singing of the Rhine;[3] a shaft of red light on the Sphinx's smile, and caravans in sandstorms, and an icy wind at sea, and gold in mines that no man knew, and mothers sitting at their doors in valleys singing babes to sleep, and women in dank cellars selling souls for bread, and the whir of wheels in giant factories, and a single prayer somewhere in a den of death,—I could not find it, though I searched,—and the smoke of battle, and broken music, and a sense of lilies alone beside a stream at the rising of the sun—and, at last, your face, dear, all alone.

I discovered then, that the walls and roof of the room had vanished quite. The night-wind blew in. The maple in the yard almost brushed my cheek. Stars were about me, and I thought the rain had stopped, yet seemed to hear it, up on the seeming of a window which I could not find.

One thing only hung between me and immensity. It was your single, awful, haggard face. I looked my last into your eyes. Stronger than death, they held and claimed my soul. I feebly raised my hand to find your own. More cruel than the grave, your wild grasp chained me. Then I struggled, and you cried out, and your face slipped, and I stood free.

I stood upon the floor, beside the bed. That which had been I, lay there at rest, but terrible, before me. You hid your face, and I saw you slide upon your knees. I laid my hand upon your head; you did not stir; I spoke to you: "Dear, look around a minute!" but you knelt quite still. I walked to and fro about the room, and meeting my mother, touched her on the elbow; she only said, "She's gone!" and sobbed aloud. "I have not *gone*!" I cried; but she sat sobbing on.

The walls of the room had settled now, and the ceiling stood in its solid place. The window was shut, but the door stood open. Suddenly I was restless, and I ran.

I brushed you in hurrying by, and hit the little light-stand where the tumblers stood; I looked to see if it would fall, but it only shivered as if a breath of wind had struck it once.

But I was restless, and I ran. In the hall I met the Doctor. This amused me, and I stopped to think it over. "Ah, Doctor," said I, "you need not trouble yourself to go up. I'm quite well to-night, you see." But he made me no answer; he gave me no glance; he hung up his hat, and laid his hand upon the banister against which I leaned, and went ponderously up.

It was not until he had nearly reached the landing that it occurred to me, still leaning on the banisters, that his heavy arm must have swept against and *through* me, where I stood against the oaken mouldings which he grasped.

I saw his feet fall on the stairs above me; but they made no sound which reached my ear. "You'll not disturb me *now* with your big boots, sir," said I, nodding; "never fear!"

But he disappeared from sight above me, and still I heard no sound. Now the doctor had left the front door unlatched.

As I touched it, it blew open wide, and solemnly. I passed out and down the steps. I could see that it was chilly, yet I felt no chill. Frost was on the grass, and in the east a pallid streak, like the cheek of one who had watched all night. The flowers in the little square plots hung their heads and drew their shoulders up; there was a lonely, late lily which I broke and gathered to my heart, where I breathed upon it, and it warmed and looked me kindly in the eye. This, I remember, gave me pleasure. I wandered in and out about the garden in the scattering rain; my feet left no trace upon the dripping grass, and I saw with interest that the garment which I wore, gathered no moisture and no cold. I sat musing for a while upon the piazza, in the garden-chair, not caring to go in. It was so many months since I had felt able to sit upon the piazza in the open air. "By and by," I thought, I would go in and up-stairs to see you once again. The curtains were drawn from the parlor windows and I passed and repassed, looking in.

All this while the cheek of the east was warming, and the air gathering faint heats and lights about me. I remembered, presently, the old arbor at the garden-foot, where, before I was sick, we sat so much together; and thinking, "She will be surprised to know that I have been down alone," I was restless, and I ran again.

I meant to come back and see you, dear, once more. I saw the lights in the room where I had lain sick, overhead; and your shadow on the curtain; and I blessed it with all the love of life and death, as I bounded by.

The air was thick with sweetness from the dying flowers. The birds woke, and the zenith lighted, and the leap of health was in my limbs. The old arbor held out its soft arms to me—but I was restless, and I ran.

The field opened before me, and meadows with broad bosoms, and a river flashed before me like a scimitar, and woods interlocked their hands to stay me—but being restless, on I ran.

The house dwindled behind me; and the light in my sick-room, and your shadow on the curtain. But yet I was restless, and I ran.

In the twinkling of an eye I fell into a solitary place.[4] Sand and rocks were in it, and a falling wind. I paused, and knelt upon the sand, and mused a little in this place. I mused of you, and life and death, and love and agony;—but these had departed from me, as dim and distant as the fainting wind. A sense of solemn expectation filled the air. A tremor and a trouble wrapped my soul.

"I must be dead!" I said aloud. I had no sooner spoken than I learned that I was not alone.

The sun had risen, and on a ledge of ancient rock, weather-stained and red, there had fallen over against me the outline of a Presence lifted up against the sky, and turning suddenly, I saw. . . . . .

Lawful to utter, but utterance has fled! Lawful to utter, but a greater than Law restrains me! Am I blotted from your desolate fixed eyes? Lips that my mortal lips have pressed, can you not quiver when I cry? Soul that my eternal soul has loved, can you stand enveloped in my presence, and not spring like a fountain to me? Would you not know how it has been with me since your perishable eyes beheld my perished face? What my eyes have seen, or my ears have heard, or my heart conceived without you?[5] If I have missed or mourned for you? If I have watched or longed for you? Marked your solitary days and sleepless nights, and tearless eyes, and monotonous slow echo of my unanswering name? Would you not know?

Alas! would she? Would she not? My soul misgives me with a matchless, solitary fear. I am called, and I slip from her. I am beckoned, and I lose her.

Her face dims, and her folded, lonely hands fade from my sight.

Time to tell her a guarded thing! Time to whisper a treasured word! A moment to tell her that *Death is dumb, for Life is deaf!* A moment to tell her—

First published in *Scribner's Monthly*, February 1873, 449–452, and included in *Sealed Orders* (Boston: Houghton, Osgood, 1879). In recent years the story has been reprinted in several anthologies, including Jessica Salmonson, ed., *What Did Miss Darrington See? An Anthology of Feminist Supernatural Fiction*, (New York: Feminist Press, 1989); Susan Koppelman, *Two Friends and Other Nineteenth-century Lesbian Stories by American Women Writers* (New York: Meridian, 1994); and Terry Castle, ed., *The Literature of Lesbianism: A Historical Anthology from Ariosto to Stonewall* (New York: Columbia University Press, 2003). The story anticipates Phelps's *Beyond the Gates* (1883), which is narrated from the perspective of a woman who has recently died.

Fourteen to One

A TRUE STORY

There are certain situations inherently too preposterous for fiction; the very telling of them involves the presumption of fact. No writer with any regard for his literary reputation would invent such a tale as that which I am about to relate. The reader will agree with me, I think, that the conclusive events of the story are but another evidence that truth is the most amazing thing in the world. For reasons which will be sufficiently obvious, I shall not make use of authentic names of either the persons or the localities involved in the recital of one of the most thrilling incidents in modern American history, but fold them in the film of fiction necessary to their presentation. I use the word *history* according to the best of my knowledge and belief. For that portion of the tale which is offered as such, my main witness is dead. I can only say that the testimony satisfied myself. My readers are at liberty to accept or refuse it as they choose. With this prefatory word, which may give force to the narrative, I need only proceed to record the circumstances.[1]

The Reverend Mr. Matthews was hitching up his horse to go to the post-office. The horse was old; the man was old. The horse was gray; so was the man. The wagon was well worn of its paint, which was once a worldly blue, and the wheels sprawled at the axles like a decrepit old person going bow-legged from age. The Reverend Mr. Matthews did not use the saddle, according to the custom of the region; he was lame and found it difficult to mount.

It was a chilly day, and what was once a buffalo robe lay across the wagon seat; a few tufts of hair remained upon the bare skin, but it was neatly lined with a woman's shawl—an old plaid, originally combining more colors than a rag mat, but now faded to a vague general dinginess which would recommend it to the "low tone" of modern art.[2] The harness was as old as the buffalo robe, as old as the shawl, as old as the horse, one might venture to say as old as the man. It had been patched, and mended, and lapped, and strapped, and tied, past the ingenuity of any but the very poor, and the really intelligent; it was expected to drop to pieces at the mildest provocation, and the driver was supposed to clamber down over the bow-legged wheels and tie it up again, which he always did, and always patiently. He was a very patient old man; but there was a spark in his dim blue eye.

The reins, which he took firmly enough in his bare hands, were of rope, by the way. He could not go to the post-office on Mondays because his wife had to use the clothes-line. He felt it a special dispensation of Providence that women did not wash on Saturdays, when his number of "Zion's Herald" was due.[3]

She came out of the house when he had harnessed, and stood with her hands wrapped in her little black-and-white checked shoulder shawl, watching him with eyes where thirty years of married love dwelt gently. Something sharper than love crossed her thin face in long lines; she had an expression of habitual anxiety refined to feminine acuteness; for it was the year 1870, and it was—let us call it, since we must call it something, the State of Kennessee.[4]

Mrs. Matthews stood in that portion of the house which Kennessee does not call a loggia, neither is it a porch, a piazza, or a hall. It results from the dual division of the house, which rises on each side, uniting in one boarded roof and a loft. Two chimneys of stone or of clay, according to the social status of the owner, flank the house on each side. The Rev. Mr. Matthews's chimneys were of clay, for he was a minister of the Methodist faith. His house was built of logs; through the space which cut the building the chickens walked critically, like boarders discussing their dinner. The domestic dwelling of a comfortable pig could be seen in the background. There were sheds, and something resembling a barn for the horse. All were scrupulously neat. Behind, the mountains towered and had a dark expression. A clear sky burned above, but one had to look for it, it was so far, and there seemed so small an allowance of it—so much of the State of Kennessee; so little of heaven.

"Are you going to the post-office?" asked Mrs. Matthews, softly. She knew perfectly well, but she always asked; he always answered. If it gave her pleasure to inquire, he reasoned, why not?

"Yes, Deborah," said the old man, briskly. "Want to go?"

"I don't know. Is Hezekiah tuckered out?"[5]

"Hezekiah is as spry as a chipmunk," returned the minister, confidently. Now Hezekiah was the horse, and thirty-one years old. He received this astonishing tribute with a slow revolution of his best eye (for he was blind in the other, but no one ever mentioned the fact in Hezekiah's presence) which might have passed for that superior effort of intelligence known only to the human race, and vulgarly called a wink.

"Well," said Mrs. Matthews, doubtfully, "I don't know 's I'll go."

She pronounced these words with marked, almost painful, hesitation, in an accent foreign to her environment. Her movements and dress were after the manner of Kennessee; but her speech was the speech of New Hampshire. They had been Northerners thirty years ago. Weak lungs brought him and these mountain parishes kept him. His usefulness had been so obvious, that his bishop had never shifted him far, reappointing him from term to term within a twenty-mile circuit among those barren fields. The situation was exceptional, the bishop said; at all events, he had chosen so to treat it. Thirty years—and such years!—seemed a long time to stay true to the traditions of youth and a flag. The parishioners and people whom, for courtesy, one called one's neighbors in those desolate, divided mountain homes, expressed themselves variously upon the parson's loyalty to the national cause. The Border State indecision had murmured about him critically, for the immediate region had flashed during the civil war, and remained sulky still.

The Confederacy had never lacked friends in that township. Of late the murmur had become a mutter. The parson had given offense. He had preached a sermon treating of certain disorders which had become historic, for which the village and valley had acquired unenviable notoriety,[6] and which they were slower than some other sections in abandoning, now that the civil situation supposed them to have done so.

"If I thought I could prevent anything," proceeded Mrs. Matthews anxiously, "I'd—I'd—I don't know but I'd go. Are you goin' to hold the meetin', after all?"

"Certainly," replied the minister, lifting his head. "I shall dispense the Word as usual."

"Well," said his wife sadly,—"well, I s'pose you will. I might have known. But I hoped you 'd put it off. I was afraid to ask you. I can't help worryin'. I don't know but I'll go, too. I can get my bunnet on in a minute."

Her husband hesitated perceptibly. He did not tell her that he was afraid to take her; that he was almost equally afraid to leave her. He said:—

"The lock of the back door is n't mended yet; I don't know but things need watching. That speckled bantam 's dreadfully afraid of weasels when she 's setting; I don't know 's I blame her."

"Well," returned the old lady with a sigh, "I don't know but you 're right. If it's the Lord's will I should stay at home and shoo weasels, I s'pose he can look after you without my help, if he has a mind to. Will you take the sweet potatoes along? There's a bushel and a half; and two dozen eggs."

The two old people loaded the wagon together, rather silently. Nothing further was said about the prayer-meeting. Neither alluded to danger. They spoke of the price of potatoes and chickens. The times were too stern to be spendthrift in emotion. One might be lavish of anything else; but one had to economize in feeling, and be a miser in its expression. When the parson was ready to start he kissed his wife, and said:—

"Good-by, Deborah."

And she said, "Good-by, Levi."

Then she said: "Let me tuck you up a little. The buffalo ain't in."

She tucked the old robe about the old legs with painstaking, motherly thoroughness, as if he had been a boy going to bed. She said how glad she was she had that nice shawl to line it.

"Thank you, Deborah. Keep the doors locked, won't you? And I would n't run out much till I get back."

"No, I don't know's I will. Have you got your lantern?"

"Yes."

"And your pistol?"

"No."

"Ain't you going to take it?"

"No, Deborah; I've decided not to. Besides, it's a rusty old affair. It would n't do much."

"You 'll get home by nine, won't you?" she pleaded, lifting her withered cheek over the high, muddy wheel. For a moment those lines of anxiety seemed to grow corrosive, as if they would eat her face out.

"Or quarter-past," said the parson, cheerfully. "But don't worry if I'm not here till half-past."

Hezekiah took occasion to start at this point; he was an experienced horse; he knew when a conversation had lasted long enough at the parting of husband and wife, in 1870, and in Kennessee. No horse with two eyes could see as much as Hezekiah. This was understood in the family.

A rickety, rocky path, about four feet wide, called by courtesy "The Road," wound away from the parsonage. The cornfield grew to it on each side. The tall stalks, some of them ten feet high, stood dead and stark, shivering in the rising wind. The old man drove into them. They closed about his gray head. Only the rear of the muddy blue wagon was visible between the husks.

"Levi! Levi! I want to ask a question."

She could hear the bow-legged wheels come to a lame halt; but she could not see him. He called through the corn in his patient voice:—

"Well, well! What is it? Ask away, Deborah."

"What time *shall* I begin to worry, Levi?"

To this essentially feminine inquiry silence answered significantly:—

"My dear," said the invisible husband after a long pause, "perhaps by ten—or half past. Or suppose we say eleven."

She ran out into the corn to see him. It seemed to her, suddenly, as if she should strangle to death if she did not see him once more. But she did not call, and he did not know that she was there. She ran on, gathering up her chocolate-colored calico dress, and wrapping her checked shawl about her head nervously. At the turn of the path there was a prickly locust tree. It had been burnt to make way for crops after the fashion of the country, which is too indolent to hew; it had not been well burned, and one long, strong limb stretched out like an arm; it was black, and seemed to point at the old man as he disappeared around the twist in the path where the returning-valley curved in, and the passenger found a way to the highway. The parson was singing. His voice came back on the wind:—

"How firm a foun-da-tion, ye sa-aints of the Lo-ord!"[7]

She wiped the tears from her eyes and came back through the corn, slowly; all her withered figure drooped.

"I don't know but I'd ought to have perked up and gone with him," she said aloud, plaintively.

She stood in the house-place, among the chickens, for a few minutes, looking out. She was used, like other women in that desolate country, to being left much alone. Those terrible four years from '61 to '65 had taught her, she used to think, all the lessons that danger and solitude can teach; but she was learning new, now. Peace had brought anything, everything, but security. She was a good deal of a woman, as the phrase goes, with a set strong Yankee mouth. Life had never dealt so easily with her that she expected anything of it; it had given her no chance to become what women call "timid." Yet as she stood looking through the stark corn on that cold gray day she shook with a kind of horror.

Women know what it is—this ague of the heart which follows the absent beloved. The safest lives experience it, in chills of real foresight, or fevers of the imagination. Deborah Matthews lived in the lap of daily dangers that had not alienated her good sense, nor suffocated that sweet, persistent trust in the nature of things, call it feminine or religious, which is the most amazing fact in human life; but sometimes it seemed to her as if her soul were turning stiff, as flesh does from fear.

"If this goes on long enough, I shall die of it," she said. "He will come home some day, and I shall be dead of listenin', and shiverin', and prayin' to Mercy for him. Prayer is Scripture, I suppose, and I have n't anythin' against it; but folks can die of too much prayin', as well as a gallopin' consumption or the shakes."

Only the chickens heard her, however, and they responded with critical clucks, like church members who thought her heretical. Since chickens constituted her duties, she would gratify Heaven and divert her mind by going out to see the setting bantam; who took her for a weasel and protested violently.

Mrs. Matthews came back to the house indefinably comforted, in a spiritual way, by this secular interruption, and prepared to lock up carefully, as her husband had bidden her. It was necessary to look after all the creatures first: the critical chickens, the comfortable pig, the gaunt cow, and the Rooster, for whom, as he was but one, and had all the lordliness of his race, and invariably ran away from her, and never came till he got ready, Mrs. Matthews had a marked respect, and thought of him as spelled with a capital. It took a great while that evening to get the Rooster into the pen, and while her feminine coax and his masculine crow ricochetted about the cornfield, the old lady cast a sharp, watchful eye all over the premises and their vicinity. Silence and solitude responded to her. No intrusion or intruder gave sign. The mountain seemed to overlook the house pompously, as a thing too small to protect. The valley had a stealthy look, as if it were creeping up to her. The day was darkening fast. The gloom of its decline came on with the abruptness of a mountain region, and the world seemed suddenly to shrink away from the lonely spot and forget it.

Mrs. Matthews, when she had locked up the animals with difficulty, deference, or fear, according to their respective temperaments, fastened the doors and windows of the house carefully, and looked at the clock. It was half-past six. She took off her muddy rubbers, brushed them neatly, folded away her shawl, and started the fire economically. She must have a cup of tea; but supper should wait for Levi, who needed something solid after Friday evening meeting. She busied herself with these details assiduously. Her life was what we might call large with trifles; she made the most of them; there was nothing better that she knew of to keep great anxieties out of the head and sickening terrors out of the heart.

There was one thing, to be sure: Mrs. Matthews called it faith in providence. The parson's wife had her share of it, but it took on practical, often secular, forms. Sometimes she prayed aloud, as she sat there alone, quaking in every nerve. Sometimes she pitched her shrill old voice, as she did to-day, several notes above the key, and sang:—

"How firm a foun-da-tion, ye sa-aints of the Lo-ord!
Is laid for your fa-aith in his ex-cellent word!"

But she locked the house up before she sang. She made her tea, too, and drank it.

"I always feel to get a better spiritual attitude," she used to say, "when I've had my cup of tea."

The house was so neat that its rudeness became a kind of daintiness to the eye; and the trim old lady, in her chocolate calico with its strip of a ruffle at throat and wrists, sat before the fireplace, meditative and sweet, like a priestess before an altar. She used to hate that fireplace with hot New Hampshire hatred—the kettle, the crane, and all the barbarous ways of managing; but she had contrived to get used to it now. It was the dream of her life to save money enough to freight a good Northern cook-stove over from Chattanooga. But she expected to die without it. The room winked brightly with shiny tin-ware hung above the fireplace, and chintz curtains at the windows. There were hollyhocks on the curtains which seemed like New Hampshire, if you made believe very much. There was a centre-table with a very old red and black tablecloth of the fashion of fifty years ago. The minister's writing materials adorned this table—his tall inkstand, with its oxidized silver top: his first parish in New Hampshire gave him that inkstand, at a donation party,[8] in a sleet storm one January night, with a barrel of flour and a bushel of potatoes. Beside the inkstand lay his quill pen, sharpened with the precision of a man who does not do much writing; the cheap, blue-ruled letter paper, a quire of it; and the sacred sermon paper which Mrs. Matthews would not have touched for her life; she would as soon have touched the sermons. These were carefully packed away in the corner in a barrel covered with turkey-red and surmounted with a board top.[9] The family Bible lay on the board.

Above rose the minister's "library." This was a serious affair, greatly respected in the parish and adored by the minister's wife. It took at least three poplar shelves, stained by Mr. Matthews's own hand and a borrowed paint-brush, to hold that library. Upon the lower shelf the family clock ticked solemnly, flanked by Cruden's Concordance and Worcester's Dictionary.[10] For neighbors to these there were two odd volumes of an ancient encyclopedia, the letters unfortunately slipping from a to z without immediate alphabetical connection. Upon such subjects, for instance, as alchemy or zoölogy, the minister was known to have shown a crushing scholarship, which was not strictly maintained upon all topics. Barnes's Notes on Matthew occupied a decorous position in the library.[11] The life of John Wesley,[12] worn to tatters and covered with a neat brown-paper grocery-bag, overflowed into two octavo volumes, which, after all, had the comfortable, knowing look of a biography which treats of a successful life-experience, opulent in fact and feeling, alert and happy. Beside the shriveled career of this humble disciple, what a story!

The History of New Hampshire stood beside John Wesley. A map of the State of Kennessee surmounted the library. For the rest, the shelves were fatly filled with filed copies of "Zion's Herald" and a Chattanooga weekly.

There was an old lounge in the room, home-made, covered with a calico comforter and a dyed brown shawl. The minister's slippers lay beside it; they were of felt, and she had made them. This lounge was Mr. Matthews's own particular resting-place when the roads were rough or the meeting late. If he were very late, and she grew anxious, his wife went up and stroked the lounge sometimes.

Their bedroom opened across the house-place from the living-room. It held a white bed, with posts, and old white curtains much darned. Mrs. Matthews's Bible lay on a table beside the bed. The room was destitute of furniture or ornaments, but it had a rag carpet and a fireplace. When Mr. Matthews had a sore throat and it was very cold they had a fire to go to bed by. That was delightful.

When Mrs. Matthews had taken her cup of tea and sung "How firm a foundation" till she was afraid she should be tired of it, which struck her as an impiety to be avoided, she walked about the house looking at everything, crossing from room to room, and looking cautiously after her. It was very still.

It was almost deadly still. How long the evening! Seven—eight—half-past eight o'clock. She tried to sew a little, mending his old coat. She tried to read the religious news in "Zion's Herald;" this failing, she even ventured on the funny column, for it was not Sunday. But nothing amused her. Life did not strike her as funny, that night. She folded the coat, she folded the paper, she got up and walked, and walked again.

Pretty little home! She looked it over tenderly. How she loved it. How he loved it. What years had they grown to it, day by busy day, night by quiet night. What work, what sorrow, what joy and anxiety, what economy, what comfort, what long, healthy, happy sleep had they shared in it! As she passed before the fire, casting tall shadows on the chintz curtains, she began to sing again, shrilly:—

"Home-home, dear, dear home!"[13]

Nine o'clock. Yes, nine; for the rickety old clock on the library shelf said so, distinctly. It was time to stop pacing the room; it was time to stop being anxious and thinking of everything to keep one's courage up; it was time to put the johnny-cake on and start the coffee; he would be hungry, as menfolks ought to be; God made 'em so. It was time to peep between the hollyhock curtains and put her hands against her eyes, and peer out across the cornfield. It was time to grow nervous, and restless, and flushed, and happy. It was not time, thank God, to worry.

The color came to her withered cheek. She was handsomer as an old lady than she had been as a young one, and the happier she grew the better she looked, like all women, young or old. She bustled about, with neat, housewifely fussiness. She knew that her husband thanked Heaven for her New England home-craft—none of your "easy" Southern house-keeping for Levi Matthews. What would have become of the man? As she worked, she sang unconsciously, "Dear, clean home!"

The johnny-cake was baking briskly. The candles were lighted. The coffee was stirred, and settled with the shell of an egg; it was ready to boil. It was quarter-past nine. Mrs. Matthews's head grew a little mud-dled from excitement. She began again at the top of her voice:

"How firm a foun-da-tion, ye sa-aints of the Lo-ord!
Is laid for your fa-aith in an ex-cellent home!"[14]

The clock wedged between the concordance and the dictionary struck half-past nine with an ecclesiastical tone; dogmatically, as if to insist on the point as a tenet on which she had been skeptical.

Mrs. Matthews stopped singing. She went to the window. The coffee was boiling over. The corncake was done brown. She pulled aside the curtain uneasily. The pine-wood fire flared, and blinded her with a great outburst of light. She could see nothing without, and stood for a moment dazzled. Then she began to look intently, and so accustomed her eyes to the masses of shadow and the lines of form outside. The road wound away abruptly, lost in the darkness like a river dashed into the sea. The cornstalks closed over it, stark and sear; she opened the window a little and heard them rustle, as if they were discussing something in whispers. Above the corn shot the gaunt arm of the prickly locust, burned and bare. The outlines of the mountain were invisible. The valley was sunk in the night. Nothing else was to be seen.

As she leaned, listening for the sedate hoofs of old Hezekiah, or the lame rumble of the blue wagon wheels, the Rooster uttered from his pen a piercing crow, and the bantam hen responded with an anxious cluck. She could have killed either of these garrulous members of her family for the interruption. The chickens always crowed when she was listening for Mr. Matthews. When the irritating sounds had died away on the damp air with long, wavering echoes, a silence that was indescribably appalling settled about the place. Nothing broke it. Even the cornstalks stopped. After a significant pause they began again; they seemed to raise their voices in agitation.

"What in the world are they talkin' about?" she said impatiently. She shut the window, and came back into the middle of the room. The corn-cake was burning. The coffee must be set off. The supper would be spoiled. She looked at the Methodist clock. Mr. Cruden and the Rev. John Wesley seemed to exchange glances over its head, and hers. It lacked seven minutes of ten.

"But it is n't time to worry yet!"

The woman and the clock faced each other. She sat down before it. What was the use in freezing at the window, to hear the Rooster, and the talking corn? She and the clock would have it out. She crossed her work-worn hands upon her chocolate calico lap and looked the thing in the eye.

What a superior, supercilious clock! What a theological, controversial clock! Was there even a clock so conscious of its spiritual advantages? So sure it knew the will of the Almighty? So confident of being right about everything? So determined to be up and at it, to say it all, to insist upon it, to rub it in?

Five minutes before ten—three—two. Ten o'clock. Ten o'clock, said in a loud, clerical tone, as if it were repeating ten of the Thirty-nine Articles to a Bishop.[15]

"But, oh, not quite time to worry yet!" Ten minutes past. A quarter past. Twenty minutes. The woman and the clock eyed each other like duelists. Twenty-five minutes past ten. Half-past—Deborah Matthews gasped for breath. She turned her back on the clock and dashed up the window full-length.

The night seemed blacker than ever. A cloud had rolled solemnly over the mountain, and hung darkly above the house. The stalks of corn looked like corpses. But they talked like living beings still. They put their heads together and nodded. As she leaned out, trembling and panting, a flash of unseasonable lightning darted and shot; it revealed the arm of the locust tree pointing down the road. A low mutter of distant thunder followed; it rolled away, and lapsed into a stillness that shook her soul.

She came back to her chair in the middle of the room, by the centre-table. The final struggle with hope had set in. It seemed as if the clock knew this as well as she. The ticking filled her ears, her brain, her veins, her being. It seemed to fill the world.

Half-past ten. It was as if some spirit appealed to the minister's clock: Oh, tell her so softly! Say so, gently as religious love, though you be stern to your duty as religious law. Twenty-five minutes of eleven—a quarter of—

The woman has ceased to look the clock in the eye. It has conquered her, poor thing; and, now that it has, seems sorry for her, and ticks tenderly, as if it would turn back an hour if it could. Her head has dropped into her hands; her hands to her knees; her body to the floor. Buried in the cushions of the old rocking-chair, her face is invisible. Her hands have lifted themselves to her ears, which they press violently. She herself lies crouched like a murdered thing upon the floor.

Eleven o'clock. She must not, can not, will not bear it. Eleven o'clock. She must, she can, she shall. Past all feminine fright and nervousness, past all fancy, and waste of weak vision, and prodigal anxiety, past all doubt, or hope, or dispute, it is time to worry now.

Deborah Matthews, when it had come to this, sprang to her feet, gave one piteous, beaten look at the clock, then stayed to look at nothing more. She flung open the door, not delaying to lock it behind her, and dashed out. She was as wild as a girl, and almost as agile. She ran over the rocks, and slipped in the mud, and sunk in the holes, and pushed into the cornfield, and thrust out her hands before her to brush the stalks away, and stood for a moment to get her breath underneath the locust tree. How persistently, how solemnly, that black arm pointed down the path. She felt like kneeling to it, as if it were an offended deity. All the Pagan in her stirred. Suddenly the Christian rose and wrestled with it.

"Lord have mercy!" she moaned. "He's my husband. We 've been married thirty years."

"Hain't I prayed enough?" she sobbed, sinking on her knees, in the mud, among the corn. "Hain't I said all there's any sense in sayin' to thee? What's the use in pesterin' God? But, oh, to mercy, if thou couldst take the trouble to understand what it is to be married—thirty years— and to set here in the cornfield lookin' for a murdered husband. He can't," said Deborah Matthews, abruptly starting to her feet. "God ain't a woman. It ain't in nature. He *can't* understand."

She pushed on, past the burned trees and out towards the highway. It was very dark. It was deadly lonely. It was as still as horror. Oh, there—

What tidings? For good or for ill, they had come at last. Deep in the distance the wheels of a bow-legged wagon rumbled dully, and the hoofs of a tired horse stumbled on the half-frozen ground. Far down the road she could see, moving steadily, a little sparkle, like a star. She dared not go to meet it.

Friend or foe might bear the news. Let it come. It must find her where she was. She covered her face with her shawl, and stood like a court-martialed soldier before the final shot.

"Deb-orah?"

Far down the road the faint cry sounded. Nearer, and advancing, the dear voice cried. He was used to call to her so when he was late, that she might be sure, and be spared all possible misery. He was infinitely tender with her. The Christianity of this old minister began with the marriage tie.

"Deb-orah? Deborah, my dear? Don't be frightened, Deborah. I 'm coming. I've got home."

Kissing and clinging, laughing and sobbing, she got him into the barn. Whether she clambered over the wheels to him, or he sprang out to her, whether she rode, or walked, or flew, she could not have told; nor, perhaps, could he. He was as pale as the dead corn, and seemed dazed, stunned, unnatural to her eye. Hezekiah probably knew better than either of these two excited old people how they together got his harness off, with shaking hands, and rolled the wagon into the shed, and locked the outbuildings, not forgetting the supper of the virtuous horse who rests from his labors after fifteen miles on a Kennessee road, and at the age of thirty-one.

"Lock the doors," said the minister abruptly, when they had gone into the house-place. "Lock up everything. Take pains about it. Give me something to eat or drink, and don't ask a question till I get rested."

His wife turned him about, full in the firelight, gave one glance at his face, and obeyed him to the letter. Perhaps, for the first time in her life, she did *not* ask a question. His mouth had a drawn, ghastly look, and his sunken eyes did not seem to see her. She noticed that he limped more than usual as he crossed the room to lay his old felt hat on the barrel-top beneath the library.

"You are used up," she said; "you are tuckered out! Here, drink your coffee, Levi. Here, I won't talk to you. I won't say a word. Drink, Mr. Matthews; do, dear."

He drank in great gulps exhaustedly. When she came up with the corn-cake, having turned her back to dish it, she heard a little clicking sound, and saw that his right hand closed over something which he would have hidden from her.

It was the old pistol; he was loading it, rust and all. The two looked at each other across the disabled weapon.

"It's all we have," he said. "A man must defend his own. Don't be frightened, Deborah. I'll take care of you."

"You might as well out with it," said the old lady, distinctly. "I'm ready to hear. I'm not a coward. New Hampshire girls ain't. I should think you'd know I'd been through enough, in this God-forsaken country—for that."

"Well," slowly. "Well, I suppose you're about right, Deborah. The fact is, I've had a narrow escape of it. I was warned at the meeting. We had a gratifying meeting. The Spirit descended on us. Several arose to confess themselves anxious"—

"What were you warned about?" interrupted his wife. "Never mind the anxious seat.[16] I've sat on it long enough for one night. What's the matter? Who warned you?"

"I was warned against the Ku Klux Klan, that's all," returned the parson simply, picking up the crumbs of corn-cake from his knees, and eating them to "save" the bread. "For a disbanded organization they're pretty lively, yet, round these parts. They lay in wait for me on the road home. I had to come round over the mountain, the other way. It was pretty rough. I didn't know but they'd detail a squad there. It was pretty late. The harness broke twice, and I had to mend it. It took a good while. And I knew that you"—

"Never mind me!" cried Mrs. Matthews, with that snap of the voice which gives the accent of crossness to mortal anxiety. "Tell me who warned you. Tell me everythin', this minute!"

"That's about all, Deborah. A colored brother warned me. He has been desirous of being present at all the means of grace, of late. But for the—the state of public sentiment, he would have done so. He is that convert brought to me privately, a few weeks ago, by our new brother, Brother Memminger."

"I don't know 's I half like that Brother Memminger," returned the wife. "He got converted pretty fast. And he's a stranger in these parts.

His speech ain't our speech, either. But it's a Southern name. Did he warn you?"

"He was not present to-night at the dispensing of the Word," replied the minister. "No, I was taken one side, after the benediction, without the building, by the colored brother, and warned, on peril of my life,—and on peril of his,—not to go home to-night, and to tell no man of the warning."

"But you did—you came home!"

"Certainly, my dear; you were here."

She clung to him, and he kissed her. Neither spoke for many minutes. It seemed as if he could not trust himself. She was the first to put in whispered words the thought which rocked the hearts of both.

"When they don't find you—what will they do?"

"My dear wife—my dear wife, God knows."

"What shall you do? What can we do?"

"I think," said the minister in his gentle voice, "that we may as well conduct family prayers."

"Very well," said his wife, "if you've had your supper. I'll put away the dishes first."

She did so, methodically and quietly, as if nothing out of the common course of events had happened, or were liable to. Her matter-of-fact, housewifely motions calmed him, as she thought they would. It made things seem natural, homelike, safe, as if danger were a delirious dread, and home and love and peace the foundations of life, after war, in Kennessee.

When she had washed her hands and taken off her apron, she came back to the lounge and brought the family Bible with her, and the hymn-book. They sang together one verse of their favorite hymn, "How firm a foundation," with the quavering, untrained voices that had "led the choirs" of mountain meetings for almost thirty years of patient, self-denying missionary life. Then the parson read, in a firm voice, a psalm,—the ninety-first;[17] and then he took the hand of his wife in his, and they both knelt down by the lounge, and he prayed aloud his usual, simple, trustful, evening prayer.

"O Lord, our heavenly Father, thy mercies are new every morning,[18] and fresh every evening. We thank thee that though danger walketh in darkness, it shall not come nigh us. We bless thee that thou art so mindful of thine unworthy servant and handmaiden. We thank thee that for nearly thirty years we have dwelt in conjugal love and peace beneath our comfortable roof. We thank thee that no disaster hath rendered us homeless, and that the hand of violence hath not been raised against us. We pray thee that thou wilt withhold it from us this night, that we may sleep in peace, and awake in safety"—

"*Levi!*"

A curdling whisper in his ear interrupted the old man's prayer. "Levi! There are *footsteps in the corn!*"

"And awake in safety," proceeded the minister firmly, "to bless thy tender care"—

He did not rise from his knees, but prayed on in a strong voice. So well trained to the religious habit was the woman that she did not cry out, nor interrupt him again, nor did she even arise from her knees before the old lounge.

Suddenly voices clashed, cries upsprang, and a din surrounded the house.

"Come out! Come out! Out with the Yankee parson! Out with the nigger-praying preacher! Show yourself!"

The old man's hand tightened upon the hand of his old wife; but neither rose from their knees. The confusion without redoubled. Calls grew to yells. Heavy steps dashed foraging about the house. Cries of alarm from the outbuildings showed that the animals, which were the main support of the simple home, were attacked, perhaps destroyed. Then came the demand:—

"Come out! Come out to us! Show yourself, you sneaking, Yankee parson! Out to us!"

A terrific knock thundered on the door. Steadily the calm voice within prayed on:—

"We trust thee, O Lord, and we bless thee for thy mercy to usward"—

"Open the door, or we will pull your shanty down to hell!"

"Preserve us, O Lord, for thy loving-kindness endureth forever"—[19]

"Open the door, — you, or we'll set the torches to it, and burn you out!"

"Protect us, O God"—

The light lock yielded, and the old door broke down. With a roar the mob rushed in. They were not over sixteen, but they seemed sixty, storming into the little room. They were all masked, and all armed to the teeth.

Before the sight which met his eyes the leader of the posse fell back. He was a tall, powerful fellow, evidently by nature a commander, and the men fell back behind him.

"For Christ's sake, Amen," said the parson. He rose from his knees, and his wife rose with him. The two old people confronted the desperadoes silently. When the leader came closer to them he saw that the Rev. Mr. Matthews's hands were both occupied. With the left he grasped the hand of his wife; in the right he held his rusty pistol. The hymn-book had fallen to the floor; but the family Bible had been reverently laid with care upon the lounge, its leaves yet open at the ninety-first psalm.

"Gentlemen," said the parson, speaking for the first time, "I would not seem inhospitable, but the manner of your entering has perturbed my wife and interrupted our evening prayer, which it is our custom never to cut short for any insufficient cause. Now I am ready to receive you. Explain to me your errand."

"It's a — short one," said a voice from the gang; "a rope and a tree will explain it easy enough."

"And nothing less!" cried a hoarse man. "We have n't come on any boys' play this time. We've had chase enough to find you for one night."

"That's so. It s no fool's errand, you bet. We ain't a tar-and-feathering party. We mean business."

"Gentlemen! gentlemen!" pleaded the parson. He took the hand of his wife as he spoke, and lifted it to his shrunken breast, and held it there, delicately.

It was the piteous instinct of manly protection powerless to protect.

"In the name of civil justice, O my neighbors, wherein have I offended you?"

"That 's our business. It's a serious one, too," cried the hoarse man. "Your — pious prayer meetings have been a nursery of sentiments we don't approve, that's all. You 've admitted a — darky among respectable white citizens. Come now, have n't you? Own up!"

"Certainly," replied the parson promptly. "There was one colored brother present at the means of grace on one or two occasions. I regretted that my congregation did not altogether welcome him. He was converted by the mercy of God, beneath my ministrations. Would ye that I denied him the poor benefit of my prayers? Nay, then, as God hears me, I did not, nor I would not."

The old man's dim eyes flashed. He raised his rusty pistol, examined it, and laid it down. Before sixteen well-armed men he began to comprehend the uselessness of his old weapon. He looked upon the array of grotesque and ghastly masks steadily; they rose like a row of demons before his biblically trained imagination. Mr. Matthews believed in demons, in a simple, unquestioning way.

"And you've preached against that which was no business of yours. Come now, own to it! You've meddled with the politics and justice of the State. You have preached against the movements of the Klan—what's left of it. That is n't much. It's done for. We're only a few gentlemen, looking after things on our own hook."

"I own to it," said the parson quietly. "I have delivered a discourse upon the topic of your organization. I felt called of Heaven to do it. Is that all ye have against me? I pray you, for my wife's sake, who is disquieted by your presence, as you see, to leave us to ourselves and go your way—from under my roof."

"Have him out! Right smart, now!" yelled the hoarse man. "Have him out without more words! A rope! A rope! Where's a rope?"

In a moment there was *mêlée* in the house. Cries arose to the effect that the rope was left in the corn. But a fellow who had been browsing about outside ran in with a rope in his hand and handed it to the hoarse man. The rope was Mrs. Matthews's clothesline—Hezekiah's reins. The hoarse man gave it to the leader with an oath. The leader seemed to hesitate, and conferred in a whisper with the hoarse man and with others; but he was apparently overborne in his hesitation; he took the rope, and advanced with a certain respect to the parson, death in his hand, but who knew what pity in his heart? The mask hid it if any were there. The noise from the gang now increased brutally. Cries, oaths, curses, calls to death resounded through the pure and peaceful room. The hoarse man lassoed the rope, and threw it around the parson's neck. At this moment a terrible sound rang above the confusion.

It was the cry of the wife.

She had possessed herself magnificently up to this time; the Puritan restraint set upon her white, old face; she had not said a word. No murderer of them all had seen a tear upon her withered cheek. But now nature had her way. She flung herself to her knees before the ruffians; then upon her husband's neck; back upon her knees—and so, in a passion wavering between agony and entreaty, pleaded with them. She cried to them for the love of Heaven, for the love of God, for the sake of "Jesus Christ his Son, their Saviour," so she put it, with the lack of tact and instinct for scriptural phraseology belonging to her devout, secluded life.

The phrase raised a laugh.

She cried to them for the love of their own wives, for the sake of their mothers, by the thought of their homes, for the sake of wedded love, and by his honorable life who had ministered respected among them for nearly thirty years—by the misery of widowhood, and by the sacredness of age. In her piteous pleading she continued to give to the murderers, at the very verge of the deed, the noblest name known to the usages of safe and honorable society.

"Gentlemen! *gentlemen!* For the sake of his gray hair! For the sake of an old wife"—

But there they pushed her off. They struck her hands from their knees; they tore her arms from his neck, and so were dragging him out, when the parson said in a clear voice:—

"Men!—ye are at least men,—give way to the demand of my soul before you hurl it to your Maker. I pray you to leave me alone, for the space of a moment, with this lady, my wife, that we may part one from the other, and no man witness our parting."

At a signal from the big leader the gang obeyed this request. The men hustled out of the broken door. The leader stood within it.

"Watch 'em! Watch 'em like a lynx!" cried the hoarse man. But the leader turned his back.

"Deborah! Kiss me, my dear. You 've been a good wife to me. I think you'd better go to your brother—in New Hampshire—I don't know. I have n't had much time to plan it out for you. Tell him I would have written to him if I had had time. Tell him to take good care of you. Oh—God bless you, my dear. Why don't you speak to me? Why don't you kiss me? Your arms don't stay about my neck—What! Can't hold them there—at this last minute? Pray for me, Deborah. Deborah! why don't you answer me? O my wife, my wife, *my wife!*"

But she was past answering; past the sacred agony of that last embrace. She had dropped from his breast, and lay straight and still as the dead at his feet.

"God is good," said the old man solemnly. "Let her be as she is. I pray you do not disturb her. Leave her to the swoon which He has mercifully provided for her relief at this moment—and do with me as ye will, before she awakens."

A certain perceptible awe fell upon the gang as the old man stepped around the unconscious form of his wife and presented himself in the doorway.

"He seems to be a grateful old cove," said one man in a low voice. "I don't know's I ever heard a feller in his circumstances give God a good name before."

"No sniveling!" cried the hoarse man. "Have it over!"

They took him out, and arranged to have it over as quickly as might be. It must be admitted that the posse were nervous. They did not enjoy that night's work as much as they had expected to. They were in a hurry now to be done with it and away.

The old man offered no useless resistance. He walked with dignity, and without protest. He limped more than usual. His head was bare. His gray hair blew in the rising wind. The rope was around his neck.

Some one had wheeled out the blue wagon and rolled it under the locust tree. As this was done the old horse whinnied for his master from the stall. The parson was pushed upon the cart. Short work was made of it. As the leader of the gang stooped to help the hoarse man fling the rope over the burned bare limb of the tree, and to adjust the noose about the old man's neck,—which he made insistence on doing himself,—a mask dropped. It was the face of the chief himself which was thus laid bare, and alas, and behold, it was even no other face than the face of—

"Brother Memminger!" cried the old minister, speaking for the first time since he had been dragged from the house. The leader restored his mask to his downcast face, with evident embarrassment.

"*You!*" said the parson. "I thought," he added gently, "that you had found a Christian hope. You communed with me at the Sacrament two weeks ago. I administered it to you. I am—sorry, Brother Memminger."

The fellow muttered something, Heaven knew what, and fell back a step or two. Some one else prepared the rope to swing the old man off. He who was known as Brother Memminger dropped to the rear of the gang, surveyed it carefully, then advanced to his place at the front, nearest to the victim. Every man awaited his orders. He was their chief. They had organized and they obeyed, even in their decline, a military government. There was a moment's pause.

"I would like," said the doomed man gently, "a moment to commend my soul to God."

This was granted him, and he stood with his gray head bowed. His hands were tied behind him. His face was not muffled; it had a high expression. His lips moved. Those who were nearest thought they heard him murmur the first words of the Lord's Prayer. "Hallowed be Thy name," he said, and paused.

He said no more, nor seemed to wish it. So they ranged themselves, every man of them, to swing him off, each standing with both hands upon the rope, which had been spliced by another to a considerable length. He who was called Memminger stood, as he was expected, to give the final order. There were fourteen of them—and Memminger the chief. Beside him stood an idle fellow, masked like the rest, but apparently a servant, a tool of Memminger's, who had especial service for him, perhaps. If the old man struggled too much—or an accident happened—it was well to have an unoccupied hand. Memminger, in fact, had been well known in the gang for a good while, and was implicitly trusted and obeyed.

In putting their hands to the rope every man of them had of necessity to lay down his arms, both hands being clenched upon the rope, for a strong pull. They meant to break the old man's neck, and be done with it. Really, nobody cared to torture him.

"We're ready," said the hoarse man. "Give the signal, Cap'n. Hurry up."

The light of their lanterns and torches revealed the old man clearly—the long arm of the locust above his head—the stormy sky above. Death was no paler than the parson, but he did not struggle.

His lips moved still in silent prayer. His eyes were closed. The men bent to the rope. The chief raised his hand. The last signal hung upon his next motion.

Then there was a cry. Then his mask dropped, and from the face of the man beside him another fell, and it was the face of a negro, obedient and mute. Then the powerful figure of the leader straightened. His familiar eye flashed with a perfectly unfamiliar expression. Two muscular arms shot out from his body; each hand held a revolver sprung at full-cock and aimed.

"*Boys!*" he cried in an awful voice, *"I am an officer of the United States! and the first man of you who lets go that rope,* DROPS*!"*

In an instant, armed as he was, he covered them, every man of them unarmed and standing as they were. His negro servant sprang to his aid.

"The first man of you who stirs a muscle on that rope dies!" thundered the quasi Brother Memminger. "I am a deputy marshal, authorized by the National Government to investigate and hasten the disbanding of the Ku Klux Klan, and, in the name of the Stars and Stripes, and law and order, I arrest you, every man!"

And, in the name of simple wonder and astounding history, it was done. The negro servant, whose person bulged with hidden handcuffs, bound the men, one at a time, fourteen of them, while his master's experienced weapons covered the gang. They behaved with the composure of intelligent and dumfounded men. One of them ventured an observation. It was the hoarse man. He said: "— — — — you — to —," struggled mightily with his handcuffs, and then held his tongue.

The whole posse, by means of this simple stratagem, and by the help of that cowardice elemental in all brutes, was marched to the nearest sheriff; then delivered intact to the power of the law which the great mass of Kennessee citizens were ready to respect and glad to see defended. The country rang with the deed. Then whispers arose to hush it, for shame's sake. But it crept to Northern ears, and I record it as it was related to me.

"How is it, Parson?" said Deacon Memminger with a bright, shrewd smile, as he cut the old man down, and helped him, trembling as he was, to dismount the shaky cart. "How is it, sir? Are you sorry I came to church at your place—now? I thought—under the circumstances—and I was bound to save you. I and my darky boy have been ferreting out this thing for a hundred days. I joined 'em the first week I came down here. I came on from Washington to do it. We mean to make a thorough job of it—and I guess we've done for 'em, this time. You'll excuse me, sir, but I've got to get 'em to the sheriff, and—I'd go back and see my wife, if I were you."

She came to herself and to her misery soon enough, lying there upon the floor beside the lounge. The first thing which she saw distinctly was the Bible, opened at the psalm which has calmed more souls in shocks of danger, and in the convulsions of lawless times, than any other written words known to the literatures of the race.

But the first thing which she heard was his precious voice, pitched low, and modulated tenderly, so as not to frighten her.

"Deb-orah! Deb-orah! Don't be scared, my dear. They have not hurt me—and I'm coming back to you."

This story first appeared in two periodicals, the *Century Illustrated Monthly Magazine*, December 1890, 300–310, and *Methodist Magazine* 36 (1892). Phelps later made it the title story of the collection *Fourteen to One* (Boston: Houghton, Mifflin, 1891). It appeared again in the *Speaker*, December 1907.

The Rejected Manuscript

The ten minutes past three train was due at Cantelope Corner. At Cantelope Corner the great P. and Q. Railroad Company is on time. The corporation looks upon punctuality as a duty to this fattening suburb; while the citizens thereof regard it as a sacred privilege which the corporation underestimates.

Cantelope Corner should not be confounded with Cantelope Heights, with Cantelope Cascade, or with Cantelope-on-the-Saint-Henry; least of all with Northwest Cantelope, the newest, and therefore the most pretentious, of all the Cantelopes. For Cantelope is old enough to aspire; it purposes to achieve distinction. In the broad sweep of all the beautiful, bountiful Boston suburbs, none cultivates such ambition. It has been whispered, indeed, that Cantelope aims at nothing less than the rivalry of the Newtons.

The Cantelope Corner grocer (there was but one, and he was so dangerous an autocrat that we hasten to speak of him respectfully)— the grocer's driver stood on the back-door steps of the Queen Anne house belonging to Mr. W. H. T. Wire, vaguely understood to be "in electricity." The grocer twirled between his finger and thumb a clean new pass-book. He delayed to offer some pleasantries to the cook, of the sort popular in Cantelope kitchens, before he made known his errand; for this was not his hour for taking orders from the imposing and imperious back door known in the arcana of trade as "We-Hold-the-Wireses."

The grocer explained that he had come for the key of the house opposite, adding that his orders were twelve o'clock sharp, with a bag of flour and a few such. He mentioned incidentally that it was three now.

"Did n't they order a *barrel?*" asked the pretty cook, as she handed the new tenants' keys to the grocer. That gentleman contemptuously shook his head. If it had been a barrel, did she think he would be found "this late"?

"But I did hear at the coal-yard, on the way round, that the new folks are literary. That puts another face on it, Molly, my dear. Literary folks are darn hard up—Lord knows why, poor devils. But I never got a bad debt out of one of 'em yet."

"Shure, then," observed Molly, with an air of crushing intelligence, "the people opposite has wrote a book, for I see it on the top shelf of the waste-paper cupboard in my lady's room."

"What's the name of it?" asked the grocer, with some interest, as he slipped the keys upon the pass-book string. "Was it 'The Innocent Sin'?[1] I've heard of that volume. It's very famous. If it's her that wrote 'The Innocent Sin,' I don't know but I'd better change the butter before they get here."

"Noa," said clever Molly, who was quite equal to the literary situation, "I heard my folks talkin' about that to the tea table. My lady says it is n't her at all at all. This one did n't write 'The Innocent Sin.' It's another woman of the same name."

"Then this butter will do," said the grocer, snapping the cover of the pass-book to. "I never heard of anything *she* wrote. She can't be of no importance. If she'd been the writer of 'The Innocent Sin' it would be another matter."

The grocer drove away to deposit his poor little order in the cold and empty house. With heavy indifference he left the pass-book behind him—the first occupant of the new home. It hung on a nail by the rusted sink, and fell conspicuously open at the page which bore the too legible legend, "Demosthenes Hathorne, to————, Debtor."[2]

The name really was Demosthenes. No trick of fiction would dare invent such an improbability, and I hasten to verify the assertion. Nay, more; the unfortunate man was baptized Aristotle Demosthenes; but experience of life, chiefly in the form of two hundred schoolboys, had elided a half of this portentous cognomen. Mr. Hathorne had been fain to reduce his too heavy personal share of the classic, at the end of the first year which he spent in guiding the fortunes of the famous Mount

Zion Academy. Nobody but the principal and his wife knew what he had suffered from the infinite capacity for the infliction of torment residing in the nature of American youth. A teacher bearing the delicious fatality of such a name was foredoomed to failure at Mount Zion. Aristotle Demosthenes Hathorne, after enduring four years the wittiest cartoons, paragraphs, caricatures, and serenades that had distinguished New England academy life in his day, resigned his first name and his position.

He had not been a very successful principal for other reasons, no one knew quite why; not even his trustees, who accepted his resignation without undue protest, and engaged a Reverend Mr. J. Smith to fill the vacancy with no perceptible delay.

The disappointed man, at the age of forty-two cast adrift to begin the world anew, tossed about Boston for a time in one of those wretched interludes of fate which professional people know too well, and which no others can understand. He waited for invitations which did not come. He listened for "calls" which he never heard. He applied for positions which had engaged the other man the day before. He snatched at chances which slipped through his shaking fingers. He lay in wait for opportunities which turned and fled at the sight of his gaunt and anxious face. He was a shy man, and that did not help him. It used to be said at Mount Zion—after he resigned—that he was not quite up to the times in his methods of teaching. He had the physique of the sensitive and the conservative. He was a belated scholar, an old-time student without modern "go." He ought to have been the pastor of a colonial parish, or the scholastic of a mediaeval controversy. He was lost in the New England scramble for a salary. He was a vellum volume out of print. He was a mistake in life's recitation. He was an anachronism.

There were two children,—and the wife,—and they had come to desperate straits. It was over a year since the salary stopped, and all her pretty expedients and brave inventions had come to an end with the little store which she had proudly saved from her own earnings for a day like this. In her heart she had always expected it some time. She had the practical sense of the two, although she did write poetry and love-stories; and when, one day, he had the chance to take two Latin School boys to tutor at reduced rates, she gently persuaded him to do so. He went to his first lesson with hanging head, and a look about the mouth so piteous that she cried all the morning. But he went.

On the strength of this prospect, and of another which they did not talk much about, and by the immediate means of the very little legacy which fell to her from her father's desultory estate, they had rented this house in Cantelope Corner. Her father had been a literary man, too; he seldom saved, and often lost; he did not understand business; it did not run in the family to be rich.

They came on the ten minutes past three train, that November afternoon, as they had planned. They came alone. They had hired their boarding-house keeper to take the children for a couple of days, till the house could be warmed and put into habitable shape.

"We'll make the most of our freedom," she said to her husband, laughing nervously as tired-out women do. "It's quite like a honeymoon, is n't it?"

He glanced at the parcels that encumbered her; at the fat shawl-strap bundle (it held his winter overcoat and the children's) which she lugged along, while he carried the valise; at her faded gray "spring and fall" pongee dress;[3] at the much-mended fingers of her old kid gloves; at the portly and expensive pile of packing-boxes marked D.H., which the baggage-master was smashing about on the platform with running commentaries not of a sacred nature.

"Ye-es," said Demosthenes Hathorne. "Yes, my dear. Quite like it."

He felt at that moment as he had sometimes done on other occasions in his life, that he was deficient in imagination when compared with his wife.

"I'll stop at the post-office," she said irrelevantly, "and you go up with the baggage, won't you? You are very tired. Here, dear. You get into the coach with the bundles. I'll see to everything."

He obeyed her mechanically; then recollected himself, and backed out of the muddy coach, knocking off his tall hat as he did so.

"*You* must ride," he urged contritely. "You must have—ah—become wearied yourself."

"He can go on the baggage-wagon," observed the driver of that vehicle, with an accent of good-natured patronage. "You do look beat out, both of you. Folks generally do, that come here—the first time."

Cantelope Corner is still so rural that a new-comer is an object of interest, while it is yet so urban that its hackmen are liable to have a grammar-school or even a high-school education, and are not expected to double their negatives. Mrs. Hathorne noticed both these little facts, with the quick eye of one whose occupation has accustomed her to take running notes of the most unpromising situations, as she jolted off in the coach with the fat shawl-strap, which jounced from her knees to the seat opposite and back again, like a passenger who had lost his balance.

"It is a town with a country heart, out here," she thought. But she was restless and disappointed about the post office. She wanted to ask the coachman to stop. She was afraid he would charge an extra fare, and meekly abandoned the idea. She was used to going without; it had become a second nature now.

Her first nature was quite another matter. She thought of it sometimes, but not often: she did not dare. They are the few and the blessed among us who dare dwell on that bright wraith who began life with us, and whom we used to call I. There seems to be a kind of antagonism between that lost dreamer and the toiler who has ousted it. Let be. Do not bring them too near each other. The children cry. The doorbell rings. The customer calls. Here are the quarter's bills.

Mary Hathorne had married her scholar for love of him, with her big blue eyes wide open; but they were the eyes of a girl who had never had to count a carriage-fare, or wear dyed dresses, or go without a popular book. She had never heard the price of roast beef. She had never dressed in a cold room on winter mornings. She had all the new magazines; for her father brought them home. She had bought her gloves by the dozen.

Poverty she had read about. Poverty—with the assurance of ignorance and youth—she had written about; for she began to send little things to her father's paper when she was quite a girl; but personal poverty, biting, blinding poverty, such as comes to the rich in mind and spirit, the kind of poverty which holds a delicately reared, finely organized creature sheer over the precipice of cold and hunger and pauperism—of this she knew no more than she did of the Simian vocabulary,[4] or the amusements of a London slum.

She had trained herself not to think much, or often, now, of her father's home. (There had been one of those large salaries which stop when the managing editor does, and which are responsible for the habits of ease that have no backers in accumulation or inheritance.) Sometimes now, on a dark morning, she would wake and put out her hand instinctively to find the electric bell, and ring for Kathleen to bring the hot water, and light the cannel fire in the grate; and to put her rose-lined wrapper and slippers beside the bed. Then she would remember that she must go, shivering, and call her new maid-of-all-work, or crawl downstairs herself to shake the kitchen fire, if the old cook had "given notice," as was more likely, because of an objection to children, or a preference for cream in her coffee.

Mrs. Hathorne had been an easy, happy city girl, one of the fortunate; the motherless, only child, the adored idol.

When her father died, a year after her marriage, life had hardly begun to undeceive her vigorous, hopeful heart. They had quite a comfortable home at Zion's Hill, and she explained the absence of things by saying, We are in the country.

This November afternoon, when she crawled up the steps of the pert little suburban house of seven rooms, and her husband had gone to start the furnace fire, she drew up the shades in the cold kitchen where the grocery-book hung, and looked out. The sky was darkening over the Queen Anne house opposite. She glanced at the big gravel-pit at the foot of the street. Then the luggage came crashing up the steps, and she wondered how she was going to unpack it all with such a backache, and then remembered that if she cried she would be good for nothing. It was one of those moments when the terrible inadequacy of power to necessity overwhelms us.

"Poor Papa!" she said. Only a woman will understand that irrelevant little cry. She was glad he had not lived to see how hard it all was.

Then her strong voice rang cheerfully through the empty house:—

"Are the *book*-boxes all right—all here? The rest are less valuable. Dear! Come up and see how beautifully everything has come through. . . . Oh, it is better than boarding!"

She turned, when the expressmen had left them alone, and clung to him in a wave of passionate tenderness.

"Oh, it is a *home*. Dear, don't worry. We will keep it. I will work. We will work—when we get settled. And there is my new book. You *shall* have meat enough, and all the new reviews!"

She managed to slip away from him that evening, as, with soft feminine obstinacy, she had meant to, all along. There was no kerosene. They needed tacks. There was nothing for his breakfast.

"And you are so tired. There, dear! I will run to the stores."

"I *am* tired," acceded the teacher, sinking heavily upon the cheap lounge which he had drawn up beside the register. He let her go—she smiled to think how easily, as she hurried down in the windy November night, as straight to the post office as her aching feet could carry her.

With fire on her white cheeks, and breath panting through her delicate lips, she snatched the evening mail from the postmaster. Her agitation attracted the attention of the postmaster's sister, who watched her as she tore open the only letter addressed to herself. She sat down in the show-window (the post office had been built for a shoe store) and read the letter, which ran:—

MRS. M. L. HATHORNE:

Dear Mrs. Hathorne,—We are in receipt of your MS. entitled "Love's Daily Bread." We should have acknowledged it some weeks ago, but in the pressure of business it has been overlooked. We beg to say that we will give it our consideration at our earliest convenience. We hope that it may prove as satisfactory as the novel which we had the pleasure of publishing for you some years since. We regret to say that the excellent sales of "A Platonic Friendship" have come to a practical end. We hope that the tale which we have in hand will prove to be of a more permanent interest to the public.

We are, madam, yours very truly,

BIND & BLOW, Publishers.

Mary Hathorne had stumbled upon what is called literary success as softly and with as much surprise as she stumbled now, for very exhaustion, upon a rolling pebble in the concrete sidewalk. She had written a book, and people read it. That was all she knew about it. Editors had fought upon it, women had cried over it, and men smoked over it; libraries took twenty copies of it; her dearest poet wrote to her about it, and her most dreaded critic recognized her for it—all these facts had puzzled as much as they pleased her. She was too modest, too naïve, too spontaneous a woman to analyze or to train herself. She had written the book as naturally as she had fallen in love. She had accepted her success as simply as she sang to her babies. It had been a dizzy experience, short-lived and intoxicating. She was, in brief, one of too many American writers who are the victims, not the masters, of what we call fame; who are caught to the clouds and dashed to the ground on the whirl of the same tornado. She was a "one-book author." She had flashed and puffed out. She was threatened with the fate that meets the gift which has no sustaining power. She knew by instinct—for she had genius enough to possess fine instincts—that her new book would not move easily. But she had not expected as much suspense and delay as if she were a new author.

"And oh, we need the money—we need it so!" she cried.

For the proceeds of "A Platonic Friendship" were gone long ago: she had, in fact, sold her copyright for a trifling sum. Yet she had really expected her new novel to make them comfortable for a while. A chilly doubt was sinking into some quicksand in her mind. She was not used to being slighted by publishers. She tore the letter of Messrs. Bind & Blow into twenty pieces. Her husband need not see it. He seemed to be asleep on the lounge when she got in; by-and-by he turned, and asked if she had the tacks. No mention was made of the publisher's letter. If there were good news, she would have run up the steps, and dashed in to tell him. He knew, before her footfall turned the corner. But it was not necessary to say anything. Had he not let her go to the post office on purpose? No matter what she thought of him for doing so. He rolled over on the lounge like a lazy brute, while his heart was wrung for her. He knew that he spared her something harder to her than an aching back or blistered feet. He had begun already to deceive her in this matter with the divine deceit of love.

"I can't go to bed yet," she said at half-past ten o'clock. "You'd better go. The mattresses are warm enough now, and we *cannot* work any more to-night. I must sit up awhile over those proofs which came this morning. There are twelve galleys—a double lot. They should have caught the return mail."

These were the proof-sheets of a little Sunday-school book, written over a year ago to meet a doctor's bill. The book had been paid for on receipt of the manuscript; it had not gone to press until this time.

Now proof-sheets, as none but their slaves and victims know, easily take high rank in that class of inanimate things which is possessed of the Evil. The essentially modern imagination might call them the electric cars of the literary profession. Without regard to life or limb, they roll crashing into that margin of existence which is reserved for other human exactions. They lie in wait for one's hour of maddening preëngagement. They lurk, watching for one's direst emergency. They select the confusing occasions of public amusement, and are well known to prefer a houseful of company. They delight to hit the eve of a journey. They meet the exhausted traveller at the door of his hotel. In the house of his friend he becometh a hermit, and sitteth solitary, correcting his galleys in the face of the offended host, who is a recent acquaintance, and impressed with the bad manners of the literary class.

The proof-sheet delights to detain one from the reception given in honor of the author. It pursues one to the foot of the lecture platform, and to the pulpit stairs. It loveth Christmas eve and house-cleaning. It aims even at the wedding-day. It haunts the sick-room. It shows a ghoulish interest in the crises of bereavement. I have repeatedly known it to pursue funerals, and to call the mourner from the coffin, or meet him as he returns from the grave. On such timely and welcome occasions the printer's brief command, "Return immediately," stares in the face the unfortunate who has vainly hoped for the freedom of an hour of sorrow or of joy.

Therefore, when her proof-sheets must needs select her moving-day to add their fire to her whirling brain, poor little Mrs. Hathorne felt no undue surprise. It did indeed occur to her that if she had been a washerwoman her day's work would have been done by this time, possibly even been deferred or omitted in view of the circumstances. But this white-handed daughter of toil was a patient little woman, and more accustomed to do her work than to complain of it. She sat till midnight, then crawled up and threw herself on the bed in her clothes. She was too exhausted to undress, and Aristotle Demosthenes Hathorne was too sound asleep to know it.

The children came out when the house got warm, and life in Cantelope "set in," as we say of a snowstorm. They were pretty, pleasant children enough; gentle and shy, and not inhumanly noisy—scholars' children; easily amused with picture-books, and accustomed not to play auction or tally-ho while their parents read and wrote. But they had the defects of their temperaments; being sensitive, they were not strong; they were ailing a good deal; the autumn was cold; the boy had the croup, and so on; and their mother did not get to work, as she had hoped, upon her novelette for the "Pacific."[5] It would have made them all quite easy for the winter if it could have been finished; and then, if it had been paid for in advance.

"I seem to be too tired to write," she said, apologetically, when her husband came home, gloomy and bitter, from his two cheap pupils and told her that one of them was about to prefer a Harvard tutor, being the son of a lime-contractor, who thought Mr. Hathorne behind the times.

"I am sorry I can't seem to be stronger and get at it. We must depend upon my book this year. Never mind, dear!"

"You say that every time," he muttered. "You'd say 'Never mind, dear,' if we were ordered to Siberia, or providing a dinner for the Spartan's fox."[6]

His soft dark eyes filled. He looked at her with the adoring hunger of a man who is cheated by fate out of his natural right to protect from toil and responsibility the woman whom he loves. Then he went upstairs and locked his study door.

She listened for a few moments to his heavy footfall, nervously pacing overhead and shaking the thin floor.

"Come, Popsy! Come, Boy!" she called merrily to the children. "Come down to the post office and get a good-luck letter!"

This nervous journey to the post office had become both the open and the secret occupation of her restless days. A singular silence had fallen upon the house of Messrs. Bind & Blow. When before had the author of "A Platonic Friendship" been kept waiting by a publisher? The book should have been in press by this time. The "good-luck letter" did not come.

"I fink it's nuffin but Sandy Close or a Bible story,"[7] confided Boy to Popsy, with masculine and modern skepticism as to the occult.

"Oh, Boy!" rebuked Popsy, on a high moral throat tone. "Ve Bible *came*."

"I fought a man to-day, mamma," observed Boy, as he cantered to the post office. "It was ve grocer-man; I pitched into him, I bet you!"

"Dear me, Boy! Why in the world should you fight the grocer?"

"'Cause I was engaged to his little sister, who sits on ve cart," explained Boy, serenely. "She said Tennyson was a bigger writer van you, mamma.[8] So I broke ve engagement. I *could n't* fight a girl, you know. So I fought ve grocer. She's nuffin but a step-sister, anyhow."

"Mamma! Has you' good-luck letter come? *Mamma!*"

"Run home, Popsy," she said faintly. "Run on, Boy. I'll overtake you."

She sank down on the show-window. The office was empty. The sun streamed in all over the steam-heated, suffocating room. Mrs. Hathorne slowly opened the letter of Messrs. Bind & Blow. Her fingers shook so that the postmaster's sister could see them. Her eyes dashed over the words:—

". . . We regret to be obliged to decline the publication of your novel, 'Love's Daily Bread.' We have submitted the MS. to three of our best readers, which accounts for our delay in forwarding to you the result of our consideration. There is a diversity of opinion among them, but the odds are against the wisdom of our undertaking the work at the present time. It does not present itself to the judgment of the house as possessing the popular qualities of your former book; and we fear that its publication would disappoint both yourself and us.

"Hoping to receive from you at some future time a novel calculated to maintain the enviable literary reputation which you have already acquired, we are, dear madam, yours very truly,

"BIND & BLOW."

The children came trotting back for her, she stayed so long; and the postmaster's sister asked her if she did n't feel a little faint.

"Don't arx her, Boy," whispered Popsy, with the quick intuition of a little woman. "Don't arx mamma for luck letters to-day. It is n't coming till annover mail."

When she got home her husband met her. His thin jaws worked unsteadily. He came down the steps and helped her in.

"He knows," she thought. "He sees. I need not tell him."

Neither said anything to the other about the manuscript; and dusk came on. She left her last domestic experiment, hopefully imported at extra wages from Cantelope-on-the-Saint-Henry, to provide such a supper as the gods might decree, and went away upstairs alone.

"You ought to be too proud to cry, you poor gray-haired thing!" she sobbed. She tossed her things about to find a pink ribbon that brightened up her worn black "afternoon dress"; she added a bit of fine lace and an antique bracelet that her father gave her. She had a grim notion of making herself gay, so nobody should notice that she had been crying. Searching for a fresh handkerchief (on such trifles hangs our fate), she opened her husband's bureau drawer by mistake.

There, face down upon his collars and cuffs, lay a fat brown parcel. She turned it over. It was the manuscript of "Love's Daily Bread." It had come by express while she was at the post office; and Mr. Hathorne had hidden it, like the poor masculine ostrich that he was, with stupid, blundering, precious tenderness, that she might not know, till he could get up courage to tell her.

It was days before either of them mentioned the matter. But when she went down to tea in the pink ribbon and antique bracelet, carrying herself in her poor dress as no woman can but one who has once known the ease and the manner of the world, the disappointed author went up to her unsuccessful scholar and put both arms around his thin neck.

"Never mind, dear," she said; "never mind!"

"Oh, I shall secure more pupils, without a doubt," he answered quickly. He thought himself a tactician of a high order.

The history of that first winter in the hired house at Cantelope Corner was the history of a manuscript.

Doubtless the neighboring Cantelopers bore their share of the universal human struggle; but sometimes it seemed, by comparison, an easy share. How fared it with the clerk, the carpenter, the baker, and the electrician in the Queen Anne house? Not one of them but knew more of daily creature comfort and less of harrowing anxiety than our two students; who, if they suspected the truth, that the grocer at their back door went to a better dinner and a warmer house than theirs, never admitted it, even to each other. The house of the electrician came to seem to them by bitter contrast a place of degree. They had been so used to the standards by which professional people judge of society that it was a moral shock to them to find themselves "looking up," as the phrase goes, to a man who ordered his coal by the dozen tons, and assaulted the English in which he addressed the expressman who brought out his game-dinners from the town markets.

"Wire has offered me a place in his what-you-may-call-it," said the ex-principal of Mount Zion Academy one day, with an ironical smile. "He has taken the notion that he would like a 'professor' attached to his concern. He suggested it on the 8.10 train yesterday, in everybody's hearing."

"You declined, of course!" The daughter of Boston's distinguished literary editor lifted her head. She was a sensible little woman, but the scorn of "trade" was in her blood.

"I—that is—I waived the question," replied Demosthenes Hathorne, with a haggard look. "I have one pupil left."

"And I, my book!" she cried, hotly. "I have sent it off again. It *must* be printed! I shall keep on sending it—till I die."

She was sitting by the window in the full light of their only sunny room when she spoke; and he looked at her closely. It occurred to him for the first time that she did not look as well as usual; but, being an instructed man, he reasoned that the impression was probably the result of a sub-conscious cerebration, acting automatically upon the brain-cells by the conduit of her last three words. This explanation was quite satisfactory to him.

Now it chanced that a week from that day she found herself too tired to go for the evening mail, and he somewhat reluctantly took the pathetic little walk upon which both of them had come to look with a kind of misery not to be understood in Cantelope Corner. The grocer and the electrician were spared that subtle anguish. The postmaster and the expressman, unconscious agents in the fate of the author who was outliving her popularity, looked upon the tragedy of that higher, sadder lot with the perplexity of beings from another world.

"Mummer's deaded," announced Popsy, calmly, when her father came home with the mail that night. The little girl was engaged in pouring the contents of the syrup jug upon the face of her mother, who lay unconscious upon the rude lounge.

It happened to be one of those interregna so common in country and suburban life, to be most succinctly described by the two, and the too familiar, words, "No girl." There had been guests to lunch as a matter of course—one of the Mount Zion faculty, and Boston ladies. Our friends could not wholly escape, even in Cantelope, the fate of the refined poor. They must meet the demands of cultivated society upon less than the income of a good mechanic.

This delicate woman, who had scarcely had a broom in her hands till she was married, had dropped, after the dishes were "done," in an attempt to mop the kitchen floor.

Demosthenes Hathorne was frightened. He looked vacantly about the womanless house, then sent, for the love of Heaven, to his nearest uneducated neighbor. Molly the cook ran over with the heartiest, prettiest Irish sympathy in the world, and between them they got the poor lady to bed.

In the bustle consequent upon this incident, Mrs. Hathorne did not ask her husband, nor did he tell her, whether he had heard from the manuscript of "Love's Daily Bread." He put away the letter, which was hidden against his throbbing heart; he tucked it between the leaves of Burton's "Anatomy of Melancholy."[9] Her book had been, somewhat curtly, refused.

When she came to herself she sent the story out again courageously enough. She had begun to expect it back by this time. They now fell into the way of avoiding the subject altogether. Neither asked, "Have n't Scowl & Critic acknowledged the manuscript yet?" Neither said, "Have you tried Vellum & Volume's Sons, as you meant to?" She ceased to haunt the post office. She winced when the expressman drove down the north side of their little street.

One bright morning, when Messrs. Frisky & Flourish had returned the book, with the objection that it was too "earnest" for their trade, Mary Hathorne stoutly put on her bonnet and rather a thick veil, and went in to Boston by the next train, bearing a rising determination in her heavy heart, and the rejected manuscript in her trembling hand.

She went straight to the private office of that prince of American publishers, who will be remembered longer for his great, good heart, and for exquisite courtesy to timid and troubled authors, than he will for the high quality of the success which gave him his unique position in the advancement of American literature.[10]

Her courage was born of her despair. She had never dared to approach him before. Her own publishers, selected with her natural timidity and in youth, had been but second-rate folk; and of the firms that had rebuffed her since, not one presumed to compete with the distinguished house to which, at last, so to speak, she crawled.

"I will never try again," she said, as she tottered into the elevator.

The publisher glanced at her card. "You do me honor, madam," he said, with that high-bred but wholly human manner of his. "'A Platonic Friendship' deserved the success it met. I shall examine your book with sympathy—I knew your father," he added gently.

The tears started behind her thick veil; she choked like a school-girl sending in a prize essay. In her effort to control her emotions her veil dropped, and his deep-set, observant gaze rested upon her sunken face. She had a beautiful face.

"That is a dying woman," thought the man of fine eyes.

"I have been—discouraged," she breathed impulsively.

Then, like the unworldly being that she was, half-child, half-woman, she dashed headlong, and told him the whole story.

"I may as well take my manuscript back now," she gasped. "You won't want it—now I have told."

She held out her shaking hand.

But he who was wisest of the wise in the mysterious laws that govern the great freshets of public taste and whim—the great publisher shook his gray head, and snapped the lock of his awful safe upon "Love's Daily Bread."

"Dear Mrs. Hathorne," he said firmly, "I do not conduct my house according to the judgments of other publishers. You are tired out, I see, and disheartened, as you say. You forget that, while it is not uncommon for a popular author to meet apparent failure after a first success, there sometimes comes what athletes call a second wind. Whatever happens, you may feel sure that your manuscript will have been read by a friend to your best possibilities and to yourself. Even if this book should fail— what of that? You have a dozen better in the brain that conceived your first novel. Take heart. Believe in yourself—for the public believes in you; and so do I."

"She needs roast beef—and cream—and a nurse for the children," he thought, with swift compassion, as he watched the color dash her deathly face.

The grocer left his cart standing where it was, and ran over to Mr. We-Hold-the-Wires' Queen Anne back door. He ran fast, and entered breathless.

"Molly! Molly, my dear! Hurry over to Hathorne's for the Lord's sake; and maybe Mrs. Wire would go; they need women there! She's taken very dangerous, and nobody to home but the young ones and that Tom-fool of a Swede, who can't speak a word of Christian English, from Northwest Cantelope. And do be quick about it!"

It was hours, it was days, it was years, for aught she could have told them, when she lifted her conscious eyes to their watching faces.

"Kathleen!" she breathed.

She thought she was in her father's house. But it was not Kathleen. Irish Molly was there, crying as the women of her race cry from the bubbling sympathy of their kind and easy hearts. Mrs. W. H. T. Wire was there, so gently and so deftly serving this stricken neighbor that one would never think to ask whether her husband had been to college. And then there was a doctor, from Cantelope Cascade. A voice somewhere spoke of "such an excellent nurse."

"Has n't my husband come home from Boston yet?" asked Mary Ha-thorne, feebly.

Then she perceived that arms held her, and that they were his. Great burning tears fell on her face.

"Oh, Thene," she said, "it will give you such a headache!"

She did not say anything more then; she did not ask about the baby; and it was not till the next day that they told her that the little creature—born long before it was expected—had breathed and cried and died.

She did not express any sorrow, but only said to her husband: "I'm afraid I was n't quite strong enough to take care of it. And how could we have sent another through college?"

Midwinter sank heavily into the windy climate of Cantelope Corner. Do the best they might, the house was cold. She could not leave her room, and indeed she showed no inclination to do so.

"I shall be better next week," she said. But next week she was not any better. She did not talk much, even to her husband. But he could see that anxiety did a deadly work upon her. It was the moral anxiety of a woman who has borne the heavy end of life for her beloved so long, and so bravely, that death appeared to her like the return of the universe to chaos.

"Boy must go to Harvard, you know," she said one day. "I don't see how it is ever going to be done—without me," she added, in a dull voice. But when he tried to answer her, she stopped his trembling lips with her little, shrunken fingers, and sank away into a weak sleep.

She talked affectionately of Irish Molly now and then. "Give her some of my clothes. I have one or two dresses left that she would be willing to wear. And then there is dear Mrs. Wire. I never understood such sorts of people before. She has done things so—so delicately. I wish you could find some way to repay our obligation."

Then he plucked up courage to tell her that he had accepted the position in W. H. T. Wire & Co. He hoped to cancel any obligation they were under by serving the science of electricity, as represented in that particular firm, with the honor and the intelligence of an educated gentleman.

"I will give him more than my salary's worth!" he said, proudly. "It is only on trial," he pleaded. "I have n't committed myself for more than six months. And I've about concluded, Mary, that if a man can't do one thing, it is no disgrace to him to do another. Besides, the fact is, my darling, I have parted with my last pupil."

"Oh, never mind!" she sighed, with the phantom of her old smile.

All this while she had never alluded to her book. She had not once asked him if he brought anything for her from the evening mail. Into a silence as deep as that other silence down which she was sinking, she dropped the subject of "Love's Daily Bread" forever.

"It has been rejected," she told herself quite plainly, "and he can't bear to tell me."

Only once she said to him: "My work is over, Thene, don't you see? My day is done. I've run my race, and I'm not fashionable any more. I don't suppose I write after the new style. And I have n't been very strong, you know. And oh, we've had such a hard pull!"

The tears did not start in her dry, bright eyes. She looked on, over his head, out of the window, at the cold sky that overhung the gravel-pits. She did not seem to see him. The children ran in and called her, kissing and laughing, but she responded vaguely to them.

He felt at the bottom of his heart that she was so worn out, she needed rest so much, that she was not altogether sorry to die. He perceived that she was not making the full fight. And yet, God knew! she loved him. But she was sinking for lack of a stimulant which he could not give. Already the awful distance of death seemed to have crept in between the husband and the wife.

"Kiss me on my cheek, dear," she said. "Don't keep away the air. Oh, I've tried—to do my share—to help along. But it is n't easy doing . . . so many things. Don't let Popsy take to writing."

Popsy and Boy went to the morning mail, for their father had gone in on the early train; it was his first day's work in the service of W. H. T. Wire & Co. It wrung his heart so to leave her from eight o'clock till five, that he forgot that it was otherwise afflicting to "go into trade."

So Popsy and Boy went to the mail. The nurse and the Swede remained in the house. It was a sunny day.

The children cantered down and trotted back. She lay idly on the lounge, vaguely looking over at the Queen Anne house, and did not see the little things when they ran down the northern sidewalk. They rushed, and bounded in.

Popsy carried the papers, and Boy hugged the letters to his breast. There were several of them, and she looked them over idly; two from Mount Zion, for Mr. Hathorne; a bill; another bill; a receipt; a few pages of pretty feminine sympathy for herself from a Beacon Street friend; last in the pile, a letter in a strange hand. The envelope bore the crest of the great publishing house, to whose threshold she had crept with the rejected manuscript which she had threatened to send somewhere "till she died."

She did not show any emotion now. She felt too near the real world to be shaken by the phantasms of this. What could happen? What could matter now? The book had been refused weeks ago. The great publisher was sorry she was dying, perhaps. He would say some kindly thing—for her father's sake. She cut the letter slowly, with a little pearl letter-opener which the children gave her on Christmas.

A folded paper dropped from it, which fell to the floor. She read the letter leisurely.

"My dear Mrs. Hathorne," so it ran, "I owe you an apology for my delay in writing. A somewhat serious illness must be my excuse. Being now quite well again, I have myself read your novel, 'Love's Daily Bread,' and shall take much pleasure in publishing the same. I regard it as a story of a high order, and a great advance upon your first. I shall be happy to publish it upon the usual ten per cent. royalty. But I am so confident of its success that I take the liberty of enclosing our check for a sum in advance, which, I hope, you may feel an interest in receiving, as a test of our faith in the book. When your profits upon the sales shall have reached the limit of this sum, your royalty upon all subsequent sales will begin. If these terms are agreeable to yourself, we will send contracts to that effect for your signature, and put the book to press at once.

"I anticipate for the novel a rousing sale. *You have found your second wind.* I predict for the book a literary success which will inspire you to write us a dozen more.

"I am, dear Mrs. Hathorne,

"Yours sincerely,

"_____."

"Mummer," said Popsly, severely, "You've dwopped a good-luck letter. Boy was making a cannycupio of it. I took it away, for he don't know any better; 'n' now he's playing cut his froat wiv you' Christmas letter-scutter."

The child put the folded paper into her mother's transparent hand. It was a check for one thousand dollars.

She took her first walk to the post office one divine spring day, and the children cantered on before. Hope had done its hearty work. The wine of success sprang to her head and bounded in her veins. Care fled, and death followed the footsteps of care.

What a day! The early suburban robins and blue jays swooped upon the lightning-rod of the rented house, and swayed away, chattering and trilling joyously. The very sunshine seemed to say: "Well again! Well again!" Even the quartz in the gravel-pits glittered like something precious.

The Queen Anne house opposite was all alive with neighborly interest. Mrs. Wire came down the steps and offered her a glass of wine, and Molly ran out bareheaded and over the street, and gave the convalescent lady a good hug before everybody, for she said she could n't help it.

Then the expressman drove up, and said how glad he was to see her out again. And the postmaster's sister said she was quite a stranger, and welcome back! But the grocer stopped his cart, and lifted her in, and took her home, for she said she was n't fit to walk it. He was definitely deferential, and asked her how she liked the butter. He talked about "Love's Daily Bread." He said there was a piece about it in the Cantelope "Weekly Telephone." He said he heard it was a bigger thing than "The Innocent Sin." In the course of the little journey he confided to her that he hoped to marry Molly in July. And all the neighborly, pleasant place, the "town with the country heart," seemed to her to shine that day; and she felt as if her own happiness were something which had brimmed over till it flooded and filled the world.

Her husband came home by an early train. When he saw her watching for him at the window, looking like a new wife in her new cream-white gown, but leaning, pale and sweet, in her old place in her old way, the children, all faces and no bodies, like the cherubs in the pictures, cuddling behind her, he choked, and bowed his face, and blessed God; and then he ran up the steps, and caught her.

By and by she showed him the letter which she had kept all day. "We will read it together," she said. "I thought I'd rather wait for you."

It was the letter of the publisher who was so wise in the wiles of the world of books, and so tender in the world of the broken of spirit and of hope.

"The book is moving grandly," so he wrote.[11] "The orders are coming in by telegraph. 'Love's Daily Bread' will be the novel of the year. When you are quite well, give us another."

"I wonder if *I* might take another?" said Demosthenes Hathorne, slowly.

He turned his wife's face to his; and if he was prouder of the kiss than he was of the book, who would blame him?

First published in *Harper's New Monthly*, January 1893, 282–94 and collected in *The Empty House* (Boston: Houghton, Mifflin, 1910).

The Oath of Allegiance

It was the time of great purposes and small hopes; it was the time of grand deeds and dark dreams; it was the time of glory and madness, of love and despair; it was the time of the greatest motives and the noblest achievement, the truest praying and the bitterest suffering that our land and our day have known.[1]

The story which I have to tell, in so far as it is a story at all, is a tale of the war, and therefore not in the fashion. It is in such important particulars true that it may ask a respectful hearing, since, in the matter of which I have to speak, it will be found that the fact rather than the way of putting the fact is the source of interest.[2]

It was the summer of the year 1862, in the New England university town which let us call Bonn upon these pages. The year and the term were at their bloom; the elms were in rich leaf, and stood stately, like unconscious pagan divinities, august, in groups and ranks upon the college greens. The paths were weeded and clean. The grass was long and luxuriant; for this was before it was thought necessary to shave one's lawn to fighting-cut. The June air melted delicately against the cheek. The proper cultivated flowers grew in the proper places, as such things do in well-directed towns. The white Persian lilac was in blossom in the sedate gardens of the faculty. The well-trimmed honeysuckle clambered over the well-painted porch. The June lilies, in rows, stood decorously dying on the edges of the graveled paths. No one ever did anything indecorously in Bonn,—except, of course, the boys.

One of the boys had been dangerously near an indecorum in one of those highly cultivated gardens on the June day of which we speak. It had been a merry day, full of sun and winds and spices, full of the essences of growth and blossom and of reaching on to that larger life which precedes a glowing death; and the sturdy boy felt it, as he ought to, restlessly; not as the serene elms did, and the white lilac. The elms always seemed to him to belong to the faculty.

As he sat in the shade of the particular elm that overhung the southeast corner of Professor Thornell's garden, on the rustic seat (of iron, painted, not at all rusty) against the high stone wall, the arms of the tree swooped over him vigilantly, and gave him an uneasy sense as of one who would be requested to stay after that recitation if he forgot himself. Nature herself always seemed, in Bonn, to be appointed by the trustees.

His companion on the painted rustic seat did not say "swooped." She said "swept,"—the branches swept. She was the only daughter of Professor Thornell.

The young man, it was easy to see at a glance, was of a sort known in college circles as the popular fellow. This may mean almost anything; it sometimes means the best of things, as perhaps in this instance. He had a happy, hearty face. His eye was as direct as a noon sunbeam, and at times as bright; at others, it withdrew, like the eyes of a much older man, into a subdued cloud, blue, or gray, or violet, or one knew not what. He had bright brown hair, curly, and beneath the boyish mustache the cut of a firm, rather full, but remarkably delicate mouth was agreeably visible. He had the complexion and hands of carefully reared but athletic boys. He did not look as if he had ever done a stroke of work in his life outside of a campus or a schoolroom. One smiled on glancing from his cheek, ruddy and fair as a girl's, to his palms, gnarled with the knocks of baseball, and his iron wrists. He had a round, Greek head, well set upon his shoulders. Seen for the first time in a crowd, an experienced teacher would have said of him, "There goes a promise,—a well-born, well-balanced promise."

The girl beside him was a trifle older than he, by the shade of a year, perhaps. At their age each camel's-hair stroke of the brush of time tells. This little circumstance added dignity to her carriage and appearance. She hardly needed it. To some of the students she would have been more charming with a touch less of stateliness, but Harold Grand liked her the better for it. Deep in his young heart he was proud of the fact that the fellows used to say that you could not get near her with a ten-foot pole. This ancient and obvious figure of speech was the final college tribute to the distance, the modesty, and the sweet haughtiness of womanhood. Young Grand rated it accordingly.

In the pleasant, delicate fashion with which our best young people conduct such comradeships they had been friends for a long time, as university time goes, since junior year; and he was about to graduate. They talked friendship, as young folks do. Of love they had never spoken.

We speak of language as if it depended upon the lips to utter. What does the heart say, and what the turn of the head, the touch of the hand, the fall of the foot, or the mood of the eyes? He sat looking at her that day steadfastly, with the bright, fearless, masculine gaze before which her own drooped. She leaned against the painted seat, and stirred uneasily. "Will you have the rest of the song?" she said. She reached around without turning her head, and lifted her guitar from the grass to her lap. Miriam did not play the piano, like the other girls. To please her father she had accomplished herself in the use of this old-fashioned instrument, her mother's guitar. She played for Harold now and then because he liked it. Little dashes of light from the elm branches overhead flecked her sensitive face. She was not a beautiful girl, but she had the prophecy of a noble face.

She wore the "spring-and-fall dress" of a well-regulated professor's daughter, who must always appear as pretty as possible on the least possible sum of money. The dress was gray, trimmed with dark blue. Her eyes played between the two colors. She wore a drapery sleeve, in the fashion of the day, with a wide, full white undersleeve finished with a narrow linen cuff; a linen collar bound her throat: both were fastened by plain gold studs. Her hands, like her playing, were different from the other girls', for she wore no rings.

Young Grand was quite familiar with the details of this severe little costume, for it was not new this spring. It seemed to him a kind of celestial uniform created for her, but he had never said so. She mourned sometimes that she could not "dress" when Harold called. She would have liked to put on a new gown every time he came to see her, and so be a new girl on each occasion; but she had never said that, either. She did not feel so when the other boys called. Now, when Tom Seyd came it was quite different.

"Yes, play to me, please," said Harold Grand.

She struck a few notes, and stopped.

"I can't!" she pleaded.

"Why not?"

"It's because—it's the way—it's the way you look at me."

He did not look at her any the less for this. She began to tremble, and her cheek blazed. Then he took a swift, manly pity upon her, and folded his arms and turned his head, staring at the stone wall and the elm tree. He had never touched her in his life; beyond the conventional grasp of meeting and parting, his hand had never met her hand. He would as soon have dared to touch the Ludovisi Juno.[3] But now his moment of weakness overtook him, as it overtakes most of us at some unexpected time. His fingers strolled to the edge of her gray dress; his arms ached to take her, so he folded them, like the young gentleman that he was, and nodded at the faculty elms as who should say, "No, sir! You don't keep me after this recitation!" And Miriam began to sing.

Thus ran the scene of their simple courtship; so plain and pure and young, one might say so primitive, that it seems almost too slender to re-set, in these days when our very boys and girls coquet with the audacity and the complexity of men and women of the world. And that was all.

Call the memory on wings through the upper air, move the sympathy gently, and summon the imagination softly, and possibly, then one may understand what one has forgotten or what one never understood. We keep ourselves supplied with superior, slighting phrases for the loves of boys and girls. It would become us to preserve our respect for, and our comprehension of, experiences which may be the tenderest and the truest of life.

And Miriam, under the elm tree in her father's garden, to her mother's guitar, began to sing:—

> "Under the floods that are deepest,
> Which Neptune obey;
> Over rocks that are steepest,
> Love will find out the way."[4]

She had a sweet, not a strong voice; and she sang as the young and the happy do. Harold Grand unfolded his arms. He became curiously aware of the pressure of his mother's ring upon his finger. His eyes dropped from the elm to the white lilac; then they strayed to the drooping yellow lilies. The end of the long blue ribbon at her throat blew in the warm air against his wrist. He restrained it softly with his hand.

"Go on," he whispered; for the girl had stopped.

"Over the mountains
And over the waves,
Under the fountains
And under the graves,"

sang Miriam,—

"Over the mountains,
And under the graves,
Love will find out the way."

Her voice fell and ceased; her ringless hands strayed over the strings of the old-fashioned instrument; she looked as if she had come out of a picture of the date of her mother's youth. He watched her profile, with the braid of brown hair low in the neck, and the silver arrow piercing the coil above. The air began to cool a little in the hot garden. The bees whispered sleepily to the honeysuckle, disdaining the lilies, which had left their prime behind them. The afternoon sank.

"Yet I like them," said Miriam abruptly. "I love those yellow lilies as long as they live, and when they die I love their ghosts. You never could think how they look by moonlight! I come out sometimes and walk up and down that path, quite late, to see them."

"You are changing the subject," suggested the young man, but not with the self-possession that the little sally might have implied.

"I have forgotten what the subject was," said Miriam mischievously; for she had recovered herself the first of the two, as women do.

"Oh—it is one as old as—older than we are—older than earth is, for aught I know," the boy said, passing his hand over his eyes. "And I was going to say—to try to say—"

Then the color burned the girl's fine, reserved face from brow to throat. Then she caught her breath, and thrust out her hand as if she would have interrupted him. But she was spared her pretty maiden trouble.

Professor Thornell, accompanied by Professor Seyd (of the Scientific Chair), came down the garden walk. The two learned men walked ponderously between the rows of yellow lilies. They discussed the unfortunate friction at the last faculty meeting, and the probable course of pedagogical harmony at the meeting of that night. They were absorbed in these great themes. They looked vaguely at the young people on the painted iron settee. Professor Thornell smiled affectionately at his daughter and passed on, and forgot her at once.

It no more occurred to him that she and young Grand needed matronizing than that he should offer a chaperon to the busts of Apollo and Minerva in the college library.[5] But when he had paced to the garden fence and back again, he stopped confusedly to say:—

"My dear, I forgot—we are so driven with commencement business—I forgot entirely that I had a message from your mother. She said I was to tell you—How unfortunate! It was some minor domestic errand. Professor Seyd, what *was* it that Mrs. Thornell desired to have done?" pleaded the Professor of English Letters helplessly.

"She desired a salad prepared for supper," prompted the Professor of Science accurately. "She desired, if you found Miss Miriam, that she should prepare a *potato* salad, with the addition of beets."

Miriam rose at once. She gathered her guitar to her lap, and put on her straw hat. The two heavily instructed gentlemen continued their walk up and down the garden paths; supperless and inaccessible, they discussed faculty matters till eight o'clock that night.

The two young people passed on up to the house between the rows of dying lilies. They passed in silence, and separated at the front door. The winged moment had fled. The sacred embarrassment of youth and love fell between them. For his life he could not then have finished his sentence. Nor could she, for hers, have helped him.

Now, the scientific professor, having an unscientific and emotional wife, had gone home, as her nerves exacted, to report himself to her; thus he came late to the faculty meeting at the president's house. Professor Thornell was annoyed.

"We need all hands to-night," he remarked, with the natural acerbity of a colleague.

Professor Seyd turned upon him a stiffened face; it showed an unprecedented lack of color; he was usually a red, comfortable man.

"Have you seen the bulletins?" he demanded shortly. "I am just from the telegraph office. We have been defeated again. Our losses are said to be"—He began slowly to repeat, with his own frightful, statistical accuracy, the rumors—for there were only rumors yet to turn to—of the evening: *Killed—Wounded—Missing*—a fearful table.

The faculty sprang from their chairs and gathered round him, while with pallid lips, he recounted the horrors of one of the worst days of the Peninsular Campaign.[6] The gray-haired president uttered a fierce, unscholarly exclamation, and automatically reached for his hat and cane. He acknowledged afterwards that it came into his head to go down town and enlist. For once in the history of Bonn University, commencement was obliterated from the consciousness of her professors. The quarrel in the faculty was forgotten. The Professor of English Letters and the Professor of Science shook hands with the Mathematical Chair, their chronic foe.

"The boys are beside themselves. They are unmanageable," said Professor Seyd, with evident agitation. "The whole university is in the streets. It is rumored that President Lincoln will issue a call for more troops. Five-sixths of the senior class will enlist, if he does, and—God bless them!—I would if I were they!"

He had a boy of his own in the senior class. It had never occurred to him that *Tom* could go.

"Hush!" said Professor Thornell, with a break in his voice. "Hear them, now. Listen!"

Far down the street and wide over the college green the boys were singing; not wildly, but with a restrained pathos and solemnity, strange to their young lips:—

> "And then, what'er befalls me,
> I'll go where duty calls me."[7]

The tramping of their steps fell on the smooth, hard streets like the marching of an army corps. It approached the president's house with measured tread.

"The college militia is out," observed Professor Thornell. "They have done some good drilling, our boys."

The faculty answered with proud eyes. These elderly men flung open the doors and windows, and rushed out like boys to meet the other boys as they poured upon the lawn, calling for speeches. In the centre of the crowd stood the college company, drawn up rank and file. The lights blazed upon their grave young faces. They saluted their instructors solemnly. Their captain advanced from the line. He stood apart, with his curly head bared, while he conferred with the president. Nobody had such a manner as young Grand. He had heroic beauty that night. His eyes were elate and remote. He seemed to see no person present.

But Tom Seyd, back in the ranks, looked straight at his old father.

In the house of the Professor of English Literature, half a mile down the surging street, a girl opened the window of her room, and put aside the white dimity curtain, to lean over the sill and listen. The drumbeats tapped the hot night air, and grew above the ceasing and the silenced college songs.

"It is the boys out drilling," thought Miriam. "They are having a good time. I wish I could see—He looks so handsome in that uniform! And Father will make them a speech."

Commencement at Bonn was but a broken drama that agitated year. The ceremonials began, after their usual fashion at that time and in that college, upon one of the closing days of June. But on the first of July came the yet well-remembered call of the President of the United States for three hundred thousand more recruits.

He who lived the war through in a university town knows what patriotism meant, in those large days, to our educated men. Where was found the purer motive, the braver, nobler act? What class of heroes in our smitten land offered to their country life more high and precious, or death so calm, intelligent, and grand?

The scientific professor, with his habitual accuracy, had foretold the turn of affairs in the college quite precisely. In fact, five-sixths of the senior class, in one wild burst of sacred rage, offered themselves for enlistment; and a large number were accepted. The boys exchanged their diplomas for their muskets. The professor held an impromptu faculty meeting on the platform of the exhibition hall, where, for the first time in the history of the old university, commencement etiquette was hurled to the winds. The short-breathed trustees clambered up by the winding stairs into the anteroom, and these venerable men, with streaming eyes, signed the sheepskins, which they dispatched after the young heroes who had flung scholastic honor and peace and safety down at the scorching feet of that great July. And so the senior class of Bonn was nobly and irregularly graduated, and marched away.

In those fiery days, personal tragedy was but the little tongue of flame in the great conflagration. Men swept to their doom with ecstasy, and the firm-set lip trembled only when it gave the last kiss at home. Women, old in trouble, took upon their souls one anguish more, and uttered no complaint. Girls—sometimes I think that the girls had the hardest of it. Nobody thought so then, or perhaps believes it now. Who has ever measured the depths of the possibility of suffering in a girl's heart? She is so unused to life, so young and trustful of joy! She expects to be happy; she has endured so little, she has hoped so much; she tastes of tenderness and anticipates delight; she prays to God, she adores her lover, and believes in her fair fate. Why do the gray-haired women weep? What is this prattle about trouble that she overhears? By love she is incredulous of sorrow. By youth she overcomes the world.

Miriam, in her father's house, sat dumb. In an hour, in a moment, it seemed, her catastrophe had come upon her. At the call for three hundred thousand more to fight the war out, he had given himself, without doubt or delay. The captain of the college militia had dashed into service without a commission, and came to her in his private's uniform to say good-by.

In the whirlwind of those few wild days, leisure was the inaccessible thing, and privacy impossible. He came: it was a matter of moments. He was allowed a day in which to visit his home in New York; for he had a mother and a sister. *They* had rights. Miriam had none. Who thought to leave the boy and girl alone together? It did not occur to the unimaginative mother of an unengaged daughter to force the situation, or to create a difficult tête-à-tête in a house full of company long ago bidden for the spoiled commencement, and staying over out of sheer excitement, to discuss the national emergency. It did not occur to the Professor of English Literature, who bustled in to bid his favorite student Godspeed, and to tell him that the university was proud of him. Babbling guests overflowed the parlors and library, the piazza, and the hall itself.

It was raining, and the garden was uninhabitable. The two young people, in the pitiable publicity which, forced at the crisis of fate, has separated thousands of approaching lives, said farewell. They looked miserably into each other's eyes. Miriam heard an old clergyman in the back parlor doorway talking about Arianism.[8] A professor's wife in the hall was cackling to another about the lint that she had picked for the soldiers.[9] Dully the girl was conscious that her father—dear old stupid father!—stood behind her. He was telling Harold for the third time that Bonn was proud of her noble boys. Before everybody she and Harold clasped hands. Before all those people she saw him move across the threshold of her father's door, and step out into the summer storm and leave her. She stirred into the vestibule, and stood beside him. In the garden the elm trees were tossing about; a wet gust blew against her thin dress,—she wore a white organdie muslin with a little vari-colored pattern; she shivered in the wind. From the stone wall drops were dripping on the iron seat. The yellow lilies lay over the gravel, beaten by the storm.

"I shall write to you," he said, "I shall write." He wrung her cold hand. She gave one look at his bowed face; its expression awed her. She saw him put on his military cap. He turned and lifted it when he had reached the sidewalk. All the people stood about, but he looked only at her.

Miriam made her way back through the commencement company. She felt her way upstairs by the banisters, for she seemed to be going blind. She held the muscles of her face stiff. Everybody could see her. She was only an unbetrothed girl,—she had no right to cry.

She got up to her room, thrust open her blinds, and leaned against the dimity curtain. But she could not see him. She thought she heard the tread of his ringing feet as they turned the corner.

She tottered to her white bed, and flung herself face down. And the people babbled in the parlors. But the old clergyman talked no more of Arianism. Word had just been sent him by telegraph from New Hampshire that his only son had enlisted for the war. By and by a maid knocked at Miriam's door; for young Mr. Seyd had come; he would go to camp in the morning.

"Oh, I can't—I *can't!*" moaned Miriam. "Maggie—manage somehow!" She held her arms up to the other girl, her mother's servant, the only other young thing in the house.

"An' that you sha'n't!" cried Maggie. She went up to Miriam, and out of her warm Irish heart, and on the passion of the solemn time that washed out all little human laws and lines, she kissed her young mistress, for the first and only time in her life, and went away without a question or a word.

Confused phrases ran through Miriam's burning brain: "Father and mother hast thou put far from me—in this hour."[10] Only the Irish maid understood.

From Washington he wrote to her. It was a short note, dashed off in pencil upon the journey, on a leaf torn from his diary. Already the solemn strangeness of his sacrifice had moved between them. In a day the college boy had become a man. He had other things to think of besides herself. He wrote of the national emergency; he spoke passionately of the Flag and its perils; he said that he hoped to go soon into action. He should write her a letter before then.

"This is all I can manage now. I write on my cap, in the cars. The boys are chattering about me. They are all in excellent courage. Some of them are talking about my being made lieutenant. It was too bad all those old coves were round when I came to say good-by. I wanted to see you alone.

"I shall write again, when I can collect my thoughts as I wish to. I shall certainly write before I go on the field. I have a good deal to say to you, and I want to hear from you before we go under fire."

And this was all. From the young soldier no other message came to her. The poor girl tied her thick winter veil across her hunted eyes, and shadowed the post-office, anticipating all the mails before her father got them. She knew that the regiment had been ordered to the front,—everybody knew that. She knew no more than everybody knew. There was no letter.

Days writhed by, as such days do; weeks,—how many she could not have told. She lived like a creature under vivisection, who understands what the men of science are saying around the torture-table.[11] Her mother had begun to notice how she looked, and the Irish girl watched her furtively.

The professor's wife came slowly upstairs one burning midsummer day, and pushed open the unlatched door of her daughter's room. The blinds were closed, and Miriam sat in the green darkness by the window, in the great old-fashioned chair, cushioned in white, that she had gone to sleep in when she was so little that her feet could not touch the floor. Her face was turned toward the lines of fiery light that blazed between the slats of the blinds; her head lay back against the chair.

Mrs. Thornell stopped in the middle of the room. Her countenance was agitated.

"My dear," she said, with embarrassment, "Professor Seyd has news from Tom. There has been—I think they called it a skirmish—it was not a great battle—but Tom was wounded; not dangerously, I think. They have gone on to bring him home."

Miriam opened her eyes; she did not turn her head, nor did she find it necessary to speak.

"And—there were others hurt—and—Harold Grand."

"You need not try, mother," said Miriam distinctly. "Maggie told me. She brought me the paper."

"He died nobly!" faltered the mother. "And—it was instantaneous, my dear. He did not suffer—like some."

"Thank you, mother," said Miriam. She turned her head away from the hot window, and shut her eyes. Her head lay heavily against the high white chair. Helpless and distanced, her mother stood uncertain. Then she stole away and went downstairs.

Miriam crawled across the room, and locked her door. After a little she went back and unlocked it. She had no right, she remembered, even to turn the key upon her unnamed, unauthorized, unmaidenly anguish. She stood alone in her room, and lifted her arms up once to the invisible sky. In her face was one of the challenges that God himself must find it hard to answer.

"How do women bear their lives?" she said.

God who sends them only knows. She bore hers as other women do who are smitten as she was. Perhaps, on the whole, she bore it better than many. But she was very young.

The letter did not come. At first she looked for it a little, with the defiant hopefulness of youth. It was a long time before she gave up haunting the post-office. She went in the morning sometimes, but in the evening always. Her hand shook so that the clerk noticed it, when she took her father's seven o'clock mail. In time the reaction struck, and a sick horror of the whole thing came upon her. Then she went no more. "I shall write to you," he had said. But he had not written.

They brought him to his mother's home in New York; and although it was vacation, a delegation from the college went on to his military funeral. His mother and sister, in their black dresses, tied the flowers about his sword, and the scattered students wore crape upon their arms for thirty days.

Miriam wore her gray dress with the blue trimming, and the muslin with the bright spot. She would have gone on her knees for the shelter of a black veil in which to hide her face from the eyes of people. But Miriam had no right to the sacred insignia of mourning, in those days thought as necessary to the decency of grief as tears. She pinned on her bright ribbons, and trimmed her hat with flowers; she went to merrymakings with the young people, as she must. She laughed when she had to. She did not cry: that was the worst thing about it. She had never cried since Maggie brought her the paper with the list.

After a while she stopped wearing those two dresses, the gray, and the organdie that she had on the last time she saw him. She folded them and put them away, for she could not bear to look at them. Only girls will understand this.

On the guitar, now, she did not play. She could not hide that; it must stand in the parlor, in its usual corner. But she put away the sheet of

music on which were penciled the notes of the old English song that
she had sung to him:

> "Over the mountains,
> And under the graves,
> Love will find out the way."

But he had not found out the way.

So she took up her part in the long tragedy of life, and supported it,
as her nature was. Her pride was as fierce as her love; the twain seized
her like fighting Titans, and tare her.[12] She stood her ground between
them, as strong youth does; and one day she opened her sad blue eyes
and noticed that she was young no more.

It took the most ardent lover she had ever had to call her attention to
this unobtrusive fact; which was the last thing that he had intended to
do. It was a June day, in the year 1877, when Tom Seyd spoke to her,—
fifteen years after he and Harold had enlisted. Tom had loved her all
his life; he had never loved any girl but Miriam. She was a woman now,
thirty-five years old, and he a man.

Since young Seyd had become his father's assistant professor he had
been an absorbed, ambitious man; but he had forced the leisure to see
her so often that she had become in a measure dependent upon his
evident tenderness, as he meant she should. Indeed, she would have
missed it. She cherished beautiful, preposterous ideals of friendship, as
lonely women do; dreaming of noble devotion which asked for nothing in return. She blessed Tom Seyd in her desolate heart, that he had
never "made love" to her, and never would.

So when he told her, that day, without prelude or apology, that he had
always loved her, she experienced a suffocating, moral shock.

"It won't do," said Seyd firmly. "It won't go, all this about friendship.
I do not feel the need of a friend. It is a wife I want. I love you."

"But not in *that* way!" protested Miriam.

"I love you in just that way," said the young man, as quietly as if he
had been analyzing a crystal before the sophomore class. "I do not love
you in any other, and I never have."

"Then you have deceived me!" cried Miriam, growing as pale as a pear-blossom.

"I undeceive you, then," said Seyd. "I love you, and I believe that I could make you happy, if you would let me try."

He stated his case with something of his father's scientific manner; dryly, so far as the words went. But his voice shook, and his hand. And into his gray eyes, that she had always thought so commonplace and "worthy," she could not look; for they beat and blinded hers. She felt in them that which the most lovable of women does not often see,—the loyalty of an unselfish, unswerving, lifelong love.

She knew good women who would have given their lives—it was in her heart to say, would have sold their souls—for love like this.

And for what should she fling it from her? For the memory of a memory, the shadow of a wraith, the echo of the voice of an unseen spirit flitting through a dark and ghostly realm; for an oath of allegiance to a claim that had never existed; for love of a boy who had not loved her enough to find a way to tell her so before he died.

"I have waited fifteen years," said Tom Seyd patiently. "I have not intruded on you, have I? I have not been stupid about it, I think. I understood how it was. But I have loved you all the same and all the while."

Her white cheek burned. A sacred shame, even after all these years, covered her with womanly confusion. She remembered how she used to be called the proudest girl in the college town. Did he taunt her with her pitiable love? "Let me go!" she gasped.

"No, no," he pleaded. "Sit down here beside me—for a minute. Listen to me—here."

Then she lifted her eyes, and behold, he had led her to the painted iron seat against the garden wall. The elm tree rose above it, venerable and calm. The white lilac was in blossom; the bees of Bonn sang to the honeysuckle; in rows the yellow lilies were beginning to die.

But Miriam stood rigid and tall. She looked through him and on, beyond him, as if he had been the ghost, and that dead boy the living man.

"If I ever listen to you," she breathed, "it will not be *here*."

And with this she fled and left him. But his heart leaped with hope and madness; and he went down to his father's laboratory to try a difficult experiment, in the delirium that a man knows but once in life.

Miriam went up the garden walk and into the house. She felt her way by the branches of trees and shrubs; for she had, for the second time in her life, that feeling of one about to be stricken blind. The house was still that night, and empty. The professor was at faculty meeting, and the professor's wife at a commencement tea. It was one of the rare occasions when a grown daughter in her father's home may command the freedom and solitude which become so precious as we grow old.

Maggie brought the tea-urn, but said nothing. Maggie had grown old and sober. There was a grocer's boy who never came back from Antietam.[13] But Maggie wore his ring, and shared her quarter's wages with his mother. Miriam looked with a fierce envy, sometimes, at the Irish girl.

It came on to be a moonlit night, sultry and sweet. Miriam went to her own room, but could not stay there. She caught up her straw hat and wandered out. House, garden, home, seemed too small to hold her. She struck into the street, and began to walk. Automatically her feet turned toward the post-office, as they used to do fifteen years before, when the seven o'clock mail came in. The boys were singing on the campus. All the college town was bright and alive.

"I am the only ghost in it," thought Miriam.

Her father's mail had been taken, and she came wearily back. Into the dark parlor the moonlight fell through the long muslin curtains. The guitar stood in the corner. For the first time for fifteen years she took it in her trembling hands. There was no one to listen. She played and sang:—

"Over the mountains
And under the graves,
Love will find out the way."

With the wail of the worse than dead her voice faltered through the empty house. She laid her cheek against the old guitar and patted it.

"Oh, good-by, dear!" she said.

The college boys on the campus began to sing those cruel army songs, fifteen years old. What right had *they*, these fortunate, light-hearted sons of pampered peace, to torture people who lived the war through?

"Farewell, farewell, my own true love!"[14]

Impossible! Impossible to think about Tom Seyd till the boys had finished singing! And it was imperative to think about Tom Seyd. Miriam put down the guitar, and ran upstairs with her fingers in her ears. If she should listen to this live man, dead ones must be kept still. She cried out as if the boys of Bonn could hear her, or would regard her if they did, "Oh, boys, stop that singing! . . . It murders us,—women grown so old that you have forgotten we're alive!"

When the knock came at her door, she did not hear it at the first; for she was moving through those spaces where sound is not, nor time, nor human interruption. She was lying on her bed, with her face buried in the pillows. The moonlight built a bridge straight through the middle of the dark room. She got up and crossed it, to come to Maggie, who stood upon the threshold.

"Oh, Miss Miriam!" said Maggie, with broken breath. "For the love of God, come here! Come out to me lamp and see . . . for I darsen't go into the dark to give it yez!"

In the hall, a hand-lamp was set upon the little table. Maggie tottered beside it; the cheek of the Irish girl was whiter than the paper in her shaking hand.

For she held a letter, stained and marred and time-discolored, bearing the forgotten red postage stamp of the denomination of the war; a letter as old as—O God! as old as anguish! For when Miriam dashed it up against the light, the house rang with such a cry as it would have broken his heart, in heaven, to hear.

"It is his ghost," sobbed Maggie. "His ghost has taken his pen in hand to comfort yez!"

But when has it been recorded in the heavens above, or on the earth beneath, that a ghost could write as he had written? Living was the hand and living was the love that penned those worn and faded pages.

With a clang she locked, and double-locked, and triple-locked the door, to read this message from beyond the grave. She had the right now.—She could keep the whole world off. She and her sacred joy and her holy grief were sanctified at last. He loved her. He had loved her then and always. In a few manly, ardent words, written upon the march, he had poured his heart out, and placed it in her keeping. He had meant to write differently, he said. He had waited to find a better time. But war made no way for love. Would she listen to this poor love-letter? Spoiled, he said, as so much else was spoiled,—the lives of men and the happiness of women,—by the accidents of war.

"I shall give it to one of the boys who is on the sick-list and has a furlough," he wrote, "and he will get it mailed for me,—in Washington, I hope, or even in New York. I think it will go more quickly so, and surer. Our mails are irregular, you know, and uncertain. Write to me, if there is time. We may be called into action any hour. I hope I sha'n't disgrace myself, for your sake. I think I shall behave better if I can get your answer,—either way you put it. I have never dared believe you really love me. But if you do, or if you can,—enough, I mean, to be my wife some day,—I don't think I *could* die if I knew that. I should come back all right. 'Love would find out the way,' you used to sing— it seems fifty years ago! I shall write my mother about you, if you give me the right, at once. She and my sister would want to see you. I send you that old ring of mother's you used to see me wear. It is the best I can do, on the march. Wear it for me, dear, if you do love me, till I see your face again. For I am

Your own, and only yours,
   Till death and after it,
     HAROLD GRAND."

She read. She clasped the gray and tattered paper to her bosom and buried it there. She fell upon her knees, and lifted her streaming face to heaven. And then, for the first time in all those years, she broke into terrible sobs.

So much of this story of a letter as is true I tell; and for more I cannot vouch. What was the fate of the message for fifteen years withheld from the stricken girl? Perhaps the soldier on the furlough died. Perhaps, at the time, his pockets were not searched. Was he some friendless fellow, for whose affairs nobody cared? Did the letter slip between the lining and the army blue? Did the uniform pass from hand to hand? Perhaps it was cut up some day for a veteran's son, and so the worn envelope slipped out, and some one said to one of the children. "There is an old army letter, sealed and stamped, and never sent. Run and mail it, my dear. We must not open it or keep it. It may be some poor girl has waited for it all these years." Whether in this way or in that way God's mysterious finger traced the lines by which the dead boy's declaration of love did force its way to her, who shall say? I know no more than you, no more than she; for I tell it only as it was told to me.

Only this I can append. When young Professor Seyd came to the house again, that evening, the Irish girl stood in the front door and barred the way.

"It's no use, Professor Tom," said Maggie, "an' that I takes upon meself to say. There's a dead man got ahead of yez. Me and you are nothin', Mr. Tom,—nothin' to her but just livin' folks."

Then Maggie told him what had happened. And Tom Seyd went back to his father's laboratory without a word. In this he showed the discretion of his temperament, which accepts a fact, be it what it will and lead it where it may, without an idle protest.

On that great glad night, she had forgotten him as utterly as annihilation. The Irish girl was wise. He was nothing to Miriam but a living man.

The elm tree in the garden could have taught him that; and the Persian lilac might have told him, "It was not love she gave you." But the yellow lilies kept awake to watch for her.

She came at midnight, when all her father's house was still. She wore the old white muslin dress with the little colored pattern. She held her head like a bride, and trod like the Queen of Joy. Nor God nor man could say her nay, now. Proudly she took upon her soul the oath of allegiance which binds the living to the dead,—that ancient oath, so often taken, so often broken, and sometimes kept. She stopped beneath the elm, and stood beside the iron seat against the garden-wall. The moon-light lay at the flood. There Miriam put his mother's ring upon her marriage finger; and there she lifted from the earth to heaven the solemn face of the happiest woman in the land.

Originally appeared in *Atlantic Monthly*, April 1894. 465–76. It was the title story for Phelps's last collection of short stories, *The Oath of Allegiance and Other Stories* (Boston: Houghton Mifflin, 1909). Portions of it also appeared in the *Altruistic Review* 2 (1894).

Dea ex Machina

It was a smoky sou'wester—one of the brilliant and beautiful light winds which precede the gale due on the New England coast in the dying of August or the birth of September.

The catboat careened and labored a good deal,[1] making the course with some difficulty, as if the solitary sailor were unpractised or out of practice; but the expression of the man betrayed no discomfort whatever. Rather it might be said that a species of insane joy possessed him. His muscles were tense with delight; every nerve quivered rapturously. His dignified straw hat floated about in the swash of the bottom of the boat, and his curling gray hair blew boyishly back from his heavily lined forehead. His eyes were two mad dancers; upon his parted lips clung a smile of ecstasy.

"Nothing *can* make a catboat safe!" he muttered, joyously, gulping mouthfuls of dashing salt water between his teeth. "I always used to say so when I used to sail. But then, she doesn't know the difference. Cat or Cunarder, it's all the same to her, thank God![2] Fortunately," he thought, "it's the time for her nap. She won't see."

The town was now well behind him, and the shore approaching rapidly. About the hotel beyond the pier the summer people stirred like figures seen in a fever. A lady in a dory just abeam of him rowed with a strong stroke.[3] She wore a boating-dress of white flannel; her arms were brown and athletic. She glanced at him over her shoulder.

In the amber mist the spire of his church shot up dizzily; the roof of the parsonage showed gray and distant—the southern piazza, where the woodbine would not grow because the winters were so bleak; the row of poplars in his front yard, all bent by the easterlies, like round-shouldered little old men; the windows of his wife's room, and the white curtains—drawn? or parted? It was a tremendous question. The minister felt the cold drops start on his forehead beneath the splashing spray.

Now the catboat put her nose into the water and began to prance. She keeled heavily. The water ran over the rail like a river. An expression of bliss scarcely less than maudlin settled upon the minister's face.

A partly submerged reef (it was half-tide) ran out ahead of him, like a forefinger with a sharp nail. Everybody knew this reef; none better than he (she had allowed him to row), and he tacked to escape it. As he luffed,[4] a flaw dealt the catboat a vicious box on the ear. She keeled and capsized.

When the minister found himself in the water, his first sensation was one of mortified astonishment that it was so difficult to swim with his rubber boots on. He was a good man, a religious man, a saint in his way, but when he felt himself sinking, a big, natural, human terror of death possessed him.

As the water roared in his ears and crushed his lungs, he uttered two words only,—

"Poor Nelly!"

For twenty years the sweet reasonableness of this most manly man had idealized and sheltered an unreasonable woman. He had performed his share of the pious deeds expected of his holy office; but there were not wanting among his people a few cynics who held that the chief Christian fact of their pastor's career was that he was the husband of his wife.

Now the lady in the dory, being but a summer lady, knew nothing of the natural history of the winter parson, and when her boat came leaping through the smoky sou'wester to the sinking man, and her ear, fine as some beautiful wild animal's, caught, half-asphyxiated as it was, that heartrending, soul-confessing "Poor Nelly!" she thought, "I save a lover worth saving—or having."

Down went her brown, beautiful arms, both of them, into the water. His, as he came up, clutched them with the blind grasp of his mortal emergency. The dory, behaving as a dory should, keeled but held stoutly. With two firm hands, as powerful as his own, the woman swung the man through the water till she brought him astern. He clambered up collectedly, and sat dripping upon one of the thwarts.[5] She took up her oars.

"Madam," said the minister, gravely,—"*moriturus saluto.*"

"*Qui fui moriturus,*" corrected the lady, quickly.[6]

"I defer to your finer—or your fresher—Latin," he responded. "You row an admirable stroke; you have a strong arm, a quick wit, a steady head—in short, an amount of pluck not expected of your sex. I am under obligations—"

"Omit to mention them," interrupted the lady, frowning slightly. "I am accustomed to meeting emergencies; it is part of my business in life. Put your hand in my pocket, please; there is some brandy there. I can't lay down these oars till I get you ashore—the tide is too strong; we shall drift. You will take two swallows," she added, nodding authoritatively at her passenger. "Who is Captain of this boat?" she asked, sharply, seeing that he hesitated. "Obey orders, I tell you!"

"Ay, ay, sir!" cried the passenger, promptly. The sailor in him came to the relief of the clergyman. As he thrust his dripping hand into the lady's dry, white pocket, and tipped a dainty travelling-flask to his purple lips, his brain whirled with a vision of two human faces providentially absent from this remarkable occasion. One was the countenance of his wife; the other belonged to the president of the parish temperance association.

"There now!" observed the lady, who was rowing with a vigorous, masculine stroke, "you look better. You are not young enough to stand this sort of thing without proper care."

"I'm not old enough to enjoy being told so!" said the minster, with spirit. A woman of the world would not have said that, he thought; and he was quite right in his conclusion.

"Pardon me," said the young lady, with unexpected gentleness; "I am obliged to be so blunt in my business."

She had now brought the dory alongside of the tossing float which lapped the water below the hotel.[7] It happened that the float was quite deserted, and after he had helped her up with the dory, the minister stood still, dripping and embarrassed, and looking at his rescuer.

She was a tall, firm young woman, with a direct eye and a grave mouth. She might have been what is called a handsome woman, but she lacked the pliable, deferent texture so necessary in the feminine face to the taste of man. She was bareheaded, and her hair was black, and brushed back from her temples.

She, on her part, saw a well-trained clerical figure, and a face of forty-six; the minster had the mouth of an educated saint and the eyes of a natural worldling. He stood gracefully in his rubber boots, and had pushed his drenched hair back from his lined forehead.

"My name is Luther Goodspeed," he said, abruptly. "I am pastor of the Congregational church in this village."

"And I am Eunice Thorpe," returned she of the white flannel. "I am a physician, and am staying at the hotel."

The minister bowed.

"What do you suppose has become of the catboat?" he demanded, suddenly.

"Oh, she went to the bottom like a diver," replied Dr. Thorpe, smiling.

"She belonged to my senior deacon," urged the minister, plaintively. "He lent her to me to get home in. I had taken my dory over to be examined and repaired. I grazed her bows the other day. Mrs. Goodspeed was afraid of a leak."

He turned and shot a pathetic glance at the parsonage. The curtains were drawn apart in the second-story window over the piazza; figures or a figure could be seen stirring between the curtains.

"Mrs. Goodspeed did not know," pleaded the minister, not without dignity, "that I was to return in the catboat. My wife is an invalid, madam. I spare her all possible disturbance. I—I—Dr. Thorpe!" cried the man. "I have not been in a sail-boat for twenty years!"

"And with the passion of twenty men in one, he loves a tiller and a main-sheet," thought Dr. Thorpe.

For one mute minute the sea-loving woman glanced at the sea-bereft man; a straight, compassionate womanly shaft of her brown eyes struck the sailor's heart of him.

But she spoke not as she looked—more wisely, as the world counts wisdom.

"Few men," she said, distinctly and slowly, "are so considerate. Many sick wives would recover, possessing such devotion. They need it— women; they are a pitiable lot!"

"You must understand—in your profession—" chattered the minister. He was shivering now, and for the first time conscious how wet and cold he was.

"You must go home at once," she commanded. "You are running a risk standing here. I will come over by and by and see how you are."

"Oh, pray don't!" cried the minister, with uncontrollable candor.

Now the young lady did not change color at this rebuff; and it smote him with a kind of helpless anger to see that she did not, but that she only smiled maternally.

"I will call upon you," he stammered. "I will call upon you to express my gratitude. Mrs. Goodspeed will write you a note. She will be very grateful."

"Run away home," said Dr. Thorpe, as if he had been a boy.

The Rev. Luther Goodspeed turned and went. It cannot be said that he ran. His rubber boots were still full of water, and he trod heavily across the beach and up the garden walk.

His heart was heavier than his feet. Two terrible interviews frowned before him. To face his wife or the senior deacon—which would be the crueler fate?

The minster sat in his study. It was now half past one o'clock, and all visible signs of the early parsonage dinner, abruptly and contritely eaten alone by the Rev. Luther Goodspeed, had been cleared away by Arvilla, the "house-keeper."

At the present moment the house-keeper was doing Mrs. Goodspeed's feet up in something hot and woolly. Mrs. Goodspeed moaned faintly at regular intervals, as if her suffering were a clock that must strike when it was wound. Now and then she clung to Arvilla's hand. When she was offended with her husband she was apt to be affectionate with Arvilla.

"Only a woman can understand a woman," she sighed. "No man *can.*"

"Land!" said Arvilla, dispassionately, "I wouldn't set the minster down for a minyot—not a *born* minyot.[8] He's got some brains left in his skull yet, if you give him credit for it. You'd oughter see Mis' Chickamy's husband, where I did nursin' in Salem before I come to you. You'd think you was the wife of a cherubim, that's all.

"What did Mr. Chickamy do?" asked the invalid, with unexpected interest. "You often allude so mysteriously to Mr. Chickamy, Arvilla. But you never explain what you mean."

"Nor I ainter gointer," snapped Arvilla. "All I say is that you've married a seraphim, and you'd oughter sense it."

"Was Mrs. Chickamy as sick as I am?" asked Mrs. Goodspeed, weakly.

"A sight sicker," replied Arvilla, cruelly.

Mrs. Goodspeed made no answer. In her heart she did not think it credible that any woman could be sicker than herself. The lids drooped over her eyes. She had fine eyes, and when they were not visible her face took on a certain commonness, like a cheap candlestick in which the light has been extinguished. She had been a pretty girl; she had the petulant mouth of a spoiled invalid, but the still youthful manner of a woman beloved and sheltered.

"Has he gone over to the study?" she asked, suddenly opening her eyes. "After the shock I have received?"

"Lord!" cried Arvilla, "he's *got*ter go. He's wore out same's you be. It's consider'ble of a stent to be drownded, let alon' fussin' over you afterwards. You was consid'ble to tend to for a spell along there after he capsized. My ironin's all in the basket. I ain't teched only one shimmy and two pair of his stockin's. I wish you'd perk up a little," added Arvilla, with a mournful candor.

But the invalid did not perk up. In fact, she seemed rather to be perking down. Whatever might be said of her on some other occasions, on this Mrs. Goodspeed was really ill.

No human infliction has found less generous or even judicial comprehension, either in life or in letters, than chronic illness. Its victims, who may sometimes receive fair play in fact, seldom do in fiction.

Nevertheless, the truth compels me to admit that Ellen Goodspeed, ten years an invalid in the seashore parsonage, and for twenty years the cherished wife of the Reverend Luther, belonged to that class of women who at their worst are what we charitably call impossible, and who when ill are never at their best.

The Rev. Luther Goodspeed sat in his church study. His next Sunday morning's sermon lay half written upon his table, held in its rebelliously fluttering place by a Concordance and the Revised Version;[9] for the sou'wester brushed brusquely in at the large window. It was unexpectedly a stained window, having been presented by a deceased but once sympathetic parishioner, who was understood to be under special spiritual obligations to the pastor. The design presented the figure of Christ healing the sick—a cripple. The Christ was white, the cripple was yellow; a lavender Temple on a pea-green Palestine showed beyond. The window, which moved inwards and outwards on a swivel, was open, and the minister sat in the full draught, hungrily. He still panted a little, like a man who has passed through an excessive exertion of either mind or body. His boyish curls, yet wet, clung to his temples and forehead. He had a wearier expression than he was accustomed to allow himself; he wore one of the looks that a man's wife does not see. He had taken up his pen mechanically, but he was not writing. An arrow of yellow from the tallith of the Judean cripple hit the minster's idle hand.[10] He glanced at it and his lips moved. "Poor Nelly!" he said. "Poor Nelly!" His thoughts could not get beyond this familiar stage.

The sou'wester, which was dying leisurely, suddenly set a rousing whirl of air astir in the church study and slapped the painted window. The study door opened loudly and slammed to in the draught.

"You've gotter come right over!" commanded Arvilla, shrill with unwonted excitement. "She's got *something* this time. The old doctor ain't to home, for I seen him gewhollopin' over to the harbor. I've sot out to find somebody else. You run right along and set by her till I get one!"

The minister obeyed—everybody obeyed Arvilla. In startled silence, bareheaded, he ran from the church to the parsonage, and took the stairs two at a time. His lips still moved to the familiar "Poor Nelly!" It seemed to him to justify the experience of a thousand baseless alarms and wasted wells of sympathy drawn upon for all her ailing years that he should now find poor Nelly really very ill indeed.

In fact, she was, or seemed to be, unconscious, and lay silently in the arms that clasped her with the old, sure, indefatigable tenderness which Ellen Goodspeed took as a matter of course, and for which so many wives would have exchanged life.

Mrs. Goodspeed was not, in fact, a fainting woman, and the Reverend Luther, who might have easily taken a nurse's diploma in many or most departments, was at his wit's end, when Arvilla slammed up-stairs with the only doctor she had been able to secure.

"It ain't a he doctor," announced Arvilla, "but you better b'lieve she'll beat the old one out of his boots. *She* ain't no minyot, I betcher."

When the minister raised his haggard eyes he turned sick and dizzy. How was it possible to entrust his poor and precious Nelly to a physician in a white flannel dress and a low tortoise-shell back comb?

"*You!*" he cried, with piercing candor.

"Put her down," commanded Dr. Thorpe, authoritatively. "So,—perfectly horizontal—so. You are holding her too high."

"Is she—will she—die?" asked the husband, with white lips.

"Oh dear no," said the woman doctor.

Then, thus and there did the care of the minister's wife go over into the professional charge of Dr. Thorpe.

A new earth, if not a new heaven, now evolved in the parsonage. The invalid went captive at once and altogether to the girl doctor.

"The doctor understands my case perfectly," she confided to Arvilla.

"Shouldn't wonder!" retorted Arvilla, with an accent the invalid—who was not a dull person—felt to be ambiguous.

"It takes a woman to understand a woman," she repeated, sharply. A flicker of carmine brushed her pale lips; she showed a pleased color not infrequently in those days.

Her naturally fine eyes assumed a deep inward brilliance. That fretful carving between her brows had cut too deep to be recalled. You can fill and level a grave, but not those moral cañons in the human face. But a gentle cheerfulness or expectancy now suffused her expression and manner.

The truth was that the minister's wife had found that which may surcharge a nervous invalid into late recovery, and for lack of which many have died—a new absorption.

"She's got an interus'," said Arvilla.

Beneath the bruising cross Mr. Goodspeed felt another shoulder—how gentle and how strong! Manifold and mysterious were the steps by which the girl doctor interpaced the parsonage life. She wove a magic web around, across, and through the cheerless household.

Every day the minister thought of her in a new metaphor. She was climate. She was atmosphere. She was escape. She was freedom. With her came uncounted respites and reliefs; through her accession opened little vistas of rest, something that he dared not call hope, and yet for which there seemed no duller name.

The exactions of the sick-room upon the overwearied man were melting—who could say how? For three nights now he had slept undisturbed; all day he had been summoned but twice. Last week he spent a day in the city. Yesterday he had a long bicycle ride. To-day his poor Nelly herself asked him to invite his classmates from the hotel to supper.

To-morrow she thought a horseback ride somewhere would be good for him. Next week, she said, in her prettiest way—and no one had a prettier way than Nelly when she was young and well:—

"Those people at the hotel with the automobile are going to take the doctor for a trip around the Cape. They want another gentleman. If they *should* invite you—would you like to go, Luther?"

"It would not do at all for both of us to be away from you all day," replied the Reverend Luther, promptly; but the dash of fire in his eyes betrayed him.

"I didn't know you cared so *much*," replied the invalid, not without pathos. "Arvilla can take care of me quite well. Dr. Thorpe wishes me to depend on myself. The doctor likes to have me do things without people. The doctor—Oh, what should I do without the doctor? God bless her!"

"*Amen*," said the minister, solemnly.

He sat in the automobile like a beatified spirit flying through the mysteries of ether.

When he came home his wife had got down-stairs. She crept up from the study sofa and came to meet him. She wore a pretty, white, loose gown; it had bright autumnal ribbons;—the doctor had given her those ribbons.

"She makes her take an interus' in how she looks," observed Arvilla.

The minister kissed his wife adoringly. In the chariot of fire, all the blazing autumn day, a comrade had shared his flight; he returned to a dependent. He thought of the girl doctor's splendid color and vigor—

the look of her red cheek beneath her veil, her free step in her long automobile coat, the profile of her bare, brown hand upon her lap. He thought of his immeasurable obligations to her.

He looked at his invalid wife with fond returning eyes; her wasted face lay upon his breast; she lifted her thin hand to his cheek; she did not fret or complain; she hoped he had a good time.

These simple words filled him with admiration. He thought her heroic, and told her so.

"I'm glad you went," she answered, restlessly. "Isn't the doctor coming in?"

A vague jealousy stirred within the minster's heart. To his poor Nelly he had so long been the world and all that was therein!

He went out and sat on the porch alone when Dr. Thorpe came in to see how her patient had passed the day. The voices of the two women came to his ear, confusedly—the one plaintive, appealing, and delicate; the other, ringing and strong.

They grappled some duality in his own nature, hitherto submerged in his consciousness. He had the singleness and simplicity of a devout boy. He was troubled by some of his thoughts.

It was a cold September evening, and Dr. Thorpe came out buttoning her automobile coat. She wore her white flannel dress and a little white felt hat.

"Finished your cigar?" she said.—"Oh, I forgot!"

The minister looked so like a man who ought to have had the smoke which he denied himself that she was tempted to run across to the apothecary's and get him one.

"Poor fellow!" she said. "Is it Nelly? or the senior deacon?"

The minster returned her a straight, steady look, before which the mischief in her brown eyes wavered. In his the natural worldling and the acquired saint contended silently.

"Call it the Junior Endeavor," he replied.[11]

"There is to be some deep-sea fishing to-morrow—the automobile party," observed Dr. Thorpe, abruptly. "Mrs. Goodspeed has suggested that you should join us. We have engaged *The Arrow*. We sail at eight o'clock."

"*I!*—Mrs. Goodspeed!—The *Arrow!*" ejaculated the minister. "Eight o'clock!" he added, faintly. "I carry her down-stairs at ten. Dr. Thorpe, I thank you. I cannot subject my wife to such a strain. You do not know what she suffers when I am on the water.—I told you—I have not sailed for twenty years."

"As you please," replied Dr. Thorpe, sharply; her face had its professional look. "I think it well for her to make sacrifices—to exercise self-control. You obstruct my management of the case."

"I will discuss the matter with my wife," replied the minister, stiffly. The husband and the physician parted with coldness.

He felt unhappy to have quarrelled with her. His debt to her was so large that little estrangements seemed a kind of spiritual bankruptcy.

"I shall not go on her fishing trip," he said. But the next morning he was at the wharf with the rest of the party.

As *The Arrow* dashed out of the harbor, the too long sea-denied man forgot the solid earth and all that was thereon—his senior deacon, the Junior Endeavor, parish politics—yes, and his poor Nelly. Clearly Dr. Thorpe perceived that he had forgotten herself. She reflected that she should take pleasure in that fact.

Circumstances forced him to remember her unexpectedly. When the wind died, and *The Arrow* wallowed in the swell beyond the Light, the other lady of the party fell a victim to a severe attack of *mal de mer*—surrendered the excursion, and demanded that she be put ashore to walk home.[12] Her husband dutifully accompanied her. Thus it befell that the minister and Dr. Thorpe returned with the skipper.

It was late September, and the bay had the glitter of its calendar. All through the morning, while the southerly lasted, the water had presented a sheet of white fire and seemed to smoke. The wind had been good-humored, sinking to the calm that had disrupted the party, and the harbor flickered with sails. Most of these had now disappeared. *The Arrow*, alone of her class, was still beyond the bar.

Her skipper, who was of the talkative, tourist's variety, had grown unnaturally silent.

"We're goin' to have a breeze o' wind," he said, slowly.

As he spoke the words, the wind veered with an incredible swiftness, and one of the fierce autumnal northerlies, with whose temper no man may reckon, smote an unprepared and writhing sea.

The Arrow keeled and lay over as if she had been knocked down by a gun. In a moment the little pleasure-boat was quivering between whirlpool and whirlwind—her landing two miles off.

"Lend a hand, parson!" bellowed the skipper, wrestling savagely with his tiller. "If you know *anything*,—drop that mains'l, and be—quick about it!"

"Ay, ay, sir!" cried the minister, springing.

As the little sail came rattling down beneath his alert and intelligent fingers, he gave one glance through the smoky spray at the shore. He could make out the roof of the parsonage, and the row of stunted poplars bent like weather-beaten old men.

"You ain't no such pious fool, either!" yelled the skipper through the blast. "You dropped her quite toler'ble well."

Dr. Thorpe had not yet spoken.

"I can help too," she said, quickly. "I understand a boat. I can steer if you'll trust me."

"When I trust my hellum to a woman," replied the skipper, "I'll be d—d,—or a parson, either."

The passengers were both as white now as the foam in which *The Arrow* weltered. The minister looked at the doctor. Her eyes answered his steadily. In them he saw an infinite and dumb anguish. If by flinging herself overboard at that moment she could have landed him alive and in the arms of his wife, she would have done it; and he felt that she would.

"*Bail!*" thundered the skipper, suddenly. "Bail like the devil, or we'll be in hell afore we can say damn!"

The northerly had now become a hurricane. *The Arrow*, trembling from stem to stern, spun and whirled like a dead leaf. The water rushed over the rail in cataracts.

Only a few people on shore had observed the position of the little boat. These gave her up for lost, with easy unanimity. Only one of them, an old offshore fisherman, with a slimy green dory, did anything.

He took his pipe out of his mouth, picked up his oars with big, gnarled, experienced hands, and rowed out into the caldron.

Between whirlpool and whirlwind the three in *The Arrow*, drenched and gasping, clung to the last moments of consciousness in the silence with which most human souls face probable death. Even the skipper had ceased to damn. The minister sat with set teeth, and eyes staring shoreward and homeward.

"She asked me to take a tender," he muttered;[13] "it was the only thing she *did* ask."

For the first time a groan ground its way through his quivering lips.

"Shut up there!" cried the skipper, roughly. "Keep up your courage, same's you sot out to. *Bail*, I tell ye! Bail! Look here," he added, in the next breath; "I won't fool ye no longer. 'Tain't no use . . . bailin' . . . nor nothin'.—Parson, I guess it's your turn to take the hellum."

The skipper, still wrestling with his tiller as Jacob wrestled with the angel,[14] jerked off his dripping hat and made as if he would fall upon his knees.

"Come, parson," he said; "you pray. It's time."

As the minister's voice, responding with the quickness of a life's training and a life's faith, rose pleasing to Heaven and the hurricane, *The Arrow* quietly swamped.

At this moment the tempest yawned, and out of its throat dropped a slimy, green dory, rowed by an old fisherman, bent and drenched and dominant, son of the sea and of the storm, as powerful and as incredible as leviathan.

When the green dory landed her passengers the whirling shore was throbbing with people. Pre-eminent among them, a lanky figure against the frowning sky, Arvilla ornamented the cliff top. She was gesticulating wildly, and seemed to be shouting unheard words. The minister and doctor looked at her in heavy silence. Neither of them had addressed the other since they were dragged out of the foam into the dory.

To her own soul Eunice Thorpe spoke the unsparing words of an ardent and high-minded woman who believes herself conscientiously to have veered to the verge of a grave mistake.

"I meant to help them! I meant to help them!" she repeated, piteously: "I have done them an irreparable hurt!"

She dared neither forecast nor ignore the probable consequences of this day's events. She felt the sense of immaturity in human experience, or aloofness from the plan of life, which comes at times to every unwedded woman.

"They are married," she thought; "I am not. I should not have interfered. I should have let them alone."

Her spirits sank so that she did not bear the drenching very vigorously, and suffered rather a serious chill. The fisherman offered her his oil coat, and the Reverend Luther tried to wrap it about her, but she declined it.

"I am no colder or wetter than you," she said. "Put it on yourself."

He dropped the coat, and it lay in the bottom of the dory; whence the skipper promptly picked it up and threw it over his own streaming back.

"Who is that?" said the minister, abruptly, in a strained voice.— "*That?—There?*"

Her eyes followed his shaking finger.

"*It is Mrs. Goodspeed!*" she panted. "She is on the cliff. Arvilla is holding her up."

When the dory bumped on the float, the Reverend Mr. Goodspeed leaped without looking back. Everybody made way for him as he dashed like a boy up the cliff; and a low, moaning sound came from the people on the shore when he took his wife, who had not walked a rod outside her house for well-nigh a dozen years, into his dripping arms.

Eunice Thorpe turned away. She felt exiled. She experienced the isolation of the happiest solitary woman before the mysterious bond of marriage. The hotel people took care of her, the old man doctor gallantly offered her his services, and she did not look back at the two on the cliff. She allowed herself one savage thought. "If she scolds him," reflected the doctor, "I will—I will—put her in a plaster cast!"

But Mrs. Goodspeed did not scold her husband—not then. She kissed, and laughed, and cried, and blessed, and kissed again. With her invalid arms clasped around the half-drowned man, she walked steadily back to the parsonage, cooing and crooning unintelligibly all the way, as women—whether sick or well—do when they love a man or a child. And Arvilla ran on ahead to heap the fires.

The minister sat in his study. The empty church seemed muffled in more than its usual stillness. The boundings of his own heart hammered in his ears. It was a cold day, and a little fire purred in the grate. He had allowed himself this luxury, for he had coughed a good deal since *The Arrow* swamped, a week ago. His next Sunday's sermon lay before him—thirty blank, bleak pages of manuscript paper. He had not got beyond his text, which repeated the beautiful apocalyptic dream about the "first heaven and the first earth" that were "passed away."[15] He could not write. The stained-glass window was shut, and the chilly autumn sun struggled to illuminate the white Christ and the yellow cripple, but made no effort to contend with Palestine or the lavender Temple. The Rev. Luther Goodspeed had a worried look.

A low knock brushed the door, and he sprang to open it with the nervous movement of a man in unconcealed suspense. Dr. Thorpe came in without speaking, but did not take the chair which he pushed forward by the fire.

She stood with her hands upon the back of the chair, and looked—as he did—into the heart of the blaze. They began to talk at once, without ceremony or hesitation, as people do who have vital matters on hand.

"How did you leave her?"

"She's pretty tired. Arvilla is with her."

"What have you been saying to her?"

"Saying? Oh, everything, I think—that is, almost."

"You play with my suspense," he said, peremptorily. "Relieve it. It's not natural—a physician pre-empting a wife's confidence, while a husband is shut out."

"You cannot be more conscious of that than I. I purpose to put an end to it as soon as possible. She has become too dependent on me. I told her so."

"*Ah!*—That was cruel. How did she take it?"

"Like a woman—that is, with spirit. I am glad to say she showed considerable. When she was young—and well—she must have been a girl of some force of character."

"Indeed she was!" cried the husband, hotly.

"I told her," proceeded Dr. Thorpe, without meeting his eye, "that I intended to leave town next week. I have decided to practise in the city. I am going on Friday morning."

"*Going?* Friday *morning?*—I thought you meant to settle here. There are so many who—have expected it—who wish it . . . a good many ladies of my congregation—" he broke off, lamely enough.

"Such was my intention. I have changed it," replied the doctor, in a tone which admitted of no reprieve.

"How did she take *that?*" he asked, in a tone lower than her own.

"Like a lady—like a lady that she is."

"It's going to be very hard for her," he said, with an opaque, half-blind look. His gaze had returned to the fire.

"I am afraid so."

"She will miss you. She will not know how to take up—her sufferings—without you. Nor—nor I."

A sense of impending bereavement half strangled him. He wheeled and regarded her unexpectedly; he had the look of a troubled and bewildered boy.

"Steady, now, steady!" said Eunice Thorpe; but she said it to her own strong soul.

"I shall come back sometimes," she suggested in a comfortable, common-place tone. "I shall not entirely desert the case."

"*Ah!*—That will—help us out."

"I shall try to do—what is best," added the girl doctor, halting for the first time in this agitating interview.

Abruptly she turned and went to the study door. With her hand on the latch, she paused, drew a quick, deep breath, and faced him.

"Mr. Goodspeed, I think you ought to know that you do not know the details of my talk with your wife to-day. I have told her everything."

"*Everything?* I fail to—understand you, Dr. Thorpe."

Blind thoughts of things that he had read in disagreeable fiction groped for a moment through his well-ordered mind—phantoms of scenes such as did not occur in the lives of Christian clergy-men; shadowy complications of feeling, such as a gentleman, being the husband of one wife, could not suffer himself to experience. But in the dark eyes of the girl doctor he saw only that inscrutable, maternal look. A little mocking smile curved her red lips as they slowly brought out these un-expected words:

"I have told Mrs. Goodspeed that she is perfectly curable. I have told her that she has been self-deluded—that she has been an unnecessary burden upon you all these years."

"It was my privilege to assume it!" cried the husband, in a scorching tone. "It was my delight as well as my duty. My wife has been a very sick woman—"

"I have just told her that such is not the fact," interrupted the doctor, calmly. "I have told her that she has put a false diagnosis on the condi-tion. I have told her to stay out of bed and keep on her feet—that she is perfectly able. Within limits, I mean, of course. I have ordered her to walk as far as the end of that row of round-shouldered poplars every day. She has promised to do so."

"Did you ever tell her to do this before?" gasped Luther Goodspeed.

"Never."

"Why not?"

"She would not have believed me nor obeyed me. Now she can't help herself. Since she walked to the cliff to meet you, there is nothing to be said. What you call Providence shipwrecked you to disillusionize her. No therapeutics could have done it. Love did. She will never be a strong woman, or quite well. But, relatively speaking, she will recover."

"Do you mean to say," demanded the minister, severely, "that my poor Nelly—Oh, you must have hurt her! You wounded her!—I should go to her at once!"

He looked about for his hat. A shaft of the autumn sunlight struggled through the tallith of the white Christ in the window and expressed the pallor of the man's noble face. All its patient lines and conquered self were revealed, perhaps sublimated, before the doctor's steady eyes.

"You are a good man," she said, in a very low tone. "I honor you . . . above most men whom I know. I shall not deceive you about it all. She has suffered very much; she does; she must. But there has never been any lesion, nothing organic. There is a neurosis—but it is curable. I have told her—more than I shall tell you; more than she will tell you. Leave us to work it out. Leave me the management of my own case.—By the way," she added, "this bronchial irritation of yours needs attention. You have coughed ever since that first shipwreck, and two in one season have been more than your share. You are to go South for the month of March, this winter. I have told her so."

"You might have spared yourself that trouble!" cried the minister, defiantly. "When you see me ask my sick wife to spare me for a month—"

"You will not find it necessary to ask her," returned Dr. Thorpe, rather wearily. "She will propose it herself.—Don't, don't fight me so," she protested, with sudden entreaty. "Don't, *don't* make everything so hard! I am trying to do—what is best—the best I can—for her—for you—for everybody."

She held out her firm brown hand abruptly. He bowed his face above it.

"*Victurus saluto*," he said, brokenly.[16] She smiled a little, wistfully, but did not reply; and so melted from the study. He stood for a moment when she had left him; the white light from the Christ in the window passed over his face and off from it, leaving a tremulous, uncertain shadow. The minister sank into his study chair and laid his face upon his unfinished sermon. His praying lips touched the text: "*For the first heaven and the first earth were passed away.*"

In the sick-room Mrs. Goodspeed sat panting in the easy chair. Her pretty, petulant face wore a startled, something like a terrified, expression.

"Arvilla," she asked, distinctly, "what did Mr. Chickaminy do to Mrs. Chickaminy? You never told me. I really wish you would. I never knew the family, you see, and never shall. There can be no impropriety."

"Won't you *never* tell?" demurred Arvilla.

"Never, Arvilla, never!"

"Eny-meeny-mony-my,
Hold my tongue or wish I may die?"

"Eny-meeny-mony-my," echoed Mrs. Goodspeed, laughing. She was glad of a chance to laugh. Returning health had already taught her to weary of the tragic.

"Well," admitted Arvilla, sinking her voice to a hollow and unnatural whisper, "when she was so trantragious nobody *could* stand her—Mr. Chickaminy he shook her."

"Shook her! Shook his wife! A sick lady! An invalid wife! *Shook* her?" gasped Mrs. Goodspeed.

Avilla nodded solemnly. "He warn't no cherubim," she said, conclusively. "Yourn is."

There was a harvest-moon that night, and Dr. Thorpe went out to row upon the harbor. She went alone. Everybody seemed superfluous to her. She drifted up and down for an hour, and then brought her dory back to the float, and came up the ladder slowly. At the top a strong hand stretched down to meet her own.

"I meant to be in time to help you with the dory," said the minister. He spoke with some embarrassment and timidity. "My wife wishes to know—*could* you come over?" he asked, with manifest hesitation.

"Is she really in need of my services?" demanded the doctor, somewhat shortly.

"I don't think so. I think it was more a social invitation—a friendly chat—all of us together. She is trying not to go to bed so early. She is trying to please you."

"Ask her to excuse me," replied Dr. Thorpe, after a moment's silence. "I am really—pretty tired. Some other time. Tell her I will come some other time.—Go home and tell her, please. I am going to sit here on the float for a while."

It occurred to him suddenly that he might stay and sit beside her in the moonlight on the swaying float—that he must do it. Then, with a grip through his heart, like a physical pain, he perceived that he must not. He did not say, I dare not; his consciousness halted this side of the words. He obeyed her in silence. He walked, rapidly, without looking back, passed under the row of weather-beaten poplars, up the steps, and into the house.

The moon was blazing on the sea, and Eunice Thorpe buried her thoughts in gulfs of light. A woman may offer a man the highest service if she refrains from doing all she can for him. This she remembered. A noble idealization filled the delicate and upright soul of the minister. This she felt. The girl doctor meant to be glad that she had not suffered him to confuse the great counter-currents of experience. Gratitude and friendliness have the nature of the tide, and, like the tides, may rise to strange shores or ebb to familiar seas. She wondered why she was not happier that she had made this unselfish, unworldly man and that ailing and imperfect woman her lifelong and loyal friends.

Pretty soon he came to the window of his wife's room and drew the shade. She could see his shadow on the shade after it was drawn.

First published in *Harper's Monthly*, January 1904, 304–16.

ESSAYS

What Shall They Do?

The tale not long ago unfolded by "a weak-minded woman" to the "Easy Chair" has fallen upon sympathetic ears.[1]

We wish that she knew—we should like to sit down beside her in her kitchen and tell her—how our sorrowful thought has followed her through the hopeless waking, the hopeless work, the hopeless dreaming, through the whole dull, drudging day. We should like to have been there to slip the clothes upon the children, and run for the spoons and the water; we wished that we could have helped her skim the milk and make the fire—we will not offer to do the cooking, for our prophetic soul tells us that the result would be extraordinary; we make it a principle to let cooking alone, on condition that people shall let us alone, and not remind us of the typical woman who "talks French and plays the piano." But we would have gladly helped about the dusting and the dish-washing, and have planned a little that her golden hour in "the other room," in the "muslin dress," might grow into two, and the sunset find her with braver eyes and send her "strengthened on her way."

How to spend the treasured minutes, though, that is the question; we might have read to her, or we might have chatted with her; we might not, perhaps, have advised her to take the pen and paper down from the pantry-shelf. Then, perhaps, we might.

And this brings us to the point. "A weak-minded woman" is one of many, and their name is legion. Consumed with little wearing cares, their girlish dreams ended in a struggle for bread-and-butter—a steady disquiet aching through the days and nights, and a steady, baffled, disappointing effort to write it away—is not that about it?

To be sure they have not asked our advice, and may think that we don't know any more about the matter than they do, and very likely we don't; but if we think we do it answers the purpose. Perhaps the "Easy

Chair" may be right in saying: "When the feeling is so strong, yield to it."[2] Yet we venture to doubt whether this is always a safe rule.

As a general thing, it is next to impossible for a woman with the care of a family on her hands to be a successful writer. The majority of the exceptions made their literary reputation before marriage, and if they choose, may lie on their oars and drift on it. We assume that a woman at the head of a home proposes to take care of that home to begin with. If the husband and children have the go-by, and the magazine editors have the stories, we have nothing to say to her. She has no right to a place in the ranks of authorship. She has not come in by the door into the sheepfold, but has climbed up some other way.[3] Away down in some inner chamber of her heart she will find, if she make diligent search, a handwriting on the wall, but it is not our business to stop and translate it to her just now.[4]

It is no easy matter to keep the "holy fire burning in the holy place,"[5] yet never be out of kindlings for the kitchen stove, nor forget to tell Bridget about the furnace dampers, nor let the baby have the match-box to play with. It is worse than a "Conflict of Ages."[6] Women whose consciences would not let them be any thing but generous wives, and mothers faithful unto death, have had to give it up and lay by the pen forever. Women have died, too, in the struggle to bring the opposing forces into thorough, symmetrical union.

It can be done, to be sure; but it needs one or both of two things: the physical strength of an Amazon and talent of the highest order.[7] They are the geniuses of the world, as a rule, who "make it pay" in any sense. "Le jeu ne vaut pas la chaudelle,"[8] for ordinary women.

If the magazines will not publish your stories it is a natural inference that you are not exactly a genius, is it not? It is of no use to suggest Keats, or talk about "mute, inglorious Miltons," or cast glances up at Wordsworth, "knowing that he should be unpopular, but knowing too that he should be immortal."[9] All that did very well for Keats and Wordsworth, but you and I may rest content that if nobody will publish for us we don't write any thing that is worth publishing. "Unappreciated genius" may be an obsolete fact; but in these days, when it is as easy to get into print as to write a letter about—to use a bit of the boys' slang—

"played out;" and oh, Mr. Washington Moon, and Mr. Richard Grant White, if you are frowning, why don't you give us something better?[10]

So, good friend, looking wistfully up from among the children and the ironing-tables, don't depend on your pen to take away that persistent disquiet, or to hire an Irish girl. *Don't.* You run nine chances of bitter disappointment. Ah, we know all about it; taking the little yellow package out of the mail; hiding it in your pocket that no one may see; stealing away home heart-sick in the evening light, and up to your room to have a cry—you run nine chances of this where you have one of success. If, however, the Irish girl can come and the disquiet go, *without* depending on it, why, well and good.

Just here is room to say that we honestly believe that many women aspiring to authorship, and meeting with downright failure, might bring themselves a little money and a good deal of pleasure, did they not fire too high. We have seen them repeatedly; women—and men too, for that matter—who have never written any thing of a more ambitious nature than a school-composition, deliberately proposing to send, and sending, their first essay or story or poem to *Harper's Magazine* or the *Atlantic.*[11] Why, how do you expect, in your inexperience, that there will be any room for you in such quarters? Should you allow a raw cook, whom you have taken "to teach," to make her first experiments at bread-making, when you have company to dinner?

Aim lower. Send to the county papers. Lay siege to the Dailies. If they will print a story for you once in four months at three dollars a column, that is better than nothing, and will buy your summer bonnet, or take the children to the beach. If you had not exactly expected it, but brought it on rather as a side-dish in the entertainment, the success will be so much more pleasant, and the worry infinitely less. Perhaps by-and-by you will work yourself up over stepping-stones of your dead newspaper training to better things. Or perhaps you will stay where you are. In either case you will be where you belong, and should thank God and be content.

If, however, Monthlies and Weeklies and Dailies combined happen universally to "have their columns full just now, and much regret that they can not make room for your excellent article," give it up. You are only wasting time and strength and hope that, as far as money goes, would bring you in more spent in crocheting edging for the fancy stores; as far as usefulness goes, had better be given to the cheering of some other life more disheartened and crowded than your own; as far as positive, necessary comfort yourself goes, might be better employed in company with a poem, or a picture, or your little Bible, perhaps, in certain moods, out under the apple-trees, where it is cool and still.

It is not strange, but it is sorrowful, to see in what crowds the women, married and unmarried, flock to the gates of authorship. Here and there you see them with white hands of command turning back the ponderous golden hinges and entering in where the palms are, and the crowns.[12] Down below they are turning away in great sad groups, shut out.

Why will people persist in utterly hopeless efforts? And why, when one thing fails, will they not try another thing?

Women have a mania for going where they are not wanted, and then complaining that nobody makes room for them.

Authorship is but one of several favored avenues of employment, which they choke up to the brim, till no one has room to breathe, much less to turn around and take courage.

"There are comparatively few women who are taught, or who have the patience or opportunity to teach themselves, to do any thing well," wrote the editor of a certain periodical—a man who had means of knowing what he was talking about, and who, for broad, and liberal, and generous, and just views of the "woman question," has scarcely his superior. "For various reasons they only try to do a few things, and, as a consequence, those few branches are overcrowded. There are more young girls of eighteen who wish to teach than there are pupils."[13]

There is a fact, girls, for you to reflect upon. Moreover, what is true of teachers is truer of seamstresses.

Jane, for instance, is looking about for means to support herself. Jane's father is a farmer, I will suppose, or a mechanic. She has been a few terms at the neighboring school, wears pretty little lace bonnets in the summer, and is, she would like to have you understand, "as good as any body." Which, by-the-way, we should be very ready to believe were she not so anxious to explain the fact. Consciousness of worth is content with itself; it is never concerned whether other people recognize it or not. Jane has been at home for a while helping her mother, but her father is in debt, and the boys are growing, and she feels that she had better be at work. What shall she do? She can not teach, for she doesn't know enough; and many bitter reflections this costs her whenever Ella, who was in the class above her at school, and is going before the District Committee for examination in August, happens to come in sight. Factory work is not to be thought of, and nothing offers, to her thinking, but plain sewing. "Plain sewing!" Oh, the dreary pictures folded up in those two words! The stooping figure, the circles under the eyes, the contracting chest and growing cough, the weary sight and weary fingers, the remorseless stitch, stitch, stitching through the summer days.

"Why not do housework?" suggests a thoughtful friend.

Jane flushes.

"Do you suppose I'd be a servant, and run at any fine lady's beck and call?"

The foolish child takes up her needle with a jerk, and the purple eyes and stealthy cough come in due time.

In the service of a considerate, courteous family she would grow round and pink and happy, and never lose a flower from her lace bonnet, nor a jot of her independence.

But all this is a hundred-times told tale. If a girl hasn't the common-sense to see that it is as respectable to bake a loaf of bread as to make a petticoat, to sweep a room as to bind a vest, it is of small use to talk to her, and perhaps about time to stop. Not that housework is her only resource; it is one, and a good one of many. She would be better and happier in a printing-office, in a crinoline-store, in a machine-establishment, than pricking her fingers there at the kitchen-window.

Ella, on the other hand (whose father was the village doctor, and who is a girl of some sound practical education, a little culture, and more refinement), plods her four miles a day to and from school, over the long, yellow, dusty road, worn by the heat, bothered by the "Committee," "kept after" with refractory, freckled girls in pink dresses till five or six o'clock, ready to cry half her disheartened time, and earning less than the factory-girls in the tenement-houses by the river.

Yet suggest to Ella the advantages of income, comfort, ease, every thing which would accrue to her if she would go into a telegraph-office or stand behind a counter, and she turns upon you as if she had received an insult. It is "lady-like" to screw his A B C's into little Pat Shay's brain, and wade through decimals with Mary Smith. It is not "lady-like" to measure off ribbon, or write a dispatch. Now, can't she see how silly that is? See? She is shutting her eyes at this very minute tight; and, as she gropes her way through this paper, wonders whom we are talking about, and if we are not saying something impertinent somehow. A keen writer in a recent number of this Magazine took for her text, "The Lord hath eyes to give the blind."[14] Can she tell us whether He has any provision for this sort of blindness?

Now, what can be done with the wide-spread evils of the "woman's wages" system as long as women will run, and crowd, and jam, and rub into two or three channels of employment?[15] What if all the men felt it necessary to their "respectability" to be doctors or lawyers? If women will underbid each other so, who is to blame that a female district school-teacher has a salary of three hundred per annum, and that seamstresses are paid fifty cents a day? The men, for going the way of all the earth, and not paying more than they can help, or we, for not going about our business in the stores, and the factories, and the nurseries, and the hospitals till the great mass of applicants is sifted down to the best, who shall have things their own way then, and set their own terms? As for the *genus homo*, we are not proposing to relieve it from its own proper scorn, on the subject of such a paragraph as this, culled within a month from a "Liberal" paper, where it stood without comment:

> In the duties assigned to females in the Treasury Department, they are much more expert than men, and accomplish more, for half the money, than could be done by masculine fingers. There are, too, among the female employées, rapid and correct book-keepers.[16]

But this article not appertaining to the "Woman's Rights" discussion, that is none of our concern at present.

To teach can be, sometimes is, as noble as to preach. They have been some of the grandest workers of the world who have had the moulding of the world's boys and girls. But when teaching is somewhat akin to starving, that is a different matter. And the teaching of district schools is always a different matter. One may undoubtedly do good; but it by no means follows that one may not do as much good somewhere else. It certainly requires good health, a hearty love of children, equable temper, nice discrimination, and tact, to say nothing of several other qualities. As to the pleasure of it, nine girls out of ten who are palpitating over the examination questions have no idea what is before them if they "pass."

"I'd rather dig potatoes!" said a young lady of our acquaintance. She did not dig potatoes, but she went to work and learned a milliner's trade, and her mother wailed that it was "beneath her." To judge from her face she has never before been so happy. At least has never so much respected herself. If one deserves one's own respect, one will never fail to gain that of other people.

Respectability is not a matter of money or of occupation. It is simply a matter of character. "A woman's a woman for a' that."[17]

If girls can be made to understand this, half the difficulty of deciding What shall they do? will be overcome. Many a refined and educated lady is spending her life in listless aimlessness for which the day cometh wherein she must give account to Him who said, "From him that hath not, I have taken away even that he hath,"[18] because no positive employment offers itself but paid employment, and dear me! it isn't "quite the thing," you know, to "work for a living."

"I should like to do something," said a girl[19] in her father's home; "I help mother and try to be pleasant to the boys, but that does not take a half of my time. If ever I should have to support myself, I should like to know how. At any rate it would be pleasant, and my conscience would be more at rest if I had something especial with which to fill up my time. But there doesn't seem to be any thing, and so I suppose it is of no use to think about it."

Having heard of a neighbor who was in want of a non-professional music-teacher to give lessons on the piano to a few little girls, we suggested the plan to her. She was capable of filling the position. It would be doing a service. It would occupy her time, etc., the advantages were numerous.

"Why, what an idea!" she exclaimed, "I had just as lief earn money if I could do it in some nice way; if I could write now as you do—but giving music-lessons! Why, *it would look so!*"

There are exceptions though, and noble ones, to the foolish rule.

We once knew a lady,—a lady of culture and of excellent education, qualified to fill a high and lucrative post as a teacher, who, for reasons known to herself—and you may be sure that they were good ones, and sensible ones, and noble ones, perhaps—chose a clerkship in an office in a city, riding two hours daily in the cars through sun and storm, from year to year. Now is any body any the less a lady for that? Any less fitted to be an ornament to your soirée when she comes home? In any way inferior to you, who have been playing croquet and making ruffles all day? You may be sure not.

We used to honor that woman from afar off. We respected her with our whole heart's respect. We sighed for an opportunity to shower society with a little of her spirit and good sense. Next to ill-heath, the principle cause of women's unhappiness—for women are not happy—is the want of something to do. Now don't arch your incredulous eyebrows, you tired creatures, sitting down to read this at the end of the long day's washing, or mending, or "doffing,"[20] for we don't mean you. But other women will listen whom we do mean, and they know it. Whether for self-support, or for the pure employment's sake, the search for work—for successful work, for congenial work—is at the bottom of half the feminine miseries of the world. Mental hunger is quite as clamorous as the need of bread-and-butter, and neither should be hushed up with stones.[21]

If a girl, for any reason, wants a positive, outside object for her days—premising that no nearer duty lays the veto on it—it is her business to find one, and it is the business of her friends to help her. We have known fathers, not a few, forbid their daughters to seek paid employment because it was paid, and we have seen the poor girls grow sick, and thin, and miserable, and "blue," and cross, and selfish in consequence, living a life without aim or animus, moved by no necessities greater than the trimming of a walking-dress, and burdened by no higher cares than the dusting of the parlor.

Who art thou, O man! daring thus to starve and cramp and dwarf a human soul, because it happens to be a woman's soul? Who ever heard of your treating your boys so? Verily, verily it shall be said unto you, that for all this you shall enter into judgment.[22]

"But a woman's place is at home, my dear," he proses complacently. "At home; shielded and protected by the paternal care. You will be marrying before long, you know, and had better be fitting yourself to be a wife and a mother?"

But she isn't a wife and mother yet, is she? And whether she marries in one year or ten—it is quite as likely to be ten—has nothing whatever to do with the question. Because a woman hasn't a baby to rock, is no reason why she should be useless in her day and generation, a burden to herself and other people. One need not necessarily go to sleep while one is waiting for the Prince. Especially if he tarrieth long upon the mountains, while the usurpers come and go.[23]

There are women longing for the battle, whom a still, small voice has pointed to some still, small duty down in the lowlands,[24] where it is very quiet, and where the shouts of victory never come. We know them. We have seen them. God, who knows and sees, shall prove them soldiers, too, some day. Our little word can have no message to such. We would come rather as learners, sitting at their feet.[25]

But meantime there is a good force ready for the ranks. Girls, do something. Don't be afraid, ashamed, discouraged, deceived. Go to work, and go to work in the right way, and keep at work.

What shall you do? The choice is wide. The perplexity is what not to do. Has God dropped any one golden gift into your heart? Can you make statues or poems? Can you recreate the glow of sunlight upon the mountain and down the slope? imprison the human face with the "light that never was on sea or land"?[26] make the wild-flowers bloom in winter? illuminate texts? give drawing-lessons? Can you vie with Parepa?[27] sing in a choir? help to swell a chorus? teach a child his do-ra-mi's? If you can be a Parepa or a Church, very well.[28] If you can sing in the choir, or give the drawing-lessons, very well. Every thing is beautiful in its season,[29] and both are something to do.

"But I haven't any golden gift; I haven't even a special fancy for any one thing."

Well; can you teach? Or *can't* you teach? Can you measure alpaca? trim bonnets? run a machine? go on an agency? There, by-the-way, is a pleasant, varied, healthful, appropriate occupation for any body. Yes, for any body. We see no reasons why a lady is not just as much a lady if she travels with a little sale-bag in her hand, and a picture, a pen, a book in charge, as when she goes to Saratoga with her seven trunks and her servants. She may, if she be so minded, enjoy herself more with the little bag than at Saratoga, and as for the uses of the thing—why, think of the kind of people one might meet, and the good one might do them! It is as good as a parish in the jungles of Borrioboola.[30]

Then can you keep a ledger? write book notices for a busy editor? fill out insurance policies? Be a city missionary? Read to an old lady? Take care of an invalid? Go into the hospitals? Be a doctor? and be sure that you could be few things more womanly or more notable. The brave pioneers—God bless them for it!—have broken the way for you. It is an easier way now than the path of the idle or the ill-paid. The day is coming, yea, and now is perhaps,[31] when strong, and generous, and refined women will be as anxious to crowd into it as they have been to keep out of it.

Is there not after all a goodly list for pondering? And but the half has been told you. Choose ye this day whom ye will serve.[32]

First published in *Harper's New Monthly Magazine*, September 1867, 519–23, this bracing essay was recently included in an anthology on female authorship: Anne E. Boyd, ed., *Wielding the Pen: Writings on Authorship by American Woman of the Nineteenth Century* (Baltimore: Johns Hopkins University Press, 2009).

The Higher Claim

....

"Seriously speaking, this is nonsense."

Fifty years hence will it be credited, without reference to the filed language that a leading New York paper, of pre-eminent literary connections and fair practical sense, actually dispose of the entire demand for the right of Womanhood Suffrage in these five words?

The time is past for this. Whatever else may be said of the movement for enfranchising women, it has reached a point at which it commands respect; from which it claims careful consideration; and beyond which it will be justified in requiring from friends and foes alike the most conscientious, the most candid, the most patient study.

"Seriously speaking," this is sense.

When it is estimated that there are two hundred thousand names in the country already known to be connected with this movement; when the less sanguine feelers of the public pulses consider that they could count upon twenty thousand male citizens of Massachusetts to vote in favor of woman's suffrage, if a vote were taken in that state to-morrow; when it is the testimony of one of the best-informed and most judicious women publicly interested in this matter that "the *unsought* signatures to petitions for suffrage which shower upon us from *women* all over the country have reached a number and confusion that we scarcely know how to manage"; when we thoughtfully add to this the significant circumstance that the most celebrated evangelical clergyman in the country, and the statesman renowned above all others for his application of rough common sense and free Christian principle to his political views,[1] have been for no inconsiderable time publicly committed to the advancement of this claim, the time is past, we say, for looking at the subject in any but the gravest attitude and in any but the most serious light.

Lollardy failed; but penitent England honors the name of Wyckliffe only the more for that.[2] We hung John Brown; but upon the heavy lips of the negro children in their free schools his soul sings in "marching on."[3] We may manacle the Rising Woman to-day; but we shall just so surely put a scepter into the hand we maim to-morrow, and just so surely shall then belong to us shame and confusion of face. In that we laid our hands upon the Lord's anointed, Protestantism is a crowned power, color an enfranchised citizen; this is the "woman's hour." We are born into it. We cannot escape it. It is too late to ignore it. What shall we do with it? What will it do with us?

It is no figure of speech to say that the "woman question" is the most tremendous question God has ever asked the world since he asked, "What think ye of Christ?" on Calvary.[4]

If our estimate of the true character, position, capacity of woman has been hitherto one vast barbaric blunder; if her relations to man and to society have been the subject of inherited, perpetuated, fatal mistake; if her conjugal connections do not bound her purposes, nor maternity the object of her creation; if her difference from man is less than her likeness to him; if her gifts are as great as his, while her graces are greater; if the limits of human nature only are her limits, its h[e]ights her h[e]ights, its depths her depths, its rights her rights; if, in short, human nature means something more than man nature and woman nature nothing less, the world has more to retrieve and more to dare than it has ever retrieved or dared since men heard the voice of one crying in the wilderness, "Prepare ye the way of the Lord."[5]

No reform has ever struck the stratum that this movement strikes. It lies "deep in the tangled root of things." Every false soil piled above it must crumble into it. We cannot go on forever planting flower-gardens over its volcanoes.

Either the truth is in the thing or it is not. If it is, there is everything required by it. If the queen, for whom the most thoughtful men and women of the age behold "earth waiting," is an imposter, Nature itself will withhold her crown. If she be a princess of the blood, he who refuses her allegiance must count well the cost and the peril. He may do it conscientiously, he cannot do it lightly; maliciously, but he shall not do it flippantly.

He shall no longer have the chance. The world is too much in earnest about this matter. Between a zealous subject and a deliberate enemy there will soon cease to be standing-room. The splash and splatter of all secondary considerations are deepening into the great tides of eternal right and wrong.

Quietly, gradually, powerfully in the hearts of timid women and magnanimous men an "agitation" is becoming a consecration; a problem is solving into a creed. It is well for us to remember this. Whatever the struggle for the elevation of woman means, it means that which a sneer, a scowl, a threat, a *bon mot* can no longer blow away.[6]

"Ah!" said Louis XVI, looking from his palace windows, the night after the taking of the Bastile, "it is a riot."

"Sire," said the Duke de la Rochefoucauld-Lioncourt, "it is not a riot. It is a revolution."[7]

There is one aspect of this matter which is of marvelous importance, and has met with marvelous neglect from thinking people. If the movement to elevate women by means of a political existence to be no longer "fractions" but "integers" in society, is anything more than a riot, it devolves strenuously upon the *Christian Church* to espouse its interests. There never was a revolution in which the "sad friends" of the "Virgin Truth" could not find one of the "thousand pieces" of her "lovely form."[8] If he who walketh upon the earth seeking whom he may devour is suffered to soil and moil the marble flesh, upon the Christian Church shall lie the blame.[9] Wherever the pure elements of this cause succumb to the evil floating about it, the Christian Church is at fault. If oxygen yield to miasma,[10] where is the Christian Church? If the hand of God is in this thing, and the smile of Christ upon it, and the Christian Church willfully or ignorantly blinds her eyes to it, her day of repentance is as sure as tomorrow's sun.

"The Church is behindhand in this, as she has been in every other great reform."[11]

I select the words at random from the most self-possessed and it may be said the most Christian organ of the most powerful and principled branch of the Woman Suffrage party.

The fact that such a remark can ever be made with any show of justice is food for thought to Christian people; and how often it is made we have but to listen to remind ourselves.

It is a question whether the course which we took in regard to the anti-slavery reform is one which we can well afford to repeat in this.

Published in the *Independent*, October 5, 1871.

Unhappy Girls

Upon a candid examination, I believe it would be found that there is more down-right misery among young women, between the ages of eighteen and thirty, than among any other class of people.

So far from this being a surprising condition of things, the wonder is rather that it should be so seldom credited, so imperfectly understood, and so unwisely received by the more fortunate portions of the world.

The ordinary lot of the ordinary young woman is one of the most miserable and unnatural things in comfortably civilized life; and society will never adjust its distorted angles with any approach to proportion till some radical change is effected in it.

"You are quite right," writes a friend.[1] "I have known women myself who have repeatedly refused to marry because they will not reproduce in the lives of their daughters the sufferings of their own early years."

A wide-eyed creature, with a smile like a wild-brier bud, and a voice like a canary's, comes peeping over your shoulder to read these words; and you lift, perhaps, your fond paternal eyes: "Unhappy girls, indeed! What will you do with *her*?" What I do with wild-briers and canaries—nothing more. You show me the joy of birds and roses—only that. I grant you the charm of a perfume and the strength of song—nothing else. Your little daughter is happy as babies and bees are happy—not otherwise. Let her hum about your declining days and coo in your fond ears. It almost seems as if bird or bee or baby would do as well. But let her be. Perhaps the world has need of her. I admit her as I admit a kitten. But it is not with her that I have to deal. She does not happen very often. More generally the kitten answers in her stead. She is not the ordinary girl.

Let me say, in passing, that a young woman who really finds in the common lot of young women genuine happiness does so in one of two ways. Either she is too frivolous to appreciate anything truer, deeper, more worthy—in other words, she does not know any better than to like it; or she gains, by means of that sheer sacrifice of self-culture and self-reliance, which is inculcated upon her as the chief end of woman,[2] around which all the sanctities of her affections and authorities of her religion are trained to grow, the compensation which always attends the dignity of even mistaken service. She is happy by simple virtue of self-abnegation. The h[e]ight and depth, the why and wherefore, the whither and where, do not concern her. She may have wasted her life; but, having lost it, she has gained it.[3] She may have misplaced it; but, having missed it, she has found it. In short, she is happy because she does not know that she ought not to be.

"God's sacred pity touched the grand mistake."[4]

But yet it is not with her that I have to deal. *She* is not the ordinary girl. The ordinary girl, I repeat, is an unhappy creature.

If any man doubt this, let him try it. Let him pause in his education four years, five, six before he ought. Let him come home from the school-room with his young head half full of the love of great deeds and great men, great principles and great facts, and his young heart high with great hopes and dreams. (The smallest of us see this world so large when we step into it, like the burning face of a magnified moon, seen through a forest on an eastern hill!) Let him put away his books upon the shelf; he may quite as well. To-morrow his mother will make cake, and he shall stone the raisins. No, nor need he take them down the next day. Why, my dear sir, there is pickling on Wednesday! Will he snatch an hour to refresh his Horace?[5] But it is washing-day. Will he secure that last review of Darwin before the magazine goes to Cousin Maria?[6] There is nobody to set the table, my dear. Can't you just step down? Will he be off for a tramp in the woods on this wiry morning, every vein aglow and every nerve in tension for a breath of wild life to strike him through? We have the sewing-circle today. There are one hundred biscuits to be buttered first. Run and get your apron, please. Will he go to sea, or on a mission, make shoes, study medicine, banking, law, Gospel, trade? Will he make a million or a poem? A statue or a carpet-sweeper? Sir, your mother has been looking forward for years to the time when she should have you at home to relieve her of her care. Your father cannot spare you. Your little sisters are growing up, and need a brother's guidance. Charity begins at home—yes, and duty, and all zest, hope, dreams, aspirations; yes, and end there. Take up your cross and follow them.[7] Is not the kitchen wide enough? Will not the sewing-room contain your grandest meetings? Can you doubt that you are meeting, in the nursery, all the high intent of life?

I repeat, let any man try it. Let him find himself in a few years' lapse a wearied, worried, stiffened thing; grown into his treadmill; rushing out in brains and wearing out in body; a patient dependent in his parents' house; a mature man, with about the rights and under most of the restrictions of a child; an unpaid housemaid; perhaps (Heaven knows!) an unthanked and unconsidered drudge. Let him understand that marriage only can relieve him from his position; and that even marriage shall be to him in the main but a continuance of the same; and that even this relief it is not in his power to lift finger to bring within his horizon. Let him appreciate as only a sensitive woman can the peculiar annoyance of a situation in which one is even supposed to be in attendance upon the pleasure of a "lover loth who lingers long."[8] Let him find himself approaching thirty, without a dollar of his own, without prospect of future, self-subsistence, or acquaintance with any trade or business which can support him, or a hope of any, to preserve his old age from wretched and unwelcome dependence. Let any man try this, I say, if he wonder why women are not happy.

But it is said: The condition which you represent is not possible, for women have not the same tastes as men. A woman will not feel to be deprivations many customs which to a man would be galling in the extreme.

This I deny. Women have, in general, I believe, very much the same tastes with men. No woman ever failed to feel the deprivations of the life which I have depicted, except from pure pressure and warp of a long training to it and seclusion in it. A woman finds no adaptation to her "taste" in such a life but such as the prisoner found in "Picciola."[9] Would free man have stooped to cherish a weed in the crack of a jail pavement! "Galling in the extreme?" It *might be* to a man. The language only struggles to express what their lot is to many women. It cannot attain unto the h[e]ight of the settled hopelessness, the outraged sensitiveness, the sense of might and mishap in all their fine young purposes, the fierce questioning of Heaven and despair of earth, which I have seen in the faces of thoughtful women a hundred times.

But again it is said: All laws hit hard somewhere; every beneficence inflicts some pain; no custom can be adjusted smoothly to every member of society; and, since in general the natural position and employment of women must be in their husbands' or fathers' homes, a certain amount of ill-adaptedness and discontent cannot be avoided in the interval wherein the natural limits of the two overlap. There are rough seas between girlhood and wifehood from which no pilot can inevitably secure the sailor. In the main, a woman's duties are at home; and, in general, her happiness ought to be.

This again I deny. Whatever may be said of married women (and "that," as Mill says of the aberration of moral feeling, "is too weighty a subject to be discussed parenthetically and by way of illustration"),[10] the duties of the unmarried woman are not at home.

I do not refer now to those cases in which invalid or indigent parents require the personal presence and care of their children, except to say that such claims are no more binding upon the filial affection of a daughter than upon that of a son, and it does not devolve one whit more upon Sarah to leave her store or studio to meet them than upon William to leave his ship or sell out his oil-wells.

Housekeeping and home-staying are no more compulsory upon the consciences and lives of women as women than shoemaking upon the moral principle of men as men. On whatever ground all girls should be housekeepers all boys should be tinsmiths or fishermen. In the nature of things, there is no more claim upon a woman to be her father's housekeeper or her brother's seamstress than to be his hostler or his bootblack. If John should remain with his mother to help about the sewing, so should she; not otherwise. If it is incumbent upon him to expend a dozen of his young years in making preserves, it may be upon her; but not otherwise. It is a selfish affection, a sickly sentimentality, and a terrible error of parental judgment which says to the young man,

"Go, life is before you; cut your way; leave your mark; make for your-self an honest independence and an honored name; tax all the force, all the beauty, all the largeness of your being, that the world may help you, and you the world; no sacrifice will be too great for us to make in aiding you to this grand end; no separation too bitter; we shall watch and smile, and take our gray hairs to the grave in the joy of your success." And to the young woman: "My dear, we cannot spare you now; wait a while; wait a long while; wait a lifetime, perhaps. Give us your self— your young energies, and ingenuities, and the diversion of your brightest hours and the devotion of your gravest; your gifts and graces; your patience and smiles; your opportunities of growth and gain; your chance of usefulness or fame. Life is before *you*, too—lifting like a golden mist; your young eyes are alight with it. But turn away. Wait a while. Wait a long while. Wait till the color has faded and the chill sunk down. It is not for you. It may allure you; but we know better. You may long for it; but our sheltering roof is your abiding-place. We have need of *you*."

And this brings us back. I said that the ordinary lot of the ordinary young woman is unnatural.

"If there is anything vitally important to the happiness of human beings," it has been said, "it is that they should relish their habitual pursuits."[11]

But this is not all. Happiness is not the most natural thing in this world; nor the most important.

"Rights? Oh! yes," said an old countryman, "I won't deny but women has rights. They're human critters. I'll own they've got rights; but they ain't men's rights!"[12]

"They're human critters." We are apt to forget it. But they really are. The large abilities and disabilities, the great means and ends of life they possess in common with their kind to an extent in which the distinctions of sex are an impertinent and unimportant consideration. The pertinence and importance of these distinctions are secondary to the great family likeness of human nature. Women are made in the image of God before they are made in the image of Eve.

Now the position to which we remand young women is one contrary both to the needs and the obligations of young human nature.

The powers of self-management, self-support, and self-investment are the inherent needs of the maturing man or woman. The best and broadest use of these powers is obligatory upon them. This public opinion denies to women. Individuality is the birthright of each human soul. This society crushes out of women. "He who lets the world or his own portion of it choose his plan of life for him has no need of any other faculty than the apelike one of imitation."[13] This exalted trait the world has "expressed to gold-leaf" in its girls.[14] The delicate woof and lustrous coloring of the most delicate and lustrous web, the feminine conscience, have been wound about the bare bitterness of the thing till it has become a difficult matter to explain to a rational young woman that life not only allows but demands of her that she should follow her own judgment in the selection of her work, that she is mistress of her own faculties and queen of her own uses.

"I should like to be a doctor or a lawyer, to preach or to paint, to buy or sell or get gain, to have any place in the active world, any share of its definite struggles and rewards and helpfulness," cry the patient eyes of hundreds of these quiet "home-girls," whose praise is in the mouth of everybody. "But mother would not like it. I am not as happy as I wish I were. I feel as if there were a mistake about me somewhere. But father says I am doing right. I seem to myself to be stepping on tiptoe over a mine of something that I may not touch. I feel unused, untried, unsounded. But brother Edward says he cannot spare me. Like poor Charley Lamb, I 'once thought life to be something, but it has unaccountably fallen from me before its time.'[15] But Sarah says I'm just run down, and need quinine."[16]

This is not of nature nor of grace. It is a distortion and a wrong. In any but a woman we should not need to have it pointed out. Turn the tables. Reverse the coin. Suppose that Raphael had refused to gaze into the divine eyes of the Sistine Mary because his mother advised him not to.[17] Or that Milton had not entered Paradise because his father thought he'd better not. Or that Mr. Field had let the Cable go, to please a first cousin, who thought he had enough to do at home.[18]

It is often urged that young women, in the dependent and uneventful life of their mothers' homes, can find sufficient outlet for their "spare life," and effective anodyne for their discontent, in acts of charity.[19] Heaven knows what would have become of them, my friend, if they had not made that discovery long ago! "Outlet and anodyne!" Yes, but effective and sufficient.

I say again: Let any man try it. "To practice it [charity] usefully," says the author of the "Subjection of Women" (a book which no reading woman in the land should rest till she has seen),[20] "or even without doing mischief, requires the education, the manifold preparation, the knowledge, and the thinking powers of a skillful administrator. There are few of the administrative functions of government, for which a person would not be fit who is fit to bestow charity usefully."

"I long ago came to the conclusion," said a thinking woman, who has, as we say, tried "both kinds," "that the *natural* way of assisting the suffering and needy is through the legitimate avenues of a settled *business*."[21]

Behold, we have the poor always with us![22] Through the legitimate avenues of a settled business, if at all, we must relieve the suffering and meet the needs of young women. Their lives lack that "greatest possible centralization of information and diffusion of it from the center" which is the mainspring of all true government,[23] either of society or of the individual, and which in this work-a-day, bread-and-butter world can be generally secured only by the discipline of a work-a-day, bread-and-butter, profit-and-loss occupation.

It ought to be just as much of a disgrace of affliction to a parent not to have provided means of apprenticeship to a business for his daughter as for his son. It should be just as much of a mortification to a young woman to find herself unqualified, at a suitable age, for some kind of trade as it is to a young man. A girl ought to feel as much ashamed of every year that she passes in needless dependence upon her parents' bounty as is her brother.

To the speculative masculine minds interested in the advantages and disadvantages likely to accrue to the masculine half of the world from such a state of society instances will occur of women, trained on the "protection and dependence" theory, sinking in latter life a dead weight into the struggling youth of an overworked and underpaid man; planting their pretty, helpless feet on every growth in his prospects of ease;

tearing with their graceful, helpless finger holes that no tailor can mend in his pocket; often, in the pleasant names of pleasant kinships, turning his life to bitterness, and depriving him of its richest rights and dearest hopes—instances so numerous that I think even the political economy of such a mind will hardly be prepared to weigh against them those benefits which men may derive from the attentions and presence of such women in their homes.

Let us cease this foolish prattle about the sweet seclusion and the modest shelter of a deformed and wasted and wasting existence.

Send your girls away from home. It will do them good. Urge them into the world. "I pray not that thou shouldest take them out of the world; but that thou shouldest keep them from the evil."[24] Help them into the broad ways of active life, and into the brisk air of healthy competitions and acquisitions. They will strengthen for it, body and brain and soul. Train them from infancy to "be" something. There shall repay you no more a parody of the possibilities of young womanhood—sickly, moody, dwarfed, and twisted; but "a new creature."[25] Drop that sentimental clinging and that false fondness which grants your grown daughter only the privileges and immunities of a child in her teens. Aid her to "put away childish things."[26] Teach her that character comes of contest, fineness of friction, innocence not of ignorance; healthy womanhood—even as healthy manhood—from a hand-to-hand battle in the very thick of life.

First published in the *Independent*, July 27, 1871, 1. The essay also appeared in *Woman's Journal*, August 12, 1871, and *Logansport Weekly*, September 2, 1871.

Selections from
"Woman's Dress (In Four Parts)"

....

ii. Is It Healthful?*

The enormities of a woman's dress, having done their best to deform her body, will very naturally do their bravest to destroy it.

So far and so fast has this work proceeded, that the scholarly physician invited to address the New England Club upon woman's physical fitness to be,[1] to do, or to suffer, can find, in the realm of his cultivated thought, no more grateful or graceful thing to tell you, educated, thinking ladies, known to be hopeful of woman's future, trustfully anxious for her higher development, and absorbed in elevating her actual condition, than that your hopes are moonbeams, your anxious trust the diversion of overwrought credulity, your absorption in your work the blind enthusiasm of ignorance—that woman's constitution, being subject to peculiar conditions, must forever forbid her keeping pace with her brother or her husband in intellectual culture and entirely negative the question of her industrial success or existence. So low has the clinical ideal of woman fallen! So dark are the Doctor's spectacles! So great and growing the physical disability at least of American women!

If there were no other cause to account for the feeble physiques and prevailing ailments of the present generation of women (and their name is legion)[2] I believe that their present modes of dress alone would explain the mystery nearly all. *That a woman wears a biased dress and a long skirt is enough,[3] in itself considered, to make an invalid of her under favorable conditions, and sure to do so under disadvantageous ones.*

I put this assertion strongly because I feel and believe it in the strongest manner.

You will remind her of our grandmothers—the fabulous grandmothers, the healthy, wealthy, and wise,—they who scrubbed floors, did the family washing, wove carpets, spun their husbands' coats, and brought up fourteen children, in biased waists and long skirts. I reply that it is *because* they scrubbed floors, did the washing, wove the carpets, spun the coats, and *because* they brought up fourteen children, and *because* they did this, and the time faileth me to tell what else, in long skirts and biased dresses that American girls are what they are to-day—pallid, puny, undersized, undersouled, devoured by the backache, the headache, the heartache, a dark puzzle to the physiologist who undertakes their present relief, a sad problem to the political economist who looks to the future ideal society, the mothers of which they will be.

"Six new diseases," we are told, "have come into existence with the styles of dress which require the wearing of multitudinous and heavy skirts."[4]

Indeed, I wonder that there are not sixty. I wonder that women sustain, in even the wretched and disheartening fashion that they do, the strain and burden of their clothing. I wonder that any of us are left with unimpaired vitality for the pursuance of self-culture, for the prosecution of our business, for the rearing, care, and support of our families, for the whirling of the wheels within wheels of social duties which devolves dizzily upon us, till "the whip of the sky" has ceased to lash us into the struggle for existence.[5] No doctrine but the doctrine of the "Survival of the Fittest" will touch the problem.[6] We are of tougher stuff than our brothers, or we should have sunk in our shackles long ago. It was well said by one of your own members:[7] "Whenever I discuss this subject with the 'unawakened' I resort to the simple inquiry: Could your father or your husband live in your clothes? Could he walk down-town on a rainy day in your skirts? Could he conduct his business and support his family in your corsets? Could he prosecute 'a course of study' in your chignon?"

The prompt and ringing *No!* of the only possible answer is startling and suggestive. The muscular masculine physique could not endure the conventional burdens which the nervous feminine organization supports. The man would have yielded and sunk, where the woman has struggled and climbed.

I lay especial stress upon the close waist and long skirt as blunders in the methods of attire incumbent upon women, because when I consider the smoothness of surface which a fitted waist involves, thereby requiring that strait-jacket, fit only for a lunatic asylum, the corset, for its proper effect; when a woman whom I know puts on a basque waist such as she wore five years ago (like all women, she "never wore tight dresses!")[8] and feels her lungs contract and ache, and her breath come in uneasy gasps, and her arms, confined by solid seams, refuse to rise to the h[e]ight of a horse-car strap or a lifted curtain-tassel, and the whole system shrink and cramp itself to fit the unnatural restriction; when I see women stay indoors the entire forenoon because their morning-dresses trail the ground a half a yard, and indoors all the afternoon because there comes up a shower, and the walking-dress will soak and drabble all or nearly all of that; or when I see the "working-woman" standing at the counter or at the teacher's desk, from day to dark, in the drenched boots and damp stockings which her muddy skirts, flapping from side to side, have compelled her to endure; when I see her, a few weeks thereafter, going to Dr. Clarke for treatment,[9] as a consequence; when I find, after the most patient experiment, that, in spite of stout rubbers, waterproof gaiters, and dress-skirt three or four inches from the ground, an "out-of-door girl" is compelled to a general change of clothing each individual time that she returns from her daily walks in the summer rain; when I see a woman climbing up stairs with her baby in one arm and its bowl of bread and milk in the other, and see her tripping on her dress at every stair (if, indeed, baby, bowl, bread, milk, and mother do not go down in universal chaos, it is only from the effects of long skill and experience on the part of the mother in performing that acrobatic feat); when physicians tell me what fearful jars and strains these sudden jerks of the body from stumbling on the dress-hem impose upon a woman's intricate organism, and how much less injurious to her a direct *fall* would be than this start and rebound of nerve and muscle, and how the strongest *man* would suffer from such accidents; and when they further assure me of the amount of calculable injury wrought upon our sex by the *weight* of skirting brought upon the hips, and by thus making the seat of all the vital energies the pivot of motion and center of endurance; when I see women's skirts, the shortest of them, lying inches deep along the foul floors, which man, in delicate appreciation of our concessions to his fancy in such respects, has inundated with tobacco-juice, and from which she sweeps up and carries to her home the germs of stealthy pestilences; when I see a ruddy, romping school girl in her first long dress, beginning to avoid coasting on her double runner or leaping the stonewalls in the blueberry fields, or standing aloof from the game of base-ball, or turning sadly away from the ladder which her brother is climbing to the cherry-tree, or lingering for him to assist her over the gunwale of a boat; when I read of the sinking of steamers at sea, with "nearly all the women and children on board," and the accompanying comments: "Every effort was made to assist the women up the masts and out of danger till help arrived; but *they could not climb*, and we were forced to leave them to their fate"; or when I hear the wail with which a million lips take up the light words of the loafer on the Portland wharf, when the survivors of the "Atlantic" filed past him: "*Not a woman among them all! My God!*"[10]—when I consider these things, I feel that I have ceased to deal with *blunders* in dress, and have entered the category of *crimes*.

We should not overlook the minor sins in our confession—such as the heating of the head with false hair, the distortion of the hands and feet with tight leather, the scantiness of warm underwear, the exclusion of Heaven's air and light (as well as freckles) from the face by musty veils, exposure to the ague in winter and sunstroke in summer, and to the feverish heat of public assemblies at all times induced by those truly awful pieces of architecture which we term hats. Nor can we overestimate the mischief brought upon our sex by habitual attention to the making and mending, to the fashioning and refashioning, of our clothes. Much sewing is a weariness to the flesh, and of making many garments there is no end.[11]

A long train of doleful diseases follows upon the confinement of women to the needle or the treadle,[12] as any thoughtful physician of the sewing sex can testify. For the one stitch necessary to keep soul and body together probably twenty go in these days to frill and flounce them, to ruffle and tuck them, to embroider and braid them, till so much of soul is stitched into the body, and so much of body into soul that the task of indicating which is which becomes a prize problem to the most studious mind.

"I spent one hundred hours," said an educated and cultivated lady, recently—and said it without a blush of shame or a tremor of self-depreciation—"I spent just one hundred hours in embroidering my winter suit. I could not afford to have it done. I took it up from time to time. It took me a hundred hours."

One hundred hours! One could almost learn a language, or make the acquaintance of a science, or apprentice one's self to a business, or nurse a consumptive to the end of her sufferings, or save a soul, in one hundred well-selected hours. One—hundred—hours!

iv. What Can Be Done about It?

To incorporate with one's active views revolutionary ideas of the character of female attire is half the battle; but it is only half.

Most of us are more or less aware of the need of reform in this direction; but perhaps none of us can confidently see a rod before us through the fog which enwraps the waymarks by which the reform is to be effected.

For one thing, the average woman, on whose suffrages we must depend for all reforming force, is presumably contented with the principles upon which her sex dresses, and, for the most part, with their methods of execution. Clumsiness of detail may annoy her, for the average woman is no fool; she may lose her temper over a sash-end now and then; she is at times, however, gently put together, a veritable vixen on the subject of hemming frills; her anathemas of her drabbled dress-skirt amount to what has been termed an "angel's profanity" on a sweet, serene, slushy, March morning. Yet with the *plan* upon which women adorn themselves, and of which the most patent absurdities which afflict the soul and body of her to the verge of revolt are but the natural expression, she is, I think, wholly at peace.

To add to the difficulty of dealing with her upon this or any kindred point, the average woman is very much upon her guard to-day against encroachment upon her habits, or disturbance of her convictions. A dozen years ago she could be warily led into the atmosphere of healthy doubt, and surprised into newer if not better temperatures of thought. She is alert now, aroused. There is a surcharge of electricity in the air.

While she breathes, she thinks, suspects. The old weather records are safe and familiar. The sun rose and set, men married and women were given in marriage; children were born, died, and gathered to their fathers, and the sky was calm. If thunder-storms crouch on the brow of the hill, whose fault may it be? Yours perhaps. Under your most reticent allusion to the ballot she discerns, at the least, open Atheism and covert free love, if not an opium-fed baby, and a dinnerless and buttonless husband. Through your vaguest suggestion as to the healthfulness of shoulder-straps she sees herself walking up the aisle at church in the scantest of Bloomers and a stovepipe hat. Ah! she is as wise as a serpent; she is as harmless as a dove: she will not denounce you; she will only beware you.

Again, we are told that the love of personal adornment is inherent in the feminine constitution, and desirably so; that this involves a wider distinction between the apparel of the sexes than mere social security requires; that the native modesty of women will and must forbid the bridging of this distinction; that harmony between the sexes requires that women cultivate the beautiful for beauty's sake and their own; that, though the American mother become an extinct race, the American girl must weight her hips and curl her hair and read the fashion books.

In these, as in all errors, there is truth enough to take the nerve out of the arm that would strike them—often at an instant when a blow would shatter the amalgamate image and shiver the brass from the iron, the iron from the clay, and all from the silver and the gold.[13]

Again, we may bear about within our weekday creeds the assurance that we are conforming to an uncultivated, unhealthful, and immoral standard of action, and be checked at the very outset of an attempt to elevate it, by a series of petty perplexities puzzling in proportion to their littleness and as burdensome as they are base.

Our untrimmed dress consigns us to the sixth story of the hotel. Our mountain suit, worn upon Washington street would lodge us in the charge of the police.[14]

That it should be done is one matter. How to do it is quite another.

Now, in the first place, nothing will be done until some considerable body of women shall agree upon what they wish and will to do.

Mademoiselle may confine her creed to six frills; Madame to five and a fold; I may succumb to my dressmaker (saving time and trouble) upon the subject of overskirts; you may oppose her successfully on principle and preference; Maude will content herself with loosening her corset an inch or two; and Mabel will conceive of herself as having conceded everything to the Coming Woman in refusing to follow the inane and ill-bred custom of dragging her walking-dress in the mud whenever the fashion so to do "comes round" in turn.[15] We are in Cimmerian darkness and disquiet upon the matter.[16] We need light first, and organization immediately.

Suppose that any such body of women, of cultivated intelligence, should propose to itself some such catechism as this.

1. Are there any important characteristics of the actual which should be retained in the ideal feminine attire?

2. What are they?

3. What should be dispensed with ultimately?

4. What *can* be dispensed with immediately?

5. Is there anything in the essential modesty of a woman which forbids her so fashioning her garments as to be able to enter many active, gymnastic kinds of trade or recreation, from which public opinion, as crystallized in her costume, now excludes her?

6. Does either the essential modesty of the feminine nature or the safety of society require that a woman wear drapery below the knee?

Suppose by starting with half a dozen such inquiries such a body of women should multiply them at their leisure, and ramify them into reach of those details which thwart the sex at the root of all improvement in its condition.

Suppose that such a body of ladies—for instance, the New England Club—should call into council with itself one hundred ladies of that degree and kind of social influence which weighs in such a matter, in each of the cities of New York, Philadelphia, Washington, Chicago, St.

Louis, Cincinnati, and San Francisco. Suppose that seven hundred, let us say perhaps a thousand women, duly scattered throughout the country, should agree upon certain changes in their dress, and pledge themselves to their adoption. Suppose that, acting independently of French modes and mode-making (for I am convinced that this reform, if it ever comes about, will find its vantage-ground, with other emancipations, in America), we win the sympathy and command the prestige of our Republican Court, and that the leaders of fashion are let into the secret; that Mrs. Grant, for instance, were our president and Madame Demorest our committee on design;[17] that the Lady's Books became our Gospels and the pattern pamphlets the tracts of our new dispensation![18] Suppose, in short, that by one subtle, strong *coup d'état*, the thinking women of America could make it *fashionable* to dress like rational creatures?

Something of the nature of the American costume—the gymnasium dress, the beach suit, the Bloomer, call it what you will—must take the place of our present style of dress, before the Higher Life—intellectual, political, social, domestic, or moral—can ever begin for women. Many of us feel no more individual doubt of this than we do of seeing woman welcomed at the ballot-box or in the Christian pulpit.

But two objections are urged against it, with which we are all familiar. We are told that it is ungraceful; and that women, so sensitive to the graces of life as to wear camel's humps upon their backs and market-gardens upon their heads, will never submit to it. We are told that it is immodest, and that women who go half undressed to whirl the evening through in a young man's arms in that delicate pastime, the waltz, can never shock their finer natures so far as to sink to it.

I should like the opinion of any candid artist as to the relative beauty of the sight of a group of fresh young school-girls in their gymnasium suits, and the same girls dressed for the promenade, an hour later—or even of an active woman of sixty, fern-hunting in her mountain-dress, and the same woman in the fuss and feathers of her toilet at the hotel supper.

I should like any anxious sister to watch for a while the perfect protection and delicacy of the short-skirted, full-trowsered costume, as its little wearer leaps the bars and swings the ladders of her "exercises" or climbs the rocks that diversify her seashore rambles, and then to stand upon the corner of Washington and Winter streets upon a muddy day, and observe the shifts and exposures to which we are obliged to resort (every "maid, wife, and widow" of us)[19] to keep our skirts above the flood and filth of the streets.

It may justly be said that we cannot at one fell swoop impose such a style of dress upon the prejudices of the public. Here, I fancy, has been our most serious mistake. Because we cannot turn the river, we have not dammed the brook; because we cannot do everything at once, we have not lifted a finger to do any thing at all.

Suppose that we *begin* by shortening our skirts to a regulation distance of from four to six inches from the ground; that we dispense with the biased waist and corset, and retain the plaited gamp or little jacket which have been so popular; that we hang *everything* from the shoulders, and that we set ourselves humbly to study the "grammar of ornament."

Would not these four points alone, if carefully considered, and patiently, gracefully, commandingly insisted upon, effect a quiet opening in all due time for braver and better things?

In leaving this study for a discussion, our own hearts must remind us of what we need no speaker to suggest—the bearings of this question upon the responsibilities of *Christian* women.

Sometimes, in listening to the undertone which creeps from that direction, I seem to hear the voice of one crying in the wilderness: Prepare ye here—even *here*—the way of the Lord![20] So great a matter has a little fire kindled! So intricate and so appalling has been the injury wrought upon our sex by the sins and sorrows of our dress! So intricate and appalling appears the process of its cure!

The little Chinese monster,[21] grown from infancy in a pitcher, distorted into hideous mockery of natural proportions, changed into a thing human only because it is divine, might appeal to the instincts of the thoughtful observer with something of the quality and quantity of force with which the *woman of fashion* appeals to-day to the *woman of God.*

These are two of four essays about dress reform published in the *Independent* in 1873. The first appeared May 8, 1873, and asked, "Woman's Dress (In Four Parts): 2. Is It Healthful?" The second selection was the fourth in the series, and it focused on the question 4."What Can Be Done about It?" (May 22, 1873). Later that year the essays were expanded and published as a book, *What to Wear*, published by J. R. Osgood.

*Read before the New England Woman's Club.

A Dream within a Dream

It is a little singular to reflect upon that there should not be in existence a fully appropriate marriage service for the uses of either the church or the world.

The Episcopal service[1]—that most hallowed by churchly associations and most full of excellences—has yet egregious faults. Bad taste, bad grammar, and perjury may have their places; but a marriage service would not seem to be the place for them.

"I take thee *to* my wedded wife [or husband] . . . to have and to hold" is an awkwardness for which only long-inculcated reverence could feel so much rhetorical respect as not to mar a matrimonial ecstasy. "Till Death us do part" is a dislocation in which the most devout Church-woman must feel a pang. The inquiry "Who *giveth* this woman to be married to this man?" is, to say the least of it, an anachronism. "I pronounce you *man* and *wife*" flavors some what of the tenement-house patois,[2] as of a couple henceforth to say, "My man is abroad to-day," or "My woman is getting dinner."

"With all my worldly goods I thee endow" is a fiction so stupendous as to be more amusing than impressive.

"Do you promise to obey him and serve him? The woman shall say, I will." Herein we have the spectacle of a priest at the altar offering the most solemn and binding of vows to a woman who has not the least intention of keeping it; who will not keep it, if she has; and who ought not to keep it, whether she has or not.

The Church service was written in a bygone age, for a bygone type of society. Its real beauties cannot save it intact to the future. The Marriage To-be will demand a pledge for which this is neither speech nor language.

Outside of the apostolic succession we fare scarcely better. Most of the forms of marriage ceremony current among our pastors are mere abridgements and modifications of the old Church service. One of great beauty has, indeed, been written and circulated in private ministerial circles, with much acceptance.[3] But even this, inimitable as a literary master-piece, must something fail of reaching the temper in which many men and women nowadays find themselves moved to exchange the marriage vows. Nor does the short, slippery formula of the civil justice help the matter much.

Musing thus the other evening, Mr. Editor, I fell into a dream.

Epictetus advised his students never to tell their dreams.[4] As a general thing, nothing could induce me to depart from the advice of Epictetus; but I am convinced that Epictetus himself, had he been a contributor to the columns of THE INDEPENDENT, and had he dreamed the dream, would have straightway converted it into "copy" and sent it INDEPENDENT-ward by the earliest possible post.

For I dreamed that behold! I was invited to succeed the Rev. Mr. Murray as pastor of Park-street church;[5] and that, having accepted the call, upon conditions not to the purpose to specify; and that, having been duly (I doubled the l in that word; but discovered the superfluity just in time)—duly ordained, settled, discussed, made in every respect as self-conscious and wretched as it is quite proper to make a somewhat bashful new pastor in a perfectly self-possessed old church; having delivered my inaugural, and received my first pair of worked slippers, and declined my first donation party,[6] and denied my first ten or fifteen engagements, and quite become used to selecting housekeepers and conducting funerals, it fell to my lot, on a New Year's Eve, to marry my first couple.

Now, fifteen engagements is a small matter, and it is pure enjoyment to murder a donation party, and funerals and housekeepers have no effect upon my peace of mind, and it has been the one ungratified wish of my life that a young lady should work me a pair of slippers; but when it came to the wedding, I saw in my dream that my heart within me was troubled, for I doubted of the manner of the language in which I should perform this most difficult and delicate of duties satisfactorily to the young people and honorably to myself and my profession.

But I saw in my dream, and behold! when the youth and the maiden came before me, there were given unto me the words which I should speak, and that I married them according to the meaning of the words.

When I awoke, all particulars of that wedding had vanished from me. Whether there were cake and cards I know not; what the bride wore I cannot say; if there were bridesmaids or favors ask me not; but the words which I spoke remained unto me.

So, while they were yet fresh in my remembrance, I transcribed them, and, if you will have them, Mr. Editor, here they are. I will not stipulate that they shall be immediately adopted as the marriage formula of the Orthodox Congregational Church.[7] I am only inclined to claim (on the privilege of the dreamer) that they will be found not without interest as a psychological study to a certain class of minds.

Marriage Service

Which beginneth with the words "Let us pray."

(At the close of a brief prayer the minister shall say):

"In the presence of God and of these witnesses, we are now come to solemnize the covenant of this man and woman in marriage. Are you, Charles True, prepared, of your own free will's inclining and whole heart's desire, to take upon yourself the vows which shall make and keep you the husband of this woman as long as Death shall spare you one to the other?"

(He shall say): "I am."

"Are you, Charlotte Tender, prepared, of your own free will's inclining and whole heart's desire, to take upon yourself the vows which shall make and keep you the wife of this man as long as Death shall spare you one to the other?"

(She shall say): "I am."

"Is there to your inmost consciousness any hidden reason why you should not charge your lips with the utterance of these vows? Does the voice of your secret soul cry to you—by any reproach of memory, by any uncertainty of hope—to forbid these banns?[8] If there be such a reason, if there be such a voice, in the presence of God and of these witnesses, regard it, before it be too late."

(Both): "There is none such."

(Unto the man he shall say): "If you feel within your honest heart that any other woman ought to hold—or, in the sweet mood of your affection, that any other could hold—the place which this woman occupies to-day, for your soul's sake and for her soul's sake, acknowledge it before it be too late."

(Unto the woman he shall say): "If you feel within your honest heart that any other man ought to hold—or, in the sweet mood of your affections, that any other could hold—the place which this man occupies to-day, for your soul's sake and for his soul's sake, acknowledge it before it be too late."

(Receiving no responses, the minister shall proceed).

"Then, reverently do I offer you and loyally may you take upon yourselves the covenant of true marriage.

"Do you, Charles True, take this woman whose hand you hold to be your lawfully wedded wife?"

(He shall say): "I do."

"Do you, Charlotte Tender, take this man whose hand you hold to be your lawfully wedded husband?"

(She shall say): "I do."

"You promise to cleave unto each other in sickness and in health, in prosperity and in adversity, through trial and triumph, in temptation, peril, joy, sorrow, through life, unto death. You promise to be faithful each to the other in deed, word, and truth. You promise to be considerate each of the other's happiness, above all other earthly claims. You promise to assist each other in your mutual and individual life's work, rendering each to each such tender thoughtfulness and such large estimate of the other's nature that neither shall absorb in petty exactions or in selfish blindness the other's subject life. You recognize it to be the duty of every man and of every woman to live a life of individual service to an individual God, and you hold it to be the especial aim of marriage to assist men and women in the pursuance of such a service, by a union which brings mutual responsibility, mutual forbearance, and mutual comfort to replace solitary labors and lonely failures and unshared successes. You, therefore, promise to regard each the other's preference in all your plans of life, and to consider any claim of one to legislate for the other, as foreign to the spirit of a righteous marriage and to the letter of your vows. You believe that the sweet restraints and large liberty of mutual love shall serve you in the settlement of all difference of opinion, and that your happiness will be increased by your recognition each of the other's freedom of personal judgment and action. You promise to reverence in each other all that is essentially different in your natures, and to meet generously upon all that is common, and to elevate, each for the other and each in the other, your ideals of manhood, of womanhood, and of marriage. Do you thus believe and promise?"

(Both shall say): "I do."

"Then do I pronounce you to be husband and wife. The great necessity of love is laid upon you. Love is no longer its own, but another's. You are not any more your own, but each other's. You have set yourselves to learn the longest lessons of human experience. You have entered upon a condition of the highest duties, as well as of the deepest joys. As earnestly as you have come to it may it come to you. As solemnly as you have chosen each other may God's blessing choose out you. Even as tenderly as you are drawn to each other may his heart be drawn unto you. As sacredly as you cherish each other may his protection cherish you.

"'Love,' we read, 'is stronger than Death.'[9] Of whatever there shall be in a human love which outlives human life, may the love of this man and woman be found worthy to partake!

"For all that the love of man and woman may mean, in a world where they neither marry nor are given in marriage,[10] God grant that this earthly marriage may fit these two Heaven-born souls!

"Amen."

First published in the *Independent*, February 19, 1874, 1, the essay was included in Carol Farley Kessler, *Daring to Dream: Utopian Fiction by United States Women before 1863–1919* (Boston: Pandora Press, 1984).

What Is a Fact?

....

This is a noisy age. The dreamer can find no sacred silence in which to hide his fantasy. The thinker may double-lock his study door, but the winds of heaven will pilfer his thoughts from him through the window, and the birds of the air will carry the matter; if they do not, the world concludes that there was none to carry. The believer, too, is tremulous to the vibrations of the atmosphere. His mysticism and quietism come by the hardest. If he have a faith, he feels that he must believe aloud. On every hand the air is quick with clamors. The "advanced mind" shouts to the scientist. The theologian thunders at the infidel. The ecclesiastic menaces the liberal Christian. The philosopher sneers at each.

Representing none of these wise and urgent people, the writer of this fragment is moved to say a word concerning that considerable portion of humanity who walk outside the circle of this portentous amphitheatre, yet near enough to be alert to its contests as well as deafened by its din. To these honest, quiet, and thoughtful people, who in all militant eras press nearest to the combatants, constituting at once their busiest critics and truest friends, it seems, if I mistake not, as if the main question in dispute were one uncommonly easy to ask and uncommonly hard to answer.

It is a long time since that our great-grandfathers were crossing lances over the doctrine of imputed sin or the souls of infants condemned by predestination and foreknowledge absolute to an eternal hell.[1] A damned baby at best was a theory. Nobody ever saw one.

This is not the age of theory; hence we long since took our babies to be blessed by One who thought it worth while to mention the fact that of such was the kingdom of heaven.[2] Thus we care no more whether we are to be punished for the sin of Adam, having enough of our own to look to, to say nothing of the additional doubt whether Adam himself can be called a fact.[3] This, we find, is the age of fact. No one asks to-day, What is your theory? but, Where is your fact?

So, at least, it seems to these good people of whom I speak, who compose what we call "the masses" of the church and the world. The young man of business, who sits under your preaching from Sunday to Sunday, Reverend sir, watches you with a keen but yet with a slightly saddened eye. Whether this be an age for the encouragement of faith or the preservation of doctrine he is not sure. Whether he has fallen upon an era of inductive or deductive reasoning he does not know; it is probable that he does not care. But, that forces which he does not understand are threatening faiths that he reveres, he does know; and for this, in a downright, manly fashion, he does care very much indeed.

The thoughtful woman at the head of the crowded Bible class which has given such celebrity to your Sunday-school is puzzled, too. She no longer finds Barnes's Notes adequate to the religious difficulties of her observant, critical, restless pupils;[4] she no longer teaches, either, that the world was made in six days, or that the majority of the human race are doomed by a loving Father to an eternal struggle with a lake of material fire. She has heard the authenticity of the Fourth Gospel and even the original authorship of the Golden Rule called into question.[5] She has a general impression that Darwin is to blame, and that geology is at the bottom of the trouble.[6] She finds this, however, less satisfactory as an argument than might be, when her pet convert, nineteen wise years of age, announces that he will immediately become a free-thinker, on the ground that, next to immorality, there is nothing he so much prays to be delivered from as superstition. Perhaps she learns, as some of us have, to assume in general the uselessness of discussion with the initial moods of "emancipated minds."

So, perhaps, our friend, the young pew-owner, feeling himself unable to hold his ground with the fellows at the club, yet all the fonder of the faith which he cannot defend, as the father is of the child whom he sees surrendering to a stealthy disease, saddens a little more and more, but joins himself to the great rank and file of the silent believers, who try to be good fellows, and hope the Lord will clear things up some day. He thinks it would be natural to be able to give good reasons for believing anything so important as the Christian religion,—good business reasons, that were clear as the code of ethics on 'change, and as much to be respected, whether to be obeyed or not,—but finds no such reasons causing such respect, and gradually ceases to look for any.

It is safe to say that a part of the difficulties which our friends meet would be relieved, if they could more distinctly, or at least more clearly, define in their own minds some starting-point—without agreement upon which it is impossible to debate differences of either judgment or feeling, and for lack of which so many of our religious discussions are as wasted as the powder and blood of Malvern Hill.[7]

The average religious argument of to-day takes, perhaps, some such form as this,—the disputants, we may suppose, not having reached that stage of familiarity with each other's views at which controversy is tacitly and mutually conceded to be no accretion either to friendship or to faith.

The believer—we use this term and its opposite as, on the whole, less objectionable and more precise than any others which existing religious conflict has popularized—the believer begins by timidly expressing a hope that the unbeliever has "found Christ," or "is a Christian," or "is a man of faith." The unbeliever promptly and not at all timidly expresses his complete dissent from every point of conviction involved in these phrases. He may do this arrogantly or sadly, honestly or shrewdly, earnestly or flippantly, gently or maliciously, but he does it with decision. He speaks of the scientific paradoxes in the "poem of Genesis," of the morals of the Old Testament saints, of the physical impossibility of miracles, of the discoveries of geology, of personal imperfections in the character of Jesus, of the superior nature of Socrates, of the howling dervish, the negro revivals, and the damnation of children,—an article of faith which he asserts is generally wrought into the creeds of Christian churches of the present day, and secretly disavowed by kind-hearted but hypocritical people, who have not the courage openly to combat so monstrous a doctrine.

At this point, the believer strikes in rather warmly, and if he does not reply that such ignorance on any other vital point of contemporary difference would condemn his opponent to the strongest criticism of intelligent people, is tempted to do so, and feels a little out of temper and a little penitent, and suggests that the Bible is an inspired book, written by God for men and through men, and that we must expect to find difficulties in it, and earnestly and pointedly asks, Where will you find, on the whole, a better book for the guidance of human weakness?

The unbeliever replies that there is much fine poetry in the Bible, but more bad argument, Oriental superstition, and confused metaphor; that many men are inspired; that Goethe was a divine man; and that Browning's Paracelsus is as much a work of inspiration as the Song of Solomon, and far more moral.[8] He adds that it is impossible to reconcile God's sovereignty with man's freedom in any such make-shift manner as that adopted by the theologians, and that God either created sin, or he did not; that if he did he was not benevolent, and if he did not he was not omnipotent; and that we are made to cultivate our manhood, express our individuality, and study the secrets of nature.

The believer suggests that it may be possible we do not, as finite beings, understand all the mysteries in the nature of an infinite God; that it is not to be wondered at if we must leave some points unexplained; that this is perhaps a part of the discipline necessary to fit us for the eternal life.

The unbeliever hastens to say that of the eternal life we know absolutely nothing,—we cannot conceive of either beginning or end; that we are here and know it, but further than this we have no right to infer. We may cherish immortality only as a "solemn hope" (the believer's eyes fill, and he mentally ejaculates, "Poor fellow!"), or we may expect to be as the beasts that perish, and live on in the forces of nature, and the resurrection of the seasons, and the memories of unborn generations, and so on, but that geology is making every hour discoveries which are to revolutionize belief; that hope, faith, love, and the energies of imagination are beautiful fancies, but rocks are facts, and therefore (as nearly as the believer can understand) he urges that we cling to the rocks.

The believer suggests that rocks are cold comfort; to the bereaved, for instance, or the remorseful.

The unbeliever replies, vaguely, that he is not sure, either, that we comprehend the difference between infinite or finite—Finite? Infinite? He is not certain there is any infinite, or that he himself, in short, is finite—but that science— And so on, and so on.

Now, all this is firing wild. There is no gold in the target. There shows no target in the mist. If we set our aim in a fog-bank, who is to decide whether we have hit?

The believer may seek to "save" the unbeliever in this fashion till "the eve of the day of the Last Awakening,"—he will only irritate.[9] The doubting may try to "reason" with the trusting on this wise, till his tongue returns to the dust that he claims his kin to,—he can only depress. The disputants have swerved from the most elementary of the principles of logic. They have discovered no major premise in common. They must agree upon something before they can disagree intelligently about anything. There can be no dispute without a basis of harmony. "We may never, perhaps," as Hamilton says, "arrive at truth, but we can always avoid self-contradiction."[10]

Let us now suppose, as it is the object of this paper to suggest, that these two equally earnest people ask of each other, at the outset of all sincere and serious discussion, one simple question: *What is a Fact?*

The believer, we will assume, happens to put the query. The unbeliever hesitates. Neither of the disputants are psychological scholars. Both are intelligently educated. The unbeliever is the more accustomed of the two, probably, to sophistries of discussion. He perceives the importance of the point, and hesitates. It is one of the maxims of civil law that definitions are hazardous. After a thoughtful pause, he replies, with the blunt courage of common sense, which is quite as apt to hit the truth as the sharply refined point of the artist in philosophical language, that he should say a fact was a thing that could be verified.

To this the believer, without hesitation, agrees. All he claims, he adds, is that religion is a matter of fact as well as science. Grant this, he urges, and we can pursue our discussion. Deny it, and the sooner we agree to disagree the better. The believer's own vision has begun to clarify, with this closer exactness of definition, and his method of expression intensifies.

The unbeliever replies, with animation, that it is impossible to put religion and science upon the same foot-hold. We have, he urges, reached the age of reason—at last. It is no longer practicable for intelligent men to bend their necks to the yoke of superstition. We deal no more with a realm of fancy. Jesus was a rhapsodist. Christianity was full of poetry. It appealed to the imaginative era. We have passed by the birth-time of great poets. Literature acknowledges it. We do not now write epics. We invent the phonograph. Machinery, discovery, action, have replaced reverie, credulity, and dreams. We no longer pray. We telegraph. We have no time to sing psalms. We are engaged in the artificial propagation of fish.[11] Why should we attend church when we can observe the spontaneous generation of animaculæ in a bottle of boiled water?[12]

At this point the listener smiles, and the speaker breaks off with some irritation. He sees nothing to smile at. He is very much in earnest. These are serious subjects which he has mentioned. He is indeed more logical than he had seemed, and abruptly turning upon his opponent says,—

You ask me for my facts. I find them in the investigation of nature. Observe them. They alone are worthy of confidence. We seek, we study, we combine, we infer. The human mind was created—

By whom? Interrupts the believer.

Consistently, the unbeliever replies that he does not know. The powers of nature, formerly called God, have not yet fully revealed themselves to our ken. I believe nothing that I do not understand. I will not accept what I cannot prove. This is the first duty of the human reason. Man should receive only what he *knows*. I find myself a mysterious being in a mysterious condition. My business is to investigate my condition. Whether there be another world is none of my concern. No eye has seen it, no foot has returned from it, no voice has spoken from it; it is an absolutely unproved, and therefore unprovable, hypothesis. I find myself in the present world. I have occupation in the study of my limitations. There are mountains, the sea, the stars, the earth. There are geology, astronomy, the nautical sciences, the study of human diseases, the mysteries and *cultus* of the physical organization. I learn from fossil and the scalpel. The telescope and the microscope, the chart and the battery, command my attention. These give me the undeniable. Exact investigation presents me with my facts. Beyond a fact I am not justified in going.

Where is God? Can you handle him? What is prayer? Go weigh it for me! An immortal soul? My microscope has never revealed it. A fact is a thing revealed or revealable to my senses. Science alone is knowledge. Religion is superstition. Superstition is bondage. I decline to be fettered. Christianity is slavery. I choose freedom. Exact thought is my master.* And thus, and thus, and thus.

As the discussion waxes, the believer is oppressed more and more with the hopelessness, but not the helplessness of his effort. In proportion as he learns the difficulty of dissuading a man from views hardened as they are acquired by the friction of dissent from hereditary faiths, he gains nerve for his own processes of thought, and muscle for his own maturing belief. If nothing more comes out of the conversation, his faith at least is stouter for it. If he has not "converted" the free-thinker, he has himself become a better Christian.

He who believes much has always the advantage over him who believes little or nothing. Faith is the positive, as skepticism is a negation. He who affirms intelligently *and* earnestly carries by a sheer moral propulsion, as irresistible as the channel of Niagara, a power, not unlike the primal awe of nature, over him who denies.

Let us hope that our believer returns upon his antagonist a few ringing words, to which there can be no more convincing reply than the eternal and unassailable finality: I do not agree with you.

You seek, the believer says, the truth—the whole and holy and invulnerable truth. I seek no other. You desire a religion of facts. I also wish the same. You demand that we construct belief from reason. I, too, prefer a reason for my conclusions. You claim that you alone possess a basis of fact, since you only restrict yourself to what is known. You claim that you find the known alone in physical manifestations, their formulæ and solutions. I deny your claim.

I deny your claim, because (you will pardon me) of what seems to me its *ignorance*. You forget, or you have never learned, that truth is no niggard, and that science is a broad and bounteous term. It is not alone in the hard bosom of the rock that the Eternal rests. It is not only in the fumes of the laboratory that the breath of the devout seeker exhales.

* "He could not accept Christianity," said Renan of Spinoza (I quote from memory), at the recent celebration in honor of that philosopher's memory. "He could not thus surrender his liberty. *Descartes was his master!*"[13]

There are trained intellects that are not occupied with the germ theory, or with the latest treatise on the parasites of an unfortunate plant. There are students, as there are scholars, of other than material knowledges. You forget that there are to be found other than the physical sciences. You forget that the history of these other sciences commemorates much of the highest order of intellect, the most precise training, the most generous culture, the most candid research, and the purest sacrifice of self in the investigation of truth that human life has known.

You forget, in short (or you have never learned), that the MENTAL SCIENCES EXIST. You have not remembered that there is a philosophy of *mind*, as there is of *matter*; that there is a philosophy of *soul*, as there is of *sense*.

One need not be a very learned person to recall the facts that the sciences of ethics, of intellectual philosophy (even of theology, though for the sake of controversial comfort we may waive that irritating illustration), have still respectable positions in the world of thought, quite in rank with mathematics or chemistry. It has slipped your mind, for the moment, that there is a study of *Metaphysics* as well as of *Physics*. You have not articulately understood that a sufficient culture overlooks neither the existence of these two forms of human knowledge, nor their relative importance and adjustment to each other.

And this leads me to say (once more I pray your courtesy) that I deny your claim because of what seems to me its *arrogance*.

One need not be very learned, I repeat, to understand something of the debt which the students of matter owe to the students of the mind. You and I are not learned, only intelligent people, and the intelligent have heard something of Socrates, of Aristotle, of Bacon;[14] of him who (humanly speaking), it might be said, created exact thought, of him who developed, of him who reconstructed it. Mental science, as we know, was by centuries the elder born, and father of physical science, in any modern signification of the word; as the brain is the creator and guide of the movements of the hand or foot.*

* Indeed, the believer might add, we are told by scholars that the father of modern intuitionalism was the father of modern mathematics as well. Descartes was the first of our scientists to study mind in the dissecting-room.

To ignore the parental influence of metaphysical upon physical study is a species of filial ingratitude which it is impossible to describe by a smooth adjective. The very processes of thought by which you are trained to investigate the material fact, you owe to ancestral centuries of mental discipline and to apostles of mental sciences. You speak of conscious and sub-conscious cerebration. You deny the mental entity which you once called a human soul. What enables your prompt lip to utter the challenge? Whence comes your power to deny?

I do not express these things in philosophical language, for, as I have reminded you, we are neither of us learned people, but I desire to make you understand in a plain and direct fashion that which I desire to say. Is it becoming, I ask, is it the modesty of wisdom, for the instrument to ignore the influence? Shall the microscope and the retort say to the eye or the hand, "We have no need of thee"? Shall the probe say to the surgeon, "Go to! It is I who tear or torture, as it is I who heal and save"? Speaking of his scientific *confrères*, one of the most distinguished physicians whom this country has known said, *"They cannot account for the 'I.'"*[15]

In short, it seems to me that when a man exalts the science of things which are seen and touched over the science of that which sees and touches; when he prefers to mistake a convolution in the brain for that by which the convolution becomes able to think, feel, and act,—nay, by which alone it is *enabled to make the mistake*; when he selects the less for the greater, the lower for the loftier, matter for mind, brain for soul, he exhibits the presumption of the servant, sent by his master to cash a check of important value, who struts as if the money were his own.

I object to your claim because, once more, I perceive it to be a *degrading* one. It is not necessary to be great ourselves to know that the great natures of the earth have been believing natures. Even you and I can remember that music, poetry, art, philosophy, literature, nay, physics itself, owe something to faith. It is not easy to forget that Beethoven, Mozart, Bach, Händel, Haydn, Milton, Dante, Wordsworth, Raphael and Michael Angelo, Plato and Immanuel Kant and Leibnitz, Goethe and Shakespeare, Kepler and Newton, were believers in the existence of God and the immaterial nature and immortal destiny of the human spirit.[16] It might be comparatively easy to prove that you and I had no souls; to deny one to these people I have mentioned were to go as far as anything could, perhaps, to prove that you are right, and that we, at least, are destitute of any.

Degrading, I say,—degrading to the deeps below all that is truly fine, all that is delicately observant, all that is highly reverential, all that is nobly receptive, all that is capable of assimilating the ideal, the beautiful, the lofty, and the large in human history,—is that view of human mystery which your claim presents. It may be either the cause or the consequence of this view that you flippantly ignore the testimony of the great teachers of human life. You decline to sit at the feet of the prophets, priests, and kings of the world. You turn your back upon the heights; on art, on inspiration, on intuition, and imagination, on aspiration, on song, on the sources of all that makes men clear and keen in brain, refined and pure in heart. For remember that if you seek to share these things they are no longer properly yours. They are not, they never were, they never can be, the products of a materialistic philosophy. If this is not clear to you, it seems to me that your location quite as well as your attitude puts a finely and simply outlined truth out of perspective to you. He who climbs, sees. "To him, as to Moses," says a French scholar, "secrets unknown to the rabble are revealed upon the mountain-top."[17]

You sit, then, and adjust yourself to the valley. You burrow, you dig, you descend. Choosing the company of the lowest forms of manifestation, you will find that the influence of their atmosphere is upon you. If a human mind keeps the exclusive society of vegetables and insects and fossils, is it to be wondered at that it fails to see the transfigured cloud which veils, while defining, the motions of the eternal sun? If a man's corroding ambition is to be quoted as an "authority on potato-bugs," he *may* be a sensitive appreciator of Locke's Essay on the Understanding, or the "Excursion" of the Lake Poet,[18] or the Gospel of John; but does it surprise us if he is not?

Pardon once more my plainness if I tell you that I cannot accept your claim, because it seems to me not unlike the scoff of the demonstrator in the dissecting-room. His business leads him to handle flesh. How, then, should God be a spirit?

I have somewhat, too, to affirm. You have called my attention to your facts; I should be glad to acquaint you with mine. Yours, I accept; it is your conclusions which I refuse. I do not question the evolution of the species, or the zymotic theory of diseases, or the existence of the last comet, or the possibilities of the photophone, or the discoveries of psycho-physics as affecting the criminal or the insane.[19] Physical science is welcome to do her best or her worst by helpless spectators like yourself or me. A fact is a fact, though it deal with the lowest phases of nature, and truth is holy, whether she hide in a stalactite or an epic, a jelly-fish or an oratorio, a vivisection or a prayer. I accept your facts, retaining the liberty to draw my own conclusions. I only ask that you (retaining, of course, the same liberty) accept my facts before we close or continue this discussion.

Of this, then, I would remind you. The manifestations of mind are at least as much to be respected as the manifestations of matter. He was a real philosopher who gave to his book the title, Man *in his Connection with* the Human Body.[20] What we think and feel is as genuine as what we see and touch. If I handle a chair or table, my thought of them is as individual as the table or the chair. If I take a pen to write these words, that which creates the words is as real as the pen. "I am the soul of the music," said a musician, when his string snapped. "Though the strings are all broken, the *music is there*."[21] Let me add (for you will remind me that I do not touch the pulse of your difficulty) that my thought is as real as the brain-cells by whose activity I am empowered to think it.

Thus, if I listen to music which dissuades me from temptation, or lifts me from gloom, or leads me to despair, these emotions exist as much as the ivory of the piano keys, or the catgut of the violin, or the gray matter in the cerebrum which the piano, the violin, and the emotion set in agitation. I am at least as justified in assertion, as you in denial of these facts. Explain them as you will. I offer them as facts. As such—*until you can prove* that "thought is phosphorus and phosphorus is thought,"[22] *without the predominant action of your mind in making that hypothesis*— they ought to be by you respected.

There is a form of the mental life which we call spiritual. This is the highest, as it is the finest, phase of the mystery that we name existence.

Coleridge expressed what I mean when he said that "faith is itself a higher reason, and corrects the errors of reason as reason corrects the errors of sense."[23] As the physical life is revealed by its phenomena, as the mental life possesses its expression, so the spiritual life has its manifestation. This is a fact. As such it is to be respected.

As we depend upon the senses to make clear to us the presence of the sunrise, as we rely upon the reason to explain to us the nature of a thought, so we lean upon faith to reveal to us the nature of a spirit.

While the eye brings to us the color of the dawn, it can do no more; the optic nerve of an idiot, though it quiver in precise obedience to the laws of his physical organism, for threescore years and ten, will never reveal to him the rapture of the morning. Sense and reason must act together. So the reason, left to itself, informs us of the character of the thought or of the feeling which we have about the sunrise; then it comes, and there it must come, against its limitation. The intellect of a skeptic, though he cultivate it till he is in his grave, will never produce a prayer for the guidance, or endurance, or delight of the day that is about to be his. Reason and faith must work together. So, we might add, faith, as a disconnected faculty, cannot result in true devotion. Unless guided by reason, the devotee may become a howling dervish, or a hysteric nun. The sense, the mind, and the spirit must live together.

Like the life physical, like the life intellectual, the spiritual life, while yet confessing an interdependence upon these other forms of life, possesses, like them, an individual existence.

"My *soul* to me a kingdom is."[24] In this kingdom there are laws: there is obedience or disobedience; there is anarchy or order; there is the separation of government; there is the history of growth or decline. This is a fact. As such it is to be respected.

A broken physical law involves its penalty. A denied intellectual law implies a punishment. A defied spiritual law presumes its retribution.

Leap into the ocean; no opposing law of salvation interfering, you will drown. Defraud the hours of rest for study or for dissipation; you lose the mental power of controlling natural sleep. Contest against that surrender of the soul to its Creator which we call the religious life; the religious life withdraws itself from you. Unbelief closes over the willing unbeliever like the waves of the sea or the tides of insomnia. These are facts. As such they are to be respected.

Again: the great law of development is the law of action. Every natural power grows by exercise. Any school-boy knows that he can create the iron ball of muscle on his arm only by the use and training of the muscle. Any college girl understands that the various faculties of the brain become serviceable only through action, as they become through inaction inert. As with the brawn, as with the brain, so with the spirit.

To exercise spiritual power is to develop and strengthen it. To disuse it is to repress or extinguish it.

Now, then, I ask you to remember that we who believe, speak to you out of a condition whose government you have defied or ignored; and that we speak of a faculty whose exercise you have disused. If we mention the spiritual life, we mention that of which you are not a citizen, but an exile; whether by deliberate choice or chance misfortune is not to the immediate purpose,—you are exiled. You have not the citizen's right of judgment concerning our affairs. You are incompetent to criticise this life, because you are not in it. Thus, too, if we refer to spiritual power, we refer to that which you do not possess, because you do not train it; whether by accident or design is not at present to the point,— your spiritual faculties are uneducated. You are disqualified from apprehending truth by means of powers which you have atrophied by disuse. These are facts; as such they ought to be respected.

Within this spiritual life, by means of exercised spiritual faculties acting upon and acted upon by our reason, we who believe cherish certain spiritual facts. God is one of those facts. The immortality of human souls is another. The responsibility of conscience is yet a third. The hope of a happy life everlasting is to be counted. The reasonableness of Revelation we add. To the saneness and usefulness of prayer we have certified. To the power of the personal life of Jesus Christ we thrill to offer witness. To the facts of forgiven sin and comforted bereavement we bear testimony. Is not a penitent and christianized thief as demonstrable as a clam or a comet? Is not the ecstasy of a martyr as real as the fagots that burn him? Is not the resignation of the desolate mourner as much a matter of proof as the coffin or the marble sleeper over which he weeps?

And yet but once again. As the body has its senses, so has the soul. Burns speaks of "those senses of the mind" by which great religious truths are apprehended.[25] Spiritual truth is received by spiritual powers. Spiritual fact is perceived by the spiritual eye, heard by a spiritual ear, handled by spiritual touch. "The true saint," says Dr. Holmes, "can be entirely apprehended only by saintly natures."[26]

We share with you the experience of the exercised physical senses, by which you and we alike perceive the physical fact. You do not as yet share with us—and we lay no claim to what is called "saintship" in asserting this—the experience of the trained spiritual sense by which we receive the spiritual fact. To this extent and for this reason, are you as far qualified for making intelligent deductions from our premises as we for drawing such from yours?

In asking you to answer this, as an act of judicial fairness, we cannot refrain from adding that it would seem natural for a broad-minded and intelligent man to feel a certain discontent with the partial nature of his development. He who trains his body and exercises his brain, and *stops there*, is imperfect, unbalanced, crude. He who has not sought to develop his spiritual nature is a half-educated creature.

Spiritual power is the flower of the human growth. In spiritual character we find the highest, finest, and most complex form of the species. All other nature, whether physical or mental, is embryonic to spiritual nature. Spiritual culture is the culmination of human education.

We ask, therefore, evidences of this culture, as the first qualification in any man towards his becoming a critic of such nature, such power, such character, or their philosophy. Failing of this culture, your science should, we submit, grant to our science the respect of ignorance, if not the attention of the student.

We have known invalids, prisoners of their inert muscles during all the bloom and brilliance of life. Some late-found medical inspiration, some personal surrender of devotion on the part of a friend, some unexpected joy or unimagined grief, or even some electric alarm, has allured, or shocked, or startled the sick man to his feet.

The power of motion was not dead, but slept. Late and loath though they be, the great flexile and extensor actions of the great muscles begin. Between the grave of his life and the grave of his death the man partakes of a resurrection.

Such a discovery of blessedness, we may suppose, comes to him who, after the sluggishness, or willfulness, or disease of unbelieving years, is led by the late cultivation of his spiritual faculties to the possession of spiritual truth.

Facts before which his intellect has been a blank illuminate his consciousness. Mysteries at which he sneered become shrines before which he kneels. Powers which he has not hitherto recognized magnify his nature. Hopes which he has never known irradiate his life. Contrition that he has not understood permeates his heart. Tenderness which he has never approached gives pathos, as it gives purity, to his past. A future of which he has never dreamed intensifies and glorifies his present. He learns the value of his own being, and experiences the friendship of God. In the closing days of his history, as in the final scenes of the apocalyptic vision, there are "new heavens and a new earth."[27]

First published in the *Atlantic Monthly*, (November 1880, 676–85. This essay was subsequently included in Phelps's essay collection, *The Struggle for Immortality* (Boston: Houghton, Mifflin, 1889).

Women's Views of Divorce

I am asked a simple question which requires a complicated answer. Do I justify the right of divorce? Assuredly. When? When the question is a duel between a wrong and a right; when not to give the right is to commit an undeniable wrong. I justify divorce as I do a surgical operation—then and thus only; when it is the last expedient,[1] the final hope, the desperate venture; when there is nothing else to be done to save the social life.

A man and woman elect to tie themselves together for life, presumably because they cherish each other above all human beings. To say that the causes which practically invalidate this tie are infinite in variety is only to say that human nature exists. To insist that the causes which may legally separate the married should be limited in quantity is only to say that morality is a virtue or frailty a vice. We should go so far as to make this limitation the severest, the most strenuous, that the highest civilization will bear. I cannot believe, in this matter more than in others, in "going under," as the phrase has it, to a compromise with ideal Right. But what is ideal Right?

If a man knocks his wife down, he shatters the marriage-troth as much as if he brought an evil woman to her house. If a woman drinks away the moral nature of her unborn babe, she ceases to be a wife as surely as if she broke the Seventh Commandment.[2] "Infidelity" to the obligations of marriage is a term to which we give a too restricted use. I do not hesitate to say that personal abuse, or felony before the law, or desertion, or habitual drunkenness, or other equivalent (if there be equivalent) offences, may justify divorce as amply as the crime of adultery. But that these offences need to be identified with a legal conscience surpassing any thing yet brought to bear upon our statutes seems to me as much a matter of course as to say that the United States needs a navy. The power to *un*marry—in a state of society like ours—should be made "a strait and narrow way."[3] We have built it so broadly that "thousands go in thereat."[4] It should be made unenviable, unpopular, unlikely, and the judgment of the people should hedge it about with thorns and barbed wire. It should be made as disgraceful as crime. It should be made as hard as death.

The question whether a divorced person ought to marry again during the lifetime of the first partner is the last in, but it is the poser of the discussion. One gives an opinion on this point perfectly aware that life and time may change it; for one sees that experience modifies or creates opinion easily enough on any subject, but on none more thoroughly than on this. The personal equation affects our morality to an appalling extent; and saintly Stephen Blackpool, looking up out of the pit of death at the pure face of Rachel, in Dickens's story,[5] must have had his own views on divorce before which the comfortable judgment of a happy home ought to confess itself a blind and groping thing. But, so far as I feel qualified to form an opinion upon so tremendous a matter, I must believe that Mr. Gladstone, in this discussion, and Mr. E. J. Phelps,[6] in that of another review, have come nearest to the right of the case when they would deny to the divorced under any circumstances the right of remarriage until death shall give it.

Now, this old question is a threefold one, and ought to run like this: Shall we marry? Shall we unmarry? Shall we remarry? Clearly, it seems to me that the emphasis of the discussion has been put in the wrong place. We should slip it further along the line of interrogative. It is less important to inquire, Do they right to remarry? Were they wrong to unmarry? than to ask, Did they right to *marry?*

I have spoken of the right of divorce as a surgical expedient. Carry on the figure of thought and we may learn a lesson.

The best-instructed physicians know well that there exists to-day a subtle and powerful conflict in the professional world. On the one hand, the tendency of experiment turns terribly to surgery. Everything goes to the operating-table. Disease, like the demon in the New Testament, "coming out, tears him" who is so miserable as to trust his life to the surgical fashion.[7] Tennyson, with the fine eye of poetry for the prevailing facts of science, struck the situation when he wrote of his hospital doctor, who handled the child "gently enough, but his voice and his face were not kind."

"But they said too of him
He was happier using the knife than in trying to save the limb."[8]

On the other hand, there has intensified the solemn belief in the validity of the healing art. The materia medica[9] is trusted above the butcher's knife. The fine, the delicate, the patient remedy, the prophylactic, or the tonic, or the curative, becomes the material of absorbing study such as the medical world has never known before. The doctrine of mercy, the theory of prevention, rule the medical conscience, and the healer's intellect refines as the sensibility is saved—thus, please Heaven, the patient too.

Divorce, at best, is pure surgery; nothing more nor less; necessary at the extremity, never to be tolerated when the milder measure will save the life.

The truly scientific, and therefore the hopeful, treatment of this social disease must, I believe, consist more and more, and must some time consist entirely, in the preventive, and what we might call attentive, means of cure. What is the use—what *is* the use—in wearing out our brains to invent scalpels and probes, to cut, and sew, and carve, and bury, when a careful course of the right remedy would heal the patient?

In brief, so long as we are allowed to *marry* as we do, what right have we to expect anything else than unmarrying and remarrying to the end of this weak and wicked world?

As our laws stare us in the face, there is no man so drunken, so immoral, so brutal, so cruel, that he may not take to himself the purest, the most refined, the most sensitive of women to wife, if he can get her. There is no woman so paltry, so petty, so vain, so inane, so enfeebled in body and mind by corsets or chloral,[10] flirtation, or worse, that she may not become the wife of an intellectual, honorable man and the mother of his doomed children. There is no pauper who may not wed a pauper and beget paupers to the end of his story. There is no felon returned from his prison, or loose upon society uncondemned, who may not make a base play at wedlock, and perpetuate his diseased soul and body in those of his descendants, without restraint. There is no member of what we call our "respectable classes" who may not, if he choose, make a mock of the awful name of marriage, in sacrilege to which we are so used that we scarcely lift an eyelid to express surprise or aversion at the sickening variety of the offence.

Where is the law that prevents a titled roué from becoming the husband of a pure American girl?[11] Where is the law that saves a rich woman from the designs of a mercenary spendthrift suitor? Where is what Sophocles called "the unwritten law" that prevents a man and woman who do not love each other supremely, unselfishly, permanently, and we might almost say divinely, from *daring* to take upon themselves the sacred marriage-vow?[12]

Where is the public sentiment which calls a *mariage de convenance* by its true name?[13] Legalized prostitution are two ugly words; but nothing less will fit the case. Where is the drift of high emotion which scorns a loveless marriage as disgraceful, makes a foolish one unpopular, and a wicked one impossible? Give us the public opinion which will make it indelicate for a man to marry for a housekeeper or a woman for a home. Give us the average of judgment which shall stamp it a social blot to marry "for position" and call it a crime to marry for money. Give us the great ideal which shall create the noble fact. Give us such a comprehension of the feeling which ought to draw men and women into the marriage-tie that anything less than almighty love should invalidate marriage as much as the absence of a witness to the oath. Give us such a vision of the purity, the unselfishness, the patience, the tenderness, the loyalty through sorrow and sickness and ill fortune and fading fairness, and the clash of temperaments, which the marriage-bond requires— such a holy power as shall lift us above the social mire toward which our nation is sinking. The sheer force of relentless right ought to hold us up; but the average opinion must form the moral derrick.

Bring to bear upon our worst perplexity our highest opportunity. Make it as nearly impossible as human deficiency allows to *marry* wrong; and we make it all but unnecessary to ask if divorce be right.

Published in the *North American Review*, January 1890, 128–31, Phelps's essay was part of a forum on divorce, which also included replies by Mary A. Livermore, Amelia E. Barr, Rose Terry Cooke, and Jennie June. These forums were a popular means of addressing contemporary issues in the later nineteenth century, and Phelps contributed to them with some frequency. The forum was republished in *Public Opinion: A Comprehensive Summary of the Press throughout the World on All Important Current Topics*, October 1889–April 1890, and in David J. and Sheila M. Rothman, *Divorce: The First Debates* (New York: Garland, 1987).

The Moral Element in Fiction

Since art implies the truthful and conscientious study of life as it is, we contend that to be a radically defective view of art which would preclude from it the ruling constituents of life. Moral character is to human life what air is to the natural world—it is elemental.

There was more than literary science in Matthew Arnold's arithmetic when he called "conduct three-fourths of life."[1] Possibly the Creator did not make the world chiefly for the purpose of providing studies for gifted novelists; but if he had done so, we can scarcely imagine that he could have offered anything much better in the way of material, even though one look the moral element squarely in the face and abide by the fact of its tremendous proportion in the scheme of things. The moral element, it cannot be denied, predominates enormously in the human drama. The moral struggle, the creation of character, the moral ideal, failure and success in reaching it, anguish and ecstasy in missing or gaining it, the instinct to extend the appreciation of moral beauty and to worship its Eternal Source—these exist wherever human being does. The whole magnificent play of the moral nature sweeps over the human stage with a force, a splendor, and a diversity of effect which no artist can deny if he would, which the greatest artist never tries to withstand, and against which the smallest will protest in vain.

Strike "ethicism" out of life, good friends, before you shake it out of story! Fear less to seem "Puritan" than to be inadequate. Fear more to be superficial than to seem "deep." Fear less to point your moral than to miss your opportunity. It is for us to remind you, since it seems to us that you overlook the fact, that in any highly formed or fully formed creative power the "ethical" as well as the "æsthetical" sense is developed. Where "the taste" is developed at the expense of "the conscience" the artist is incomplete. He is, in this case, at least *as* incomplete as he is where the ethical sense is developed at the expense of the æsthetic. Specialism in literary art, as in science, has its uses, but it is not symmetry; and this is not a law intended to work only one way.

It is an ancient and honorable rule of rhetoric, that he is the greatest writer who, other things being equal, has the greatest subject. He is, let us say, the largest artist who, other things being equal, holds the largest view of human life. The largest view of human life, we contend, is that which recognizes it in the greatest way.

In a word, the province of the artist is to portray life as it is, and life *is* moral responsibility. Life is several other things, we do not deny. It is beauty, it is joy, it is tragedy, it is comedy, it is psychical and physical pleasure, it is the interplay of a thousand rude or delicate motions and emotions, it is the grimmest and the merriest motley of phantasmagoria that could appeal to the gravest or the maddest brush ever put to palette; but is it steadily and sturdily and always moral responsibility. An artist can no more fling off the moral sense from his work than he can oust it from his private life. A great artist (let me repeat) is too great to try to do so. With one or two familiar expectations, of which more might be said, the greatest have laid in the moral values of their pictures just as life lays them in; and in life they are not to be evaded. There is a squeamishness against "ethicism" which is quite as much to be avoided as any squeamishness about "the moral nude in art" or other debatable question. The great way is to go grandly in, as the Creator did when he made the models which we are fain to copy. After all, the Great Artist is not a poor master; all His foregrounds stand out against the perspective of the moral nature. Why go tiptoeing about the easel to avoid it?

This short essay is an excerpt from the chapter "Art for Truth's Sake" in Phelps's autobiography, *Chapters from a Life*, first published as a serial in *McClure's Magazine*, December 1895–June 1896, and then as a book by Houghton, Mifflin in 1896. It appeared in *Littell's Living Age* (1896) and *Current Literature: A Magazine of Contemporary Record*, January 1897.

The Short Story

One of the interesting things in the history of literature is a study of the moods that fashion takes in form.

The stately, stupid, periodical essay—the glory of the *Spectator*; the boudoir literature of the Ladies' and Gentlemen's Annuals;[1] the architectural love-poems in whose involved and dusty corridors any modern passion would lose itself forever; the epics useful to us as safe and pleasant anodynes; the unplausible romances and ponderous novels of adventure, impossibility, history and metaphysics which have each in turn led the fashion of their day, and made the most of it—these have retired to the back shelves of our too busy age. Only students, often only scholars, read these cylinders of a leisurely and bountiful past. Our modern taste is formed, is too much formed by our spasmodic methods of living. It is the fact, however reluctant we ought to be to own it, that the "Whip of the Sky" flogs us along so fast that the majority of what are called reading people do not find inclination or do not force time to read many books outside of the easy alcoves of fiction; and it is significant that even a full-grown novel is rapidly becoming too large an undertaking for the average mind.[2]

Out of our nervous conditions, our hurry and worry, our rush and push, our suburban trains and clubs, our ecclesiastical steam-power, and philanthropic whirlpools, and business tornadoes, out of our estrangement from leisure, our gaining passion for travel, and growing indifference to home, and marked lack of repose—there has been born one good thing if no other; and this is the short story.

The short story is, without question, the literary favorite of our time. The popular preference, which is usually worth counting in most matters, clearly turns in this direction. Newspaper syndicates have reported for a year or two a decline in the serial market. Even magazines are beginning to feel a lull in the demand for continued novels; while publishers record a briskly gaining sale for volumes of brief, collected tales.

In a word, the short story, which has, of course, always existed, but hitherto in an apologetic form that literature has recognized when a superior genius forced it to, has become the lion of our intellectual day. It does not require genius now, to give dignity to a short story; and the little "pastel" struts confidently among us,[3] believing itself to be a tale, and is scarcely undeceived.

It is not too much to claim that America is doing, and has long been doing her full share of the admirable work which this form of expression renders possible.

France, which has taught us so many noble and so many ignoble lessons in literature, has carried the short story to a refinement of elaboration which it is still possible to supplement by a depth of plummet and h[e]ight of purpose more naturally attainable by the sterner conscience and graver temperament of our people. From France we learn something; but we can teach her quite as much.[4]

Our ideal, and, we may say, probable short story-writer will not need narcotic stimulants; nor will he end his days in a private asylum.[5] Our purer morality will forbid the serpent that coils on the wing of so many of the gifted imaginations sprung from a society less controlled than ours by the cleanest ethics. On the whole, it is time to remember that the struggle narrows to these two nations; for no other can be said, strictly, to compete with us in this department of literary effort today. It is becoming a duel between the two great Republics. Which will produce the best of the briefest fiction?

A blatant claim would be an ignorant and idle matter. But it is quite within bounds to say that we have had, and still have some work of this kind as good as any to be found in France; and that we have the material for better. Our huge extent of territory, our startling variety of climate, our extremes of wealth and poverty, our assorted races, our feverish restlessness of temper, our sudden changes of fortune, our popular education, our enormous seaboard life, give us unique chances for swift and splendid effects. The results depend upon our patience and skill in handling our material; upon our ability to use our own capacity.

From Hawthorne to the last magazine favorite who rides the crest of the wave to-day,[6] our catalog of short story-writers is a varied and honorable one, full of quality in which a nation older and wiser than ours might glory. To compare the names and claims of one's fellow-workmen in a specialty is an unwelcome task; just here, an unnecessary one, and "I pray thee, have me excused."[7] As for these, we all know them. They are at the ends of our tongues, and in the depths of our hearts. We know where to turn for the representative attribute in each. Who has "the light touch"—who, solidity in the mysterious art of construction—who, fire in dramatic action—who, power in moral emphasis—who, glory of spiritual illumination—it is not for the critics alone to decide; for, the common sense of the common reader is an admirable classifier. The American short story offers, at least, these features to the attention of criticism to-day, and contains promise of more and better. It will be our own fault, I do not hesitate to say, if in a dozen years we do not write the best short stories in the world.

It is, perhaps, not out of place to notice that only one experienced in this form of literary expression, can conceive any idea of its difficulty and delicacy.

What it means to achieve a fine, short story of immediate influence and permanent position cannot be understood by writers in other literary departments any more than by the readers who take up the magazine and drop it after dinner.

"Those? Why, I supposed you got off *those things* in a few hours!" said a professor of metaphysics once to a successful short story-writer.

"I never give less than four weeks' hard work to a short story magazine story," answered the author, smiling; "and sometimes it is nearer six."[8]

The metaphysician pondered this reply as he would the duality of consciousness, and went away sorrowful, for he had great intellectual possessions; but the power to comprehend the art involved in the creation of good "light reading" was not among them.

If the testimony of those authors who have achieved something of value in the lines of both the long and the short story were fairly taken, I believe it would be found to unite in affirming that, of the two kinds of efforts, the short story is obviously more difficult, and, therefore, more doubtful of success. It is easier to construct a permanent novel than an eminent short story. The artistic conditions in the latter are like the definition which one of the Greek teachers gave of a poet: "Something light, and with wings."[9] They cannot be defined. They fly from the classifier; but they are as inexorable as the invisible winds.

The author of a short story has no easy work before him. He labors under laws of construction that may depend upon an adjective, and hang upon a semi-colon. He handles emotions and principles that must have the spontaneity of poetry and the discipline of science. Repression, condensation, suggestion must be carried to their highest finish. Yet that is a dull hand which cannot adjust these conditions to a flash of dramatic action as eager—and as brief—as a scene in the street, viewed from the window of a quiet home,—and dashing by.

The present tendency to turn the short story into a sketch is to be regretted; for it is not art. A sketch is not a story, and nothing can make it such.

Little studies of little subjects—etchings of local scenery, impressions in rustic character whose accuracy does not veil the lack of genuine human sympathy with which they are drawn, lessons in patois, experiments with the kodak upon social manner[10]—these it is fashionable to call "artistic." Give them the names that belong to them and they are delightful and honest work. But stories they are not. It is false art to call them so.

The short story of the future will not be a bit of bric-à-brac. It will be a work of faultless construction and of exquisite finish; but it will be a power in human conduct, and a profound study of the hights and deeps, the laughter and the tears of human life.

First published in the *Independent*, November 3, 1892, 1–2. The essay is part of a forum, "American Literature: Its Movements and Tendencies," which included contributions by Thomas Wenthworth Higginson and H. H. Boyesen as well.

POEMS

Divided

If an angel that I know
Should now enter, sliding low
Down the shaft of quiet moonlight that rests
    upon the floor;
    And if she should stir and stand
    With a lily in her hand,[1]
And that smile of treasured silliness that she
    wore.

    Should I, falling at her feet,
    Brush or kiss her garments sweet?
Would their lowest, least white hem upon me
    unworthy, fall?
    Or would she guarded, stand,
    Drop the lily in my hand,
And go whispering, as she vanished, "This is
    all"?

After publishing this poem in the *Independent*, June 6, 1872, Phelps included it in her collection *Poetic Studies* (Boston: James R. Osgood, 1875).

Apple Blossoms

Cold Care and I have run a race,
 And I, fleet-foot, have won
A little space, a little hour,
 To find the May alone.

I sit beneath the apple-tree,
 I see nor sky nor sun;
I only know the apple-buds
 Are opening one by one.

You asked me once a little thing,—
 A lecture or a song
To hear with you; and yet I thought
 To find my whole life long

Too short to bear the happiness
 That bounded through the day,
That made the look of apple-blooms,
 And you, and me, and May!

For long between us there had hung
 The mist of love's young doubt;
Sweet, shy, uncertain, all the world
 Of trust and May burst out.

I wore the flowers in my hair,
 Their color on my dress;

Dear Love! whenever apples bloom
In Heaven, do they bless

Your heart with memories so small,
So strong, so cruel-glad?
If ever apples bloom in Heaven,
I wonder are *you* sad?

Heart! yield thee up thy fruitless quest
Beneath the apple-tree;
Youth comes but once, love only once,
And May but once to thee!

First published in the *Independent*, June 11, 1874. Phelps included the poem in *Poetic Studies* (Boston: James R. Osgood, 1875). It subsequently appeared in a Buffalo, New York periodical, *The Magazine of Poetry: A Quarterly Review*, October 1893.

Stronger than Death

Who shall tell the story
As it was?
Write it with the heart's blood?
(Pale ink, alas!)
Speak it with the soul's lips,
Or be dumb?
Tell me, singers fled, and
Song to come!

No answer; like a shell the silence curls,
And far within it leans a whisper out,
Breathless and inarticulate, and whirls
And dies as dies an ailing dread or doubt.

And I—since there is found none else than I,
No stronger, sweeter voice than mine, to tell
This tale of love that cannot stoop to die—
Were fain to be the whisper in the shell;

Were fain to lose and spend myself within
The sacred silence of one mighty heart,
And leaning from it, hidden there, to win
Some finer ear that, listening, bends apart.

. . . .

"Fly for your lives!" The entrails of the earth
Trembled, resounding to the cry,

That, like a chasing ghost, around the mine
    Crept ghastly: "The pit's on fire!
      Fly!"

The shaft, a poisoned throat whose breath was death,
    Like hell itself grown sick of sin,
Hurled up the men; haggard and terrible;
    Leaping upon us through the din

That all our voices made; and back we shrank
    From them as from the starting dead;
Recoiling, shrieked, but knew not why we shrieked,
    And cried, but knew not what we said.

And still that awful mouth did toss them up:
    "The last is safe! the last is sound!"
We sobbed to see them where they sunk and
      crawled,
    Like beaten hounds, upon the ground.

Some sat with lolling, idiot head, and laughed;
    One reached to clutch the air away
His gasping lips refused; some cursed; and one
    Knelt down—but he was old—to pray.

We huddled there together all that night,
    Women and men from the wild Town;
I heard a shrill voice cry, "We all are up,
    But some—ye have forgot—are down!"

"Who is forgot?" We stared from face to face;
    But answering through the dark, she said
(It was a woman): "Eh, ye need not fret;
    None is forgot except the dead.

"The buried dead asleep there in the works—
 Eh, Lord! it must be hot below!
Ye 'll keep 'em waking all the livelong night,
 To set the mine a-burning so!"

And all the night the mine did burn and burst,
 As if the earth were but a shell
Through which a child had thrust a finger-touch,
 And, peal on dreadful peal, the bell,

The miner's 'larum, wrenched the quaking air;
 And through the flaring light we saw
The solid forehead of the eternal hill
 Take on a human look of awe;

As if it were a living thing, that spoke
 And flung some protest to the sky,
As if it were a dying thing that saw,
 But could not tell, a mystery.

The bells ran ringing by us all that night.
 The bells ceased jangling with the morn.
About the blackened works,—sunk, tossed,
  and rent,—
 We gathered in the foreign dawn;

Women and men, with eyes askance and strange,
 Fearing, we knew not what, to see.
Against the hollowed jaws of the torn hill,
 Why creep the miners silently?

From man to man a whisper chills: "See, see,
 The sunken shaft of Thirty-one!
The earth, a traitor to her trust, has fled
 And turned the dead unto the sun.

"And here—O God of life and death! Thy work,
    Thine only, this!" With foreheads bare,
We knelt, and drew him, young and beautiful,
    Thirty years dead, into the air.

Thus had he perished; buried from the day;
    By the swift poison caught and slain;
By the kind poison unmarred, rendered fair
    Back to the upper earth again—

The warm and breathing earth that knew him not;
    And men and women wept to see—
For kindred had he none among us all—
    How lonely even the dead may be.

We wept, I say; we wept who knew him not;
    But sharp, a tearless woman sprang
From out the crowd (that quavering voice I knew),
    And terrible her cry outrang:

"I pass, I pass ye all! Make way! Stand back!
    Mine is the place ye yield," she said.
"He was my lover once—my own, my own;
    Oh, he was mine, and he is dead!"

Women and men, we gave her royal way;
    Proud as young joy the smile she had.
We knew her for a neighbor in the Town,
    Unmated, solitary, sad.

Youth, hope, and love, we gave her silent way,
    Calm as a sigh she swept us all;
Then swiftly, as a word leans to a thought,
    We saw her lean to him, and fall

Upon the happy body of the dead—
    An aged woman, poor and gray.
Bright as the day, immortal as young Love,
    And glorious as life, he lay.

Her shrunken hands caressed his rounded cheek,
    Her white locks on his golden hair
Fell sadly. "O love!" she cried with shriveled lips,
    "O love, my love, my own, my fair!

"See, I am old, and all my heart is gray.
    They say the dead are aye forgot—
There, there, my sweet! I whisper, leaning
      low,
    That all these women hear it not.

"Deep in the darkness there, didst think on me?
    High in the heavens, have ye been true?
Since I was young, and since you called me fair,
    I never loved a man but you.

And here, my boy, you lie, so safe, so still"—
    But there she hushed; and in the dim,
Cool morning, timid as a bride, but calm
    As a glad mother, gathered him

Unto her heart. And all the people then,
    Women and men, and children too,
Crept back, and back, and back and on,
    Still as the morning shadows do.

And left them in the lifting dawn—they two,
    On her sad breast, his shining head
Stirred softly, as were he the living one,
    And she had been the moveless dead.

And yet we crept on, back, and back, and on.
   The distance widened like the sky
Between our little restlessness,
   And Love so godlike that it could not die.

This poem first appeared in *Harper's New Monthly Magazine*, July 1877 and later was included in *Songs of the Silent World and Other Poems* (Boston: Houghton, Mifflin, 1885).

Afterward

There *is* no vacant chair. The loving meet—
    A group unbroken—smitten, who knows how?
One sitteth silent only, in his usual seat;
    We gave him once that freedom. Why not now?

Perhaps he is too weary, and needs rest;
    He needed it too often, nor could we
Bestow. God gave it, knowing how to do so best.
    Which of us would disturb him? Let him be.

There is no vacant chair. If he will take
    The mood to listen mutely, be it done.
By his least mood we crossed, for which the heart must ache,
    Plead not nor question! Let him have this one.

Death is a mood of life. It is no whim
    By which life's Giver mocks a broken heart.
Death is life's reticence. Still audible to Him,
    The hushed voice, happy, speaketh on, apart.

There is no vacant chair. To love is still
    To have. Nearer to memory than to eye,
And dearer yet to anguish than to comfort will
    We hold him down by our love, that shall not die.

For while it doth not, thus he cannot. Try!
    Who can put out the motion or the smile?

The old ways of being noble all with him laid by?
Because we love, he is. Then trust awhile.

From *Songs of the Silent World and Other Poems* (Boston: Houghton, Mifflin, 1885). This poem was regularly selected for reprinting, appearing in Jeannette Leonard Gilder, ed., *Representative Poems of Living Poets: American and English, Selected by the Poets Themselves* (New York: Cassell, 1886); *The Magazine of Poetry: A Quarterly Review*, October 1890; Douglas Sladen, ed., *Younger American Poets, 1830–1890* (London: Griffith, Farran, Okeden, & Welsh, 1891); W. H. De Puy, ed., *The University of Literature in Twenty Octavo Volumes: A Cyclopedia of Universal Literature, Presenting in Alphabetical Arrangement the Biography, Together with Critical Reviews and Extracts, of Eminent Writers of All Lands and All Ages*, vol. 20 (New York: J. S. Barcus, 1896); John Clark Ridpath, ed., *The Ridpath Library of Universal Literature in Twenty-Five Volumes: A Biographical and Bibliographical Summary of the World's Most Eminent Authors, Including the Choicest Extracts and Masterpieces from Their Writings* (New York: Globe, 1898); James Miller, ed., *The Ministry of Comfort* (New York: T. Y. Crowell, 1901); Thomas Edward Potterton, ed., *The Comforter: A Compilation* (Boston: Eugene F. Endicott, 1903); *The Lutheran Observer*, March 27, 1903; James Mudge, ed., *Poems with Power to Strengthen the Soul* (New York: Eaton and Mains, 1907); Burton Egbert Stevenson, ed., *The Home Book of Verse: American and English, 1580–1912*, vol. 8: *Poems of Sorrow, Death, and Immortality* (New York: Henry Holt, 1915).

George Eliot—Her Jury

A LILY rooted in a sacred soil,
Arrayed with those who neither spin nor toil;[2]
Dinah,[3] the preacher, through the purple air,
Forever in her gentle evening prayer
Shall plead for Her—what ear too deaf to
  hear?—
"As if she spoke to some one very near."[4]

And he of storied Florence, whose great
  heart
Broke for its human error; wrapped apart,
And scorching in the swift, prophetic flame
Of passion for late holiness, and shame
Than untried glory grander, gladder, higher—
Deathless, for Her, he "testifies by fire."[5]

A statue fair and firm on shining feet,
Womanhood's woman, Dorothea,[6] sweet
As strength, and strong as tenderness, to
  make
A "struggle with the dark" for white light's
  sake,[7]
Immortal stands, unanswered speaks. Shall
  they,
Of Her great hand the moulded, breathing
  clay,
Her fit, select, and proud survivors be?
Possess the life eternal, and not *She?*

First published in *Harper's New Monthly Magazine*, May 1881, 927, the poem was retitled "Her Jury" when it appeared in Phelps's second volume of poetry, *Songs of the Silent World and other Poems* (Boston: Houghton, Mifflin, 1885). It was later reprinted in several collections and anthologies, particularly in England: Charlotte Fiske Bates, ed., *The Cambridge Book of Poetry and Song, Selected from English and American Authors* (New York: Thomas Y. Crowell, 1882); *Contemporary Review*, March 1896; *Eclectic Magazine: Foreign Literature*, April 1896; William Mottram, *The True Story of George Eliot in Relation to "Adam Bede," Giving the Real Life History of the More Prominent Characters* (Chicago: A. C. McClurg, 1906); George W. E. Russell, *Sketches and Snapshots* (New York: Duffield, 1910). The title "George Eliot—Her Jury" is the one most scholars now use.

Elaine and Elaine

I.

DEAD, she drifted to his feet.
Tell us, Love, is Death so sweet?

Oh! the river floweth deep.
Fathoms deeper is her sleep.

Oh! the current driveth strong.
Wilder tides drive souls along.

Drifting, though he loved her not,
To the heart of Launcelot,[8]

Let her pass; it is her place.
Death hath given her this grace.

Let her pass; she resteth well.
What her dreams are, who can tell?

Mute the steersman; why, if he
Speaketh not a word, should we?

II.

Dead, she drifteth to his feet.
Close, her eyes keep secrets sweet.

Living, he had loved her well.
High as Heaven and deep as Hell.

Yet that voyage she stayeth not.
Wait thou for her, Launcelot?

Oh! the river floweth fast.
Who is justified at last?

Locked her lips are. Hush! If she
Sayeth nothing, how should we?

Phelps published this poem in the *Independent*, June 7, 1883, 1, and *Songs of the Silent World and Other Poems*, (Boston: Houghton, Mifflin, 1885). It subsequently appeared in Jeannette Leonard Gilder, ed., *Representative Poems of Living Poets: American and English, Selected by the Poets Themselves* (New York: Cassell, 1886); Thomas William Herringshaw, ed., *Local and National Poets of America with Interesting Biographical Sketches and Choice Selections from over One Thousand Living American Poets* (Chicago: American Publishers' Association, 1890); *Magazine of Poetry: A Quarterly Review*, October 1893. It appears under an alternate title, "Oh, the Rivers!," in some instances.

The Lost Colors

FROWNING, the mountain stronghold stood,
Whose front no mortal could assail;
For more than twice three hundred years
The terror of the Indian vale.
By blood and fire the robber band
Answered the helpless village wail.

Hot was his heart and cool his thought,
When Napier from his Englishmen
Up to the bandits' rampart glanced,
And down upon his ranks again.[9]
Summoned to dare a deed like that,
Which of them all would answer then?

What sullen regiment is this
That lifts its eyes to dread Cutchee?[10]
Abased, its standard bears no flag.
For thus the punishment shall be
That England metes to Englishmen
Who shame her once by mutiny.[11]

From out the disgraced Sixty-Fourth
There stepped a hundred men of might.
Cried Napier: "Now prove to me
I read my soldiers' hearts aright!
Form! Forward! Charge, my volunteers!
Your colors are on yonder height!"

So sad is shame, so wise is trust!
The challenge echoed bugle-clear.
Like fire along the Sixty-Fourth
From rank to file rang cheer on cheer.
In death and glory up the pass
They fought for all to brave men dear.[12]

. . . .

Old is the tale, but read anew
In every warring human heart.
What rebel hours, what coward shame,
Upon the aching memory start!
To find the ideal forfeited,
—What tears can teach the holy art?

Thou great Commander! leading on
Through weakest darkness to strong light;
By any anguish, give us back
Our life's young standard, pure and bright.
O fair, lost Colors of the soul!
For your sake storm we any height.

After appearing in *Atlantic Monthly*, September 1892, 357–58, the poem was selected for inclusion in Edmund Stedman's *An American Anthology 1787–1900*
(the 1900 volume), as well as Burton Egbert Stevenson, ed., *The Home Book of
Verse: American and English, 1580–1912, with an Appendix Containing a Few Well-
known Poems in Other Languages*, vol. 6: *Poems of Patriotism, History, and Legend*
(New York: Henry Holt, 1915) and Burton Egbert Stevenson, ed., *The Home
Book of Verse for Young Folks* (New York: Holt, Rinehart, and Winston, 1929).

Notes

....

The Tenth of January

1. *Lawrence:* Located in Massachusetts, approximately one hour north of Boston, known for its factories.
2. *Simooms*: Hot desert winds in Asia and Africa.
3. *chignon*: French, "bun," a hairstyle.
4. *bleak, uncomforted*: Possibly a reference to Homer's *Iliad* (7.333), translated by Alexander Pope (1688–1744).
5. *dimmykhrats*: Democrats.
6. *Pemberton Mill*: A textile mill built in 1853; it closed temporarily in 1857 due to the poor economy, but reopened in 1859.
7. *Asenath Martyn:* A worker named Asenath Martin was employed at the Pemberton Mill.
8. *oriflamme*: The medieval French banner of red and orange carried by kings into war.
9. *Down-East:* Maine.
10. *The Avenue*: The fashionable section of a town, based on the reputation of New York's Fifth Avenue.
11. *Everett Mill*: A cotton mill in Lawrence, active in midcentury.
12. *seven thunders . . . voices*: Reference to Revelation 10:3–4.
13. *Floracita*: A character in Lydia Maria Child's 1867 *A Romance of the Republic*.
14. *to him . . . be given*: Matthew 25:29, Mark 4:25, Luke 8:18.
15. *bear all things and hope all things*: 1 Corinthians 13:7.
16. *Merrimack*: The Merrimack River runs through Lawrence.
17. *Reading*: Approximately fourteen miles from Lawrence.
18. *list slippers*: Slippers made of fabric that was generally used as the border of a garment or other textile.
19. *float*: The pillar cooled in such a way that it was not sound or even; the inquest into the disaster found that the defective pillars were to blame for the collapse.
20. *He hath . . . man*: In this quote Phelps combines Isaiah 53:2 and 52:14, which are generally interpreted as prophecies of Jesus' death.

21. *zouave*: A sleeveless jacket.

22. *nine days' wonder*: An event that draws significant attention but is then quickly forgotten; *successful candidate . . . muttering South*: Abraham Lincoln was elected on November 6, 1860, and by the time he took the oath of office on March 4, 1861, seven Southern states had seceded.

23. *architect and engineer . . . unaided*: According to *Scientific American*, February 11, 1860, a beam broke during construction of the mill, but Benjamin Coolidge, assistant to chief architect and engineer, Capt. Charles H. Bigelow, continued to use these beams anyway. An inquest following the disaster placed the blame on Albert Fuller, who was in charge of making the beams for the Eagle Iron Foundry, and Captain Bigelow for not properly testing them.

24. *Titans*: Figures from Greek mythology who ruled before the Olympians.

25. *lamb for the burnt offering*: Reference to Old Testament sacrifices, which often required an unblemished lamb to represent purity. See especially Genesis 22:8.

26. *pintles*: A pin.

27. *We're going . . . no more*: From the hymn "I'm Going Home" (1838), words by William Hunter (1811–77), arranged by William Miller (1766–1839).

28. *one stood . . . Son of God*: A story from Daniel 3 about three Jewish men—Shadrak, Meschak, and Abednego—who were thrown into a fire by King Nebuchadnezzar of Babylon for refusing to worship him. When the Son of God was seen in the fire with them, Nebuchadnezzar ordered them removed; the men were unharmed.

29. The real Asenath Martin was killed during the mill's collapse. Little is known about her, and much of Phelps's story is likely fictional. However, according to a report released by the treasurer of a fund collected for those affected by the collapse, $200 was paid to the woman's family. This indicates that, like the Asenath in this story, she was the primary breadwinner for the household.

Dr. Trotty

1. *waterfall*: A popular hairstyle that used false hair as the basis of a mass of curls cascading down the back of the head.

2. *Lill*: Trotty's older sister. After Phelps took her mother's name, she was called Lily by her family.

3. *gamboge*: Pigment of a dark yellow or orange hue that would have been used in Lill's paints.

4. *tippet*: A scarf or a cape.

5. *Pomp's Pond*: Pond located in Andover, Massachusetts, where Phelps lived when she wrote this story.

6. *Jerusalem*: Trotty's doll, introduced in "More about Trotty," published in 1868 in *Our Young Folks*.

7. *'lixy Pro*: Trotty's pronunciation of *elixir pro*, short for elixir proprietatis, a mix of herbs and ale believed to promote health.

8. *homeopathic:* Homeopathy is a medical philosophy that rejects surgery and other aggressive treatments, like bleeding or cupping, in favor of very diluted dosages of active ingredients.

9. *Aconite*: Wolfsbane, a common nineteenth-century pain remedy, safe in low doses but very toxic in high.

A Woman's Pulpit

1. *Mädchen*: A German girl or maiden.

2. *New Vealshire*: The locations in this story are fictional.

3. *Universalists*: A denomination that has since merged with the Unitarians; its members believe in doing good, God's love for all, and a strong reliance on reason.

4. *myself, Mr. Copperfull*: Mrs. Crupp uses this misappellation for the title character in Charles Dickens's *David Copperfield* (1850).

5. *to be sparing*: An unidentified, possibly fictional reference.

6. *Rev. Dr. Dagon of Dagonsville, and to Professor Tacitus of Sparta:* The mixed classical references are part of Phelps's humor: *Dagon*: a Near Eastern sky god, the Phoenician name for Cronos, and the god of the Philistines in the Bible who bowed to the Ark of the Covenant (1 Samuel 5); *Tacitus*: a Roman senator and historian; *Sparta*: a Greek city whose inhabitants were known for their martial prowess.

7. *and "found":* The society will pay for her housing and food.

8. *word . . . my mouth*: Isaiah 55:11: "So shall my word be that goeth forth out of my mouth: it shall not return unto me void, but it shall accomplish that which I please, and it shall prosper in the thing whereto I sent it."

9. *famous lady parishioner*: Likely a reference Lavinia Strickland Bartlett, who taught upward of seven hundred churchgoers each Sunday. Phelps is mistaken, however, in believing that Bartlett's students were men: she taught only women in her Sabbath school.

10. *mistaken the . . . existence*: Reference to Sir William Hamilton's (1788–1856) *Lecture on Logic* (1836).

11. *Barnes on Matthew*: Albert Barnes (1789–1870), an American pastor, published many theological books, including the commentary Phelps mentions here, *Notes on the New Testament Explanatory and Practical: Matthew and Mark* (1832); *Olshausen*: Hermann Olshausen (1796–1839), a German biblical scholar who wrote multiple commentaries on the New Testament;

Tischendorff Testament: Constantin von Tischendorff's (1815–74) Greek translation of the New Testament (1841–69); *Jeremy Taylor*: Taylor (1613–67) was a Royalist Anglican priest who, although accused of being a closet Catholic, spoke out strongly against Catholics and Presbyterians.

12. *Kamtschatka*: Kamchatka, a large peninsula off the eastern coast of Russia.

13. *non est inventus*: Latin, "The person is not to be found," most commonly used in legal contexts; *patois*: French, dialect.

14. *Among them . . . of them*: Reference to Jesus' prayer for his disciples in John 17:14–19; *Wesley*: John Wesley (1703–91), founder, with his brother Charles, of the Methodist Church; *Whitfield*: George Whitfield (1714–70), an itinerant preacher in the first Great Awakening; *Chalmers*: Thomas Chalmers (1780–1847), a Scottish preacher and intellectual; *Spurgeon*: Charles Spurgeon (1834–92), a famous Baptist pastor in London who published over three thousand sermons; *Beecher*: Phelps is referring to either Lyman Beecher (1775–1863), a Congregationalist clergyman in Connecticut and father of Harriet Beecher Stowe, or Henry Ward Beecher (1813–87), a celebrity minister at the Plymouth Church in Brooklyn with progressive values and beliefs.

15. *pas seul*: French, a solitary step.

16. *this magazine . . . comfortably*: Phelps was frustrated with periodicals that, in her mind, did not publish religious pieces in each installment, even when they claimed to have a Christian focus; she may well have had the *Independent* in mind, given complaints lodged during Theodore Tilton's tenure as editor.

17. *Somebody . . . never saw:* This reference remains unidentified.

18. *Spiritooalist*: Spiritualism presented a popular alternative to organized religion during the nineteenth century, stressing the possibility of communicating with the dead; *ain't scriptooral*: reference to 1 Corinthians 14:34–35, which states that women should be silent in church.

19. *preventive of diphtheria*: Very cold water was thought to prevent diphtheria.

20. *deeper than . . . sound*: Spoken by Prospero in Shakespeare's *The Tempest*, 5.1.56.

21. *Before the mountains . . .* : Psalm 90:2.

22. *animus*: Life-giving force.

23. *outré*: French, outlandish or exaggerated.

24. *exegesis*: Exposition or explanation of a text, particularly Scripture.

25. *Hamilton:* Sir William Hamilton, professor of philosophy at the University of Edinburgh who was particularly interested in various types of phenomena (see n11); *Strauss:* David Friedrich Strauss (1808–74), a German theologian whose 1835 book *The Life of Jesus* argued that the biblical account of Jesus contains more of legend than historical truth.

26. *Schleiermacher:* Friedrich Schleiermacher (1768–1834), a German biblical scholar; *Copernicus:* Nicolaus Copernicus (1473–1543), a Polish astronomer best known for his theory of heliocentrism.

27. *Hegel:* Georg Wilhelm Friedrich Hegel (1770–1831), German philosopher; *Hobbes:* Thomas Hobbes (1588–1679), English philosopher.

28. *Tom Paine:* Thomas Paine (1737–1809), a British thinker and proponent of both the American and French revolutions, was a proponent of deism, not Christianity. He attacked the latter in *The Age of Reason* (1704).

29. *It is Magnificent . . . :* Spoken by Pierre François Bosquet at the Battle of Balaclava (1854) in the Crimean War. This poem was the subject of Tennyson's poem, "The Charge of the Light Brigade" (1854).

30. *was not in haste . . . to say:* Phelps may have in mind Hermes' opening speech of the second scene of Exodus in Aeschylus's *Prometheus Bound.*

31. *Old Mother Morey . . . my story's done:* A short rhyme told to children who insisted that someone tell them a story.

32. *Ce n'est pas . . . noble hearts:* French, literally, "It is not the victory, but the battle"; the reference is to Charles Forbes Renée de Montalembert (1810–70), a French politician and proponent of a more liberal Catholic Church.

33. *The Age of Reason:* 1794 pamphlet by Thomas Paine (1737–1809) in which he expounded his Deistic beliefs; *Ecce Homo: Ecce Homo: A Survey of the Life and Work of Jesus Christ* (1869), a work focused on Christ's humanity, by Sir John Robert Seeley (1834–95).

34. *Webster:* Daniel Webster (1782–1852) was an American orator, politician, and lawyer. He served as a congressman from Massachusetts and New Hampshire and ran for president several times. His support for the Fugitive Slave Act damaged his reputation.

35. *righteousness . . . other:* Psalm 85:10.

Since I Died

1. *Doric column:* A grooved column in classical Greek architecture.

2. *King of Glories:* Psalm 24:7–10.

3. *Jura:* The Jura Mountains, part of the Alps, are located in Switzerland and France; *Rhine:* a river that runs through parts of Switzerland and France.

4. *In the twinkling of an eye:* 1 Corinthians 15:52.

5. *What my eyes . . . without you:* 1 Corinthians 2:9; Paul is speaking of "the things which God hath prepared for them that love him."

Fourteen to One

1. There is no record of the incident Phelps narrates in this story, although she defends the accuracy of her information in a personal letter.

2. *low tone*: Characterized by predominantly gray coloring.

3. *Zion's Herald:* Methodist periodical published from 1823 to 2006.

4. *Kennessee*: A hybrid of Tennessee and Kentucky, both border states during the Civil War. Tennessee joined the Confederacy, while Kentucky, after a brief attempt to remain neutral, sided with the Union. Tennessee was re-admitted to the Union in July 1866.

5. *Hezekiah*: A king of Judah; see 2 Kings 18–20.

6. *unenviable notoriety*: The Ku Klux Klan was established in Tennessee in 1866.

7. *How firm . . . word*: The first line of "How Firm a Foundation," a popular hymn published in many works, including John Rippon's *A Selection of Hymns from the Best Authors* (1787); it has been attributed to various authors, including John Keene and John Keith.

8. *donation party:* Parties held to raise or augment the salaries of ministers in the nineteenth century. Phelps's mother depicts one in *The Sunny Side; Or, The Country Minister's Wife* (1851).

9. *turkey-red*: A color of dye made with animal blood.

10. *Cruden's Concordance and Worcester's Dictionary:* Alexander Cruden (1699–1770) published *A Complete Concordance to the Old and New Testament; or a Dictionary and Alphabetical Index to the Bible with a Concordance to the Apocrypha, and a Compendium of the Holy Scriptures* in 1737; Joseph Worcester (1783–1865) published *A Comprehensive Pronouncing and Explanatory Dictionary of the English Language with Pronouncing Vocabularies of Classical and Scripture Proper Names* in 1830.

11. *Barnes's Notes on Matthew*: Albert Barnes (1789–1870), an American pastor, published many theological books, including the commentary Phelps mentions here, *Notes on the New Testament Explanatory and Practical: Matthew and Mark* (1832).

12. *Life of John Wesley*: Phelps could be referring either to John Whitehead's *The Life of John Wesley* (1805) or Henry Moore's *The Life of John Wesley* (1824); the British preacher John Wesley (1703–91) was one of the founders of Methodism.

13. *Home . . . dear home*: A variant of the popular song "Home, Sweet Home," lyrics written in 1823 by American John Howard Payne with music by British composer Henry Bishop.

14. *How firm . . . home*: Mrs. Matthews confuses the words of "How Firm a Foundation" with the lyrics of "Home, Sweet Home"; the second line of the hymn should end with "His excellent Word."

15. *Thirty-nine Articles*: A reference to the main tenets of the Anglican faith written in 1563.

16. *anxious seat*: The location at revival events where new converts could repent.

17. *a psalm: the ninety-first*: Psalm 91 discusses God's protection of those who trust in Him.

18. *thy mercies . . . every morning*: A paraphrase of Lamentations 3:22–23.

19. *loving-kindness endureth forever*: Similar phrases occur throughout the Bible, specifically in Psalm 136.

The Rejected Manuscript

1. *The Innocent Sin:* This novel seems to be imaginary, much like the novel William Dean Howells includes in *The Rise of Silas Lapham* (1885).

2. *Demosthenes*: Greek orator (384–322 BCE); *Hathorne*: Nathaniel Hawthorne's ancestors used this spelling of their name.

3. *pongee*: A type of silk.

4. *Simian*: Pertaining to apes.

5. *"Pacific"*: Phelps gestures to a kind of periodical, an elite literary magazine akin to the *Atlantic Monthly*, rather than any particular magazine.

6. *Spartan's fox*: In his *Laconic Apophthegms*, Plutarch (ca. AD 46–120) tells the story of a Spartan boy who hides a stolen fox under his clothes. People come looking for the animal, but the boy refuses to speak even though the fox has severely injured him. When asked why, he says it is better to die than to let people know your weaknesses.

7. *Sandy Close*: Santa Claus.

8. *Tennyson:* Alfred Tennyson (1809–92), British poet.

9. *Burton's . . . Melancholy*: Robert Burton (1577–1640), an Anglican priest, wrote *Anatomy of Melancholy* in 1621 to explore the causes of melancholy, or depression.

10. *prince of American publishers*: Phelps is referring to her own publisher, James T. Fields, who was known for his kindness toward authors. Her autobiography, *Chapters from a Life*, contains a long section on Fields.

11. *book is moving grandly:* Fields uses this phrase in a letter to Phelps about *The Gates Ajar*.

The Oath of Allegiance

1. This paragraph echoes the opening of Charles Dickens's *A Tale of Two Cities* (1859).

2. Phelps draws on her own experience of the Civil War for this story. In her autobiography, *Chapters from a Life*, she writes, "Andover was no more loyal, probably, than other New England villages; but perhaps the presence of so many young men helped to make her seem so to those who passed the years from 1861 to 1865 upon the Hill" (72).

3. *Ludovisi Juno*: Large marble statue of Juno, wife of Jupiter, in the Ludovisi Garden in Rome.

4. *Under . . . the way*: "Love Will Find Out the Way," by an unknown songwriter of either English or Scottish origin.

5. *Apollo and Minerva*: Greek god of the sun and Roman goddess of craftsmanship and knowledge.

6. *Peninsular campaign*: Under the command of General McClellan, the Union tried, and failed, to capture Richmond, April 4–July 11, 1862.

7. *And then . . . calls me*: Perhaps taken from the song "Farewell," of unknown British origin.

8. *Arianism*: The belief developed by Arius (d. 336) that there is no trinity and that Jesus and the Holy Spirit were later creations. Challenges to the Christian trinity were central to the theological rifts that led to the founding of Andover Theological Seminary, where Phelps's grandfather and father served as professors.

9. *lint*: Women collected lint for bandages as part of their contribution to the war effort.

10. *Father and mother . . . hour*: Likely a reference to Job 19:13–14.

11. *vivisection*: Phelps was vehemently opposed to the practice of performing exploratory surgery on live animals.

12. *Titans*: Figures from Greek mythology who ruled before the Olympians.

13. *Antietam*: The Battle of Antietam, one of the bloodiest of the war, took place September 16–18, 1862.

14. *Farewell . . . true love*: From "The Soldier's Farewell" by the German songwriter Johanna Kinkel (1810–58).

Dea Ex Machina

1. *Dea Ex Machina*: Feminine version of *deus ex machina*, a term that originated in Greek drama but now refers to an unanticipated agent who resolves a complicated situation; *catboat*: a type of sailboat.

2. *Cunarder*: A large steamship of the transatlantic Cunard Line.

3. *dory*: A small boat.

4. *luffed*: Putting the bow into the wind and thus making the sails flap.

5. *thwarts*: A seat designed for a rower.

6. *moriturus saluto*: Variation on the standard Latin phrase Roman gladiators recited to the emperor before fighting, "He who is about to die salutes you." *Qui fui moriturus*: The female character corrects the minister's more standard rendition to stress that he will die one day, but not today.

7. *float*: Dock.

8. *minyot*: A mispronounced word or an obscure colloquialism.

9. *Concordance*: Reference book that lists the occurrences of a word in a text; *Revised Version*: a British version of the Bible first published in 1881 that drew controversy.

10. *tallith*: A traditional Jewish fringed shawl.

11. *Junior Endeavor*: Junior Endeavor societies, dedicated to training godly children, grew out of the Christian Endeavor societies started by Reverend Francis Clark (1851–1927) in Maine in the late nineteenth century.

12. *mal de mer*: French, seasickness.

13. *tender*: A small boat or dingy that allowed passengers to ferry to shore in case of emergency or if there was insufficient depth to dock.

14. *Jacob . . . angel*: Genesis 32:22–31.

15. *first heaven . . . away*: Revelation 21:1.

16. *Victurus salute*: "He who is about to win salutes you." The minister's Latin is again in error, however, for *salute* should be *saluto*.

What Shall They Do?

1. *weak-minded . . . easy chair*: Phelps refers to a letter sent to the editor of *Harper's New Monthly Magazine* in 1867 and printed in the column "Editor's Easy Chair." The female correspondent describes the toils of her life, the solace that writing provides, and the assistance the publication of her stories could provide.

2. *the "Easy Chair". . . yield to it*: George William Curtis (1824–92) was editor of the magazine from 1863 to 1892 and responsible for the "Editor's Easy Chair."

3. *come in . . . other way*: John 10:1.

4. *hand . . . translate it*: Reference to Daniel 5:5–31.

5. *holy fire . . . holy place*: From "Moving" (1862), published in the *Atlantic* by Mary Abigail Dodge (1833–96), who wrote under the name Gail Hamilton.

6. *Conflict of Ages*: *Conflict of Ages: The Great Debate on the Moral Relations of God and Man* (1853) by Edward Beecher (1803–95), a New England minister and brother of Harriet Beecher Stowe.

7. *Amazon*: A fabled tribe of women in South America of unusual size and strength.

8. *Le jeu ne vaut pas la chaudelle*: French idiom, "The game is not worth the effort."

9. *Keats*: John Keats (1795–1821), British Romantic poet; *mute . . . Miltons*: from "Elegy Written in a Country Churchyard" (1751) by Thomas Gray (1716–71); *Wordsworth*: William Wordsworth (1770–1850), British poet, wrote similar words in his long poem *The Excursion*.

10. *Washington Moon*: George Washington Moon (1823–1909), British poet, critic of the Revised Version of the Bible, and editor of the Revised Eng-

lish New Testament; *Richard Grant Wright*: American writer and authority on Shakespeare (1821–85).

11. *Harper's Monthly and Atlantic Monthly*: Prestigious literary magazines.

12. *ponderous . . .* crowns: Heaven.

13. *For various reasons . . .* pupils: Unidentified citation.

14. *A keen . . .* blind: Elizabeth Thompson's "Our Eyes," *Harper's New Monthly Magazine*, July 1867.

15. *woman's wages*: Women were paid less than men, a practice justified in part by the fact that they did not have families to support. That this was often not the case did little to change the system.

16. *In the duties . . . book-keepers*: *The Nation* ran an essay about female employees in the Treasury Department in its December 13, 1866, issue, but its argument is more negative than the one Phelps references.

17. *A woman's . . . that*: A play on the poem "A Man's a Man for A' That" (1794 or 1795) by the Scottish poet Robert Burns (1759–96).

18. *From him . . . hath*: Paraphrase of Matthew 13:12 and Luke 8:18.

19. *a girl*: This woman, and the *neighbor* in the next paragraph, remain unidentified and are likely fictitious.

20. *doffing*: Removing fibers from a carding machine or replacing a full bobbin.

21. *bread . . . stones*: Matthew 7:9 and Luke 11:11.

22. *Verily, verily*: Jesus uses this phrase many times throughout the Gospels.

23. *tarrieth long*: The phrase draws on fairy tale or mythic imagery, as in Penelope's patience waiting for Odysseus to return in Homer's *Odyssey*.

24. *still, small voice*: 1 Kings 19: 11–12.

25. *learners . . . feet*: Phelps's readers would have thought of Mary, sister of Martha and Lazarus, who sat at Jesus' feet to learn from him.

26. *light . . . land*: From Wordsworth's "Elegiac Stanzas, Suggested by a Picture of Peele Castle, in a Storm, Painted by Sir George Beaumont" (1805).

27. *Parepa*: Scottish opera singer Euphrosyne Parepa-Rosa (1836–74).

28. *Church*: Frederic Edwin Church (1826–1900), American painter and part of the Hudson River School movement.

29. *Every . . . season*: Ecclesiastes 3:11.

30. *Borrioboola*: Fictional African country from *Bleak House* (1852) by Charles Dickens (1812–70).

31. *The day . . . now is*: A loose reference to John 5:25.

32. *Choose . . . serve*: Joshua 24:15.

The Higher Claim

1. *clergyman . . . statesman*: Phelps refers here to Henry Ward Beecher, the influential pastor of Plymouth Church in Brooklyn, and Thaddeus Ste-

vens, Republican politician; both were vocal in their support of the suffrage movement.

2. *Lollardy*: Fifteenth-century pre-Protestant movement for religious reform; *Wyckliffe*: John Wycliffe (c. 1330–84) was an inspiration for the Lol-
lards because of his criticism of the Catholic Church and his work on an
English translation of the Bible.

3. *John Brown*: An ardent abolitionist who led an unsuccessful assault on
the federal armory at Harper's Ferry in October 1859, for which he was
executed on December 2, 1859; *"marching on"*: reference to either "John
Brown's Body" or "The Battle Hymn of the Republic," two important
Union marching songs that used the same tune and some of the same
lyrics.

4. *What think ye*: Matthew 22:42.

5. *Prepare ye the way*: Isaiah 40:3, a prophecy that a forerunner of Christ
would utter these words; fulfilled by John the Baptist (Matthew 3:3, Luke
3:4, John 1:23).

6. *bon mot*: French, witticism.

7. *Ah! . . . revolution*: Popular, but probably apocryphal, exchange said to
have occurred on July 15, 1789, between the king of France and a member
of the nobility committed to social reform. A similar version punctuates a
chapter in Thomas Carlyle's 1837 *The French Revolution: A History*.

8. *sad friends . . . lovely form*: The cited passages are from John Milton's *Are-
opagitica* (1644).

9. *If he who walketh*: 1 Peter 5:8.

10. *miasma*: A poisonous vapor, believed by nineteenth-century scientific theory to be the source of contagious diseases.

11. *The Church*: Unidentified citation.

Unhappy Girls

1. *a friend*: Unidentified private correspondent.

2. *the chief end of woman:* Phelps argues that culture imposes a different purpose on women than on men. According to the Westminster Catechism,
the chief end of man is to glorify God and enjoy him forever.

3. *having lost . . . gained it*: Matthew 10:39, 16:25; Mark 8:35; Luke 9:24, 17:33.

4. *God's . . . mistake:* Misquote of Jean Ingelow's "Remonstrance," which
claims that love for Eve led Adam to choose sin.

5. *Horace*: Quintus Horatius Flaccus (65–8 BCE) was a Roman lyric poet.

6. *Darwin:* Charles Darwin (1809–82), British naturalist who developed the
theory of evolution.

7. *Take up . . . follow them*: Luke 9:23.

8. *lover . . . long:* While Phelps could be referring to lines 177–80 of *Prelude* (1850) by William Wordsworth (1770–1850), she is more likely employing rhetoric common during the Romantic era of the early nineteenth century.

9. *Picciola:* An 1865 novel by Joseph Xavier Boniface Saintine (1798–1865) about a prisoner who brings a plant to life as an ideal woman.

10. *that . . . frustration:* From "On Liberty" (1859) by John Stuart Mill (1806–73).

11. *If there . . . pursuits:* From Mill's *The Subjection of Women* (1869).

12. *Rights? . . . rights!:* Unidentified citation, probably fictitious.

13. *He who . . . imitation:* From Mill's "On Liberty."

14. *expressed to gold-leaf:* From "Farming," published in *Society and Solitude* (1870), by Ralph Waldo Emerson (1803–82).

15. *Charley Lamb . . . its time:* Reference to the British essayist Charles Lamb, "That We Should Rise with the Lark" (1826).

16. *quinine:* Medicine with many uses, including combating malaria.

17. *Raphael:* Italian painter and architect (1483–1520).

18. *Milton:* John Milton (1608–74), British writer famous for *Paradise Lost* (1667); *Field:* James T. Fields (1816–81) of Fields, Osgood, one of Phelps's publishers and an early supporter of her career.

19. *anodyne:* Pain reliever.

20. *Subjection of Women:* See note 11.

21. *I long ago . . . business:* Unidentified reference.

22. *we have . . . with us:* Matthew 26:11, Mark 14:7, John 12:8.

23. *greatest . . . center:* From Mill's "On Liberty."

24. *I pray . . . from evil:* John 17:15.

25. *a new creature:* Likely a reference to 2 Corinthians 5:17.

26. *put away childish things:* 1 Corinthians 13:11.

Selections from "Woman's Dress"

1. *New England Club:* the New England Woman's Club of Boston was founded in 1868 by Caroline M. Severance (1820–1914) to provide women with a place for social engagement and education in the arts, sciences, and foreign languages. Phelps lectured to the club about dress reform in 1873, after which members opened a clothing store that sold fashions more attuned to women's physical needs.

2. *their name is legion:* Reference to Mark 5:9, Luke 8:30, and the demons, named Legion, that can possess humankind.

3. *biased dress:* A pattern cut on the diagonal or slant to better conform to the waist.

4. *Six new diseases . . . heavy skirts:* The excessive weight of women's garments, often more than twelve pounds, was a source of concern for many health professionals during the period.

5. *the whip of the sky*: Poem published in 1871 by Thomas G. Appleton (1812–84) that is critical of the fast pace of nineteenth-century life.

6. *Survival of the Fittest:* Theory developed by Charles Darwin (1809–82) as part of the theory of evolution.

7. *one of your own members*: Phelps seems to be addressing a member of the club; the reference is unidentified.

8. *basque-waist:* A slightly dropped waist on a skirt.

9. *Dr. Clarke*: Dr. Edward H. Clarke, Boston physician, author of the controversial *Women in Education* (1873), parts of which he delivered as a lecture to the New England Woman's Club. The following year Julia Ward Howe edited *Women and Education: A Reply to Dr. E. H. Clarke's "Sex in Education,"* to which Phelps contributed a chapter.

10. *"Atlantic"*: The ss *Atlantic* ran aground and sank on April 1, 1873, during a voyage from Liverpool to New York.

11. *Much sewing . . . no end*: A reworking of Ecclesiastes 12:12.

12. *treadle:* A pedal on various machines, including the loom.

13. *shatter . . . the gold*: Daniel 2:31–45.

14. *Washington Street*: A prominent street in an affluent section of Boston.

15. *Coming Woman:* Reference to an article published in *Lippincott's Magazine* in 1870 by P. Thorne, pen name of Mary Prudence Wells Smith (1840–1930). The woman in the article is more concerned with healthy and practical clothing than with emulating Parisian fashion.

16. *Cimmerian*: An ancient tribe in Crimea who supposedly lived in total darkness.

17. *Mrs. Grant*: Julia Boggs Dent Grant (1826–1902), wife of President Ulysses S. Grant; *Madame Demorest*: Ellen Louise Demorest (1824–98) ran Madame Demorest's Emporium, an important clothing store. She was instrumental in promoting the use of paper patterns.

18. *Lady's Books*: Popular serials, such as *Godey's Lady's Book* (1830–92), that provided women with varied content, including fiction and fashion.

19. *maid, wife, and widow*: Phelps could be referencing any one of a number of popular novels, including *The Cloister and the Hearth; or, Maid, Wife and Widow* (1861) by the British author Charles Reade (1814–84); *The Maid, Wife, and Widow* (1806) by the British author Henry Siddons (1774–1815); or *Ella Cameron, Or, The Maid Wife, and Widow of a Day* (1861) by an anonymous American author. She could also be referring to the poem "The Highland Widow's Lament" (1796), which is attributed to Robert Burns (1759–96) and is based on the old Scottish song "Oh ono Chrio," sometimes also referred to as "O Hone A Rie" or "The Widow of Glenco."

20. *the voice . . . the Lord:* Isaiah 40:3, a prophecy that a forerunner of Christ would proclaim these words; John the Baptist fulfilled the prophecy (Matthew 3:3; Mark 1:3; Luke 3:4).

21. *little Chinese monster:* Phelps makes a similar reference in "A Woman's Pulpit."

A Dream within a Dream

1. *Episcopal:* American denomination with origins in the British Anglican church.

2. *patois:* French, dialect.

3. *One of great . . . acceptance:* Unidentified reference; it is likely that this proposed sermon remained private.

4. *Epictetus:* Roman philosopher and proponent of Stoicism (55–135).

5. *Rev. Mr. Murray . . . church:* Reverend William Henry Harrison Murray (1840–1904) filled the pulpit of Boston's Pine Street Church from 1868 to 1874. Phelps's father, Austin, was the minister at Pine Street from 1842 to 1848.

6. *donation party:* Parties were held to raise or augment the salaries of ministers in the nineteenth century. Phelps's mother depicts one in *The Sunny Side; Or, The Country Minister's Wife* (1851).

7. *Orthodox Congregational Church:* Phelps is referring to the more conservative branch of the Congregational Church, with which Andover Theological Seminary was associated.

8. *banns:* Announcement made in church regarding a couple's proposed marriage.

9. *Love . . . than Death:* Sentiment espoused by many influential writers and thinkers, including the poet John Milton (1608–1674) and the hymn writer Isaac Watts (1674–1748).

10. *in a world . . . marriage:* Matthew 22:30, Mark 12:25, and Luke 20:35 all reference Jesus' assertion that people will not marry in heaven.

What Is a Fact?

1. *imputed sin:* Original sin. The belief in imputed sin raised concern over the fate of babies who die before baptism or hearing the Gospel; for centuries, Christians have struggled with whether unbaptized infants go to hell or if God, knowing that they had no opportunity to choose, would allow them into heaven, or limbo in the Catholic tradition. In the 1880s Phelps's father became involved in a controversy on this subject, writing in defense of the idea of infant damnation.

2. *babies . . . heaven:* Matthew 19:14, Mark 10:14, Luke 18:16.

3. *Adam himself . . . fact:* The literal, versus the allegorical, truth of the Bible was an important point of controversy across the nineteenth century.

4. *Barnes's Notes*: Albert Barnes (1789–1870), an American minister and author of a well-known series of Bible commentaries on various books of the Old and New Testaments.

5. *Fourth Gospel*: Scholars have long questioned whether or not the Gospel of John was written by Jesus' disciple John; *authorship of the Golden Rule*: This aphorism has been attributed to Jesus for centuries, but the first account of its usage comes from Confucius.

6. *discoveries of geology*: Geological discoveries in the nineteenth century presented substantial challenges to traditional Christian beliefs. Charles Lyell's *Principles of Geology* (1830), for example, demonstrated that the world was much older than the account in Genesis suggested.

7. *Malvern Hill*: Civil War battle fought on July 1, 1862.

8. *Goethe*: German author Johann Wolfgang von Goethe (1749–1832), known for works such as *Faust* (1808 and 1832); *Browning*: Victorian poet Robert Browning (1812–89) wrote a poem about German alchemist Theophrastus Bombastus von Hohenheim, commonly known as Paracelsus.

9. *the eve . . . Awakening*: Unidentified citation.

10. *We may . . . self-contradiction:* Sir William Hamilton (1788–1856), Scottish philosopher, from Lecture 23 of the *Lectures on Metaphysics*, published 1859–60.

11. *artificial . . . fish:* In the 1840s scientists became interested in breeding fish. Particularly important in this study were Anton Géhin and Joseph Remy, French scientists, who started experimenting with trout in 1844.

12. *spontaneous . . . water:* By 1880, ideas of spontaneous generation had been mostly abandoned.

13. *Renan*: Ernest Renan (1823–92), a French thinker and author of the influential *Life of Jesus*, spoke at the bicentenary celebration of Baruch Spinoza's death on February 21, 1877, at the Hague. Spinoza (1632–77) was a philosopher from the Netherlands; although Jewish by birth, his beliefs were more closely aligned with pantheism. René Descartes (1596–1650) was French philosopher and mathematician.

14. *Bacon*: Francis Bacon (1561–1626), British intellectual and scientist.

15. *They cannot account*: Unidentified citation, but Phelps is generally referencing late-century questions about identity and the body.

16. *Beethoven:* Ludwig van Beethoven (1770–1827), German composer; *Mozart*: Wolfgang Amadeus Mozart (1756–91), Austrian composer; *Bach:* Johann Sebastian Bach (1684–1750), German composer; *Händel:* George Frideric Handel (1685–1759), German composer who did most of his work in England; *Haydn:* Franz Joseph Haydn (1732–1806), Austrian composer; *Milton*: John Milton (1608–1674), British author; *Dante:* Dante Alighieri

(1265–1321), Italian author; *Wordsworth*: William Wordsworth (1770–1850), British Romantic poet; *Raphael*: Raffaello Sanzio (1483–1520), Italian artist; *Michael Angelo:* Michelangelo Buonarroti (1475–1564), Italian painter; *Plato*: Greek philosopher (428–347); *Immanuel Kant*: German philosopher (1724–1804); *Leibnitz*: Gottfried Wilhelm Leibniz (1646–1715), German philosopher and mathematician; *Kepler:* Johannes Kepler (1571–1630), German mathematician and astronomer; *Newton:* Isaac Newton (1642–1727), British scientist.

17. *To him . . . mountain- top*: From a speech at the Hague given on February 21, 1877, by Ernest Renan (1823–92). Phelps misquotes Renan, however; in the original, the statement is in the past tense: "Secrets unknown to the rabble were revealed." It was translated into English by Phelps's brother, Moses Stuart Phelps (1849–83).

18. *Locke's Essay*: British philosopher John Locke (1632–1704) wrote *An Essay Concerning Human Understanding* in 1689; *Excursion*: ten-volume poem published by Wordsworth in 1814.

19. *zymotic theory of diseases*: Zymotic theory, which refers to contagious diseases; *photophone*: machine created by Alexander Graham Bell and Sumner Tainter that used a beam of light to send sound waves, including human speech, from one location to another; *the insane:* changing ideas about the nature and treatment of insanity emerged in the late nineteenth century, encouraging treatment in place of or addition to confinement.

20. *He was . . . Human Body*: Phelps is likely referring to *The Human Body and Its Connexion with Man* (1815), by James John Garth Wilkinson (1812–99).

21. *I am . . . is there:* Phelps gestures to a conversation in Plato's *Phaedo* about the fate of the soul.

22. *thought . . . though*: An idea espoused by the Dutch intellectual Jacob Moleschott (1822–93).

23. *faith . . . sense*: Paraphrases an aphorism of Archbishop Robert Leighton (1611–84) that Samuel Taylor Coleridge (1772–1834) examines in *Aids to Reflection in the Formation of a Manly Character on the Several Grounds of Prudence, Morality, and Religion* (1825).

24. *My soul . . . is*: Likely a play on "My mind to me a kingdom is," published in 1588 by Sir Edward Dyer (1543–1607).

25. *Burns . . . the mind*: From "No. cccxiii. To Mr. Cunningham. A Mind Diseased. 25th February, 1794," written by Scottish poet Robert Burns (1759–96).

26. *The true . . . natures*: From "Jonathan Edwards," published in 1880 in the *International Review* by Oliver Wendell Holmes Sr. (1809–94).

27. *new heavens . . . earth*: Revelation 21:1; see note 14 for "A Woman's Pulpit."

Women's Views of Divorce

1. *last expedient*: Phelps was a lifelong advocate of homeopathy, a medical philosophy that rejected surgery and other aggressive treatments, like bleeding or cupping, in favor of highly diluted dosages of active ingredients.
2. *Seventh Commandment*: Exodus 20:14, the prohibition against adultery.
3. *a strait and narrow way*: Matthew 7:14.
4. *thousands go in thereat*: Matthew 7:13.
5. *Stephen Blackpool . . . Dickens's story*: *Hard Times* (1854) tells the unhappy story of a mill hand who is prevented from marrying the virtuous woman he loves because of the difficulty and expense of divorcing his alcoholic wife.
6. *Gladstone:* William Gladstone (1809–98), four-time British prime minister in the mid- to late nineteenth century; *E. J. Phelps*: Edward J. Phelps (1822–1900), Yale law professor and author of *Divorce in the United States* (1889), which argued that divorcées should be prevented from remarrying.
7. *demon . . . tears him*: Luke 9:39.
8. *gently enough . . . the limb:* From Tennyson's poem "In the Children's Hospital," published in *Ballads and Other Poems* (1880).
9. *materia medica*: List of ingredients and directions for making medicines.
10. *chloral*: Strong-smelling oil used as a sleeping aid or to calm anxiety.
11. *roué:* French, slang for a dissolute man.
12. *Sophocles called "the unwritten law":* Sophocles speaks of *nomos* (unwritten law) in *Antigone*, although Phelps's interpretation of the play is somewhat anachronistic. The idea that it would be wrong to marry someone you did not love would have been thoroughly alien to both Sophocles and his audience.
13. *mariage de convenance*: French, marriage of convenience.

The Moral Element in Fiction

1. *Matthew Arnold's . . . life:* From preface of "Last Essays on Church and Religion" published in 1877 by Matthew Arnold (1822–88).

The Short Story

1. *Spectator:* British publication by Joseph Addison and Richard Steele which ran from 1711 to 1712, and again briefly in 1714; the magazine often contained satirical pieces related to current events in England; *Ladies' and Gentleman's Annuals:* a general reference to popular nineteenth-century gift books, sometimes associated with particular periodicals or specific reform movements.

2. *Whip of the Sky:* 1871 poem by Thomas G. Appleton (1812–84) critical of the pace of nineteenth-century life.

3. *pastel:* A short descriptive piece lacking depth.

4. *France . . . as much:* Nineteenth-century French authors were pioneers in poetry and prose, developing realism, naturalism, and symbolism. Phelps aligned herself more closely with British realism, particularly as practiced by George Eliot.

5. *stimulants . . . asylum:* French poet Charles Baudelaire (1821–67) wrote "Les Paradis Artificiels" (1860) that many read as an apology for drug use; his prose poems experimented with the distinction between poetry and prose. Guy de Maupassant (1850–93), French author noted for his short stories, died in a private asylum in Paris.

6. *Hawthorne:* Nathaniel Hawthorne, American author (1804–64).

7. *I pray thee, have me excused:* Luke 14:18–19.

8. *Those? . . . nearer six:* In *Chapters from a Life*, Phelps tells this story but identifies herself as the "successful short story-writer" and the gentleman as "a friend" (267).

9. *Something . . . wings:* Paraphrase of a statement by Socrates in Plato's *Ion*.

10. *patois:* French, dialect; *kodak:* a literary snapshot.

Poems

1. *lily:* Phelps's family referred to her as Lily after she changed her name to Elizabeth Stuart.

2. *lily . . . toil:* Reference to Matthew 6:28 and Luke 12:27.

3. *Dinah:* Dinah Morris is the heroine of Eliot's first novel, *Adam Bede* (1859).

4. *As if . . . near:* Although the phrase corresponds to Eliot's representation of Dinah's Methodism and is consistent with a scene early in the novel where she preaches to villagers, the passage does not appear in *Adam Bede*.

5. *Testifies by fire:* Baptism by fire was associated with the figure of John the Baptist and was key to the late nineteenth-century evolution of Pentecostalism. This stanza is about *Romola*, Eliot's historical novel about fifteenth-century Florence (serialized in 1862–63; published as a book in 1863).

6. Dorothea Brooke is the central character in Eliot's seventh novel, *Middlemarch: A Study of Provincial Life* (serialized in 1871–72; published as a volume in 1874).

7. *"struggle with the dark":* Phelps misquotes Dorothea's defense of religious belief from chapter 39 of *Middlemarch*: "That by desiring what is perfectly good, even when we don't quite know what it is and can not do what we

would, we are part of the divine struggle against evil—widening the skirts of light and making the struggle with darkness narrower."

8. *Launcelot*: Phelps wrote multiple poems and several stories based on Arthurian legends. This one relates to Elaine, the maid of Astolat.

9. *Napier*: Sir Charles Napier (1782–1853) served in the British army in India.

10. *Cutchee:* These hills served as a haven for groups of robbers.

11. *mutiny*: The Sixty-fourth regiment, which was composed of Bengalese soldiers, mutinied twice.

12. *From rank . . . dear*: Napier's men fought in the Cutchee Hills from January 16 to March 9, 1845, and successfully routed the robber bands.

In the Legacies of Nineteenth-Century American Women Writers series:

To order or obtain more information on these or other University of Nebraska Press titles, visit www.nebraskapress.unl.edu.

www.ingramcontent.com/pod-product-compliance
Lightning Source LLC
Chambersburg PA
CBHW060601030726
47498CB00005B/1495